RULES OF CONTRACT LAW

Selections from the Uniform Commercial Code, the Convention on Contracts for the International Sale of Goods, and the Restatement (Second) of Contracts

RULES OF CONTRACT LAW
Selections from the Uniform Commercial Code, the Convention on Contracts for the International Sale of Goods, and the Restatement (Second) of Contracts
with Material on Contract Drafting and Sample Examination Questions and Answers

Charles L. Knapp
Max E. Greenberg Professor of Contract Law
New York University

Nathan M. Crystal
Roy Webster Professor of Law
University of South Carolina

Little, Brown and Company
Boston   New York   Toronto   London

Library of Congress Catalog Card No. 92-82980

ISBN 0-316-49932-3

Fourth Printing

EB-M

Published simultaneously in Canada
by Little, Brown & Company (Canada) Limited

Printed in the United States of America

Contents

RULES OF CONTRACT LAW
Selections from the Uniform Commercial Code,
the Convention on Contracts for the
International Sale of Goods, and the Restatement
(Second) of Contracts

The Uniform Commercial Code

EDITORS' NOTE [1]

As the United States developed a national market economy during the nine-teenth century, the number of business transactions across state lines increased dramatically. Many of these transactions were cumbersome, however, because of differences among the states on commercial subjects, such as negotiable in-struments, sales, and warehousing. Recognizing these problems, a number of business lawyers suggested the need for greater uniformity among the states in commercial law.

In 1889 the legislature of New York, the leading commercial state at that time, passed a statute providing for the appointment of commissioners who were authorized to solicit the appointment of commissioners from other states for the purpose of preparing uniform state laws. In 1892 the first meeting of the National Conference of Commissioners on Uniform State Laws (NCCUSL) was held in connection with the annual meeting of the American Bar Association. At first the Commissioners concentrated on technical questions, such as standardized forms for acknowledgement of instruments, but they soon ventured into more substantive areas. By the early part of the twentieth century, the Commissioners had prepared uniform acts on a number of commercial subjects: negotiable instruments, sales, warehouse receipts, bills of lading, and trust receipts, to name just a few.

Adopted in many states, the uniform acts did foster the cause of uniformity to some extent. A number of factors, however, limited the success of the National Conference. Professor and later Judge Robert Braucher summarized the prob-

---

1. Matters covered in this Note are explored more fully in the following works: Robert Braucher & Robert A. Riegert, Introduction to Commercial Transactions 19-31 (1977); James J. White & Robert S. Summers, Uniform Commercial Code 1-6 (3d ed. 1988); and Nathan M. Crystal, Codification and the Rise of the Restatement Movement, 54 Wash. L. Rev. 239 (1979).

lems as follows:

> [The history of the uniform acts] provides an illustration of four major difficulties which have afflicted uniform legislation: (1) difficulty in obtaining original enactment, (2) a tendency toward deviation from the official text at the time of the original adoption, (3) nonuniform judicial interpretation, and (4) difficulty in promulgating and obtaining enactment of uniform amendments.

Robert Braucher & Robert A. Riegert, Introduction to Commercial Transactions 21-22 (1977).

By 1940 it was apparent that many of the uniform acts adopted early in the century required revision. At the fiftieth annual meeting of the National Conference of Commissioners, William A. Schnader, the president of the Conference, called for the creation of a uniform commercial code. The Conference quickly adopted his suggestion, subject to obtaining funding. In 1944 the Conference combined forces with the American Law Institute (ALI) to sponsor the project, with Professor Karl Llewellyn of Columbia Law School as Chief Reporter.

After a lengthy process involving circulation of drafts among advisors, business groups, and others, the National Conference and the ALI issued an official text of the proposed Code in 1951. Pennsylvania became the first state to adopt the Code, in 1953. The project received a major setback in 1956, however, when the New York Law Revision Commission, after a three-year study, advised the New York Legislature that the Code "is not satisfactory in its present form." The New York Law Revision Commission's study has been published in a six-volume set and remains an important source of information about the Code.

The New York study caused the ALI and the National Conference to reexamine the Code. In 1958 the sponsoring organizations issued a revised Official Text. New York adopted this new version of the Code in 1962, and other states quickly followed suit. By 1968 the Code was in force in all jurisdictions except Louisiana, where only certain articles have been enacted. Even to this day, however, the process of revision goes on. In 1961 the ALI and the National Conference created a Permanent Editorial Board for the Uniform Commercial Code to monitor developments in commercial law and propose revisions of the Code. Revised Official Texts of the Code were published in 1962, 1972, 1978, and 1990. The current official version is the 1990 text.

Although titled a commercial code, the name is somewhat of a misnomer because the Code fails to cover a number of important commercial subjects. Transactions involving real estate and personal services are generally outside the scope of the Code. In addition, even for transactions subject to the Code, many aspects are regulated by other bodies of law. For example, Article 8 of the Code deals with title and transfer of investment securities, such as common stock. Most of the law governing transactions in securities, however, lies outside the Code. Moreover, common law principles continue to govern transactions to which the Code is applicable unless specifically displaced by Code provision. UCC §1-103.

Rather than a comprehensive code of commercial law, the UCC instead consists of a loosely related collection of revised versions of the most significant uniform acts adopted earlier this century by the National Conference of Commissioners. The Code is divided into 13 articles, the last two of which deal with effective date, repealers, and transition from prior law. Article 1 covers a number of general matters; it includes a section containing definitions that apply throughout the Code. UCC §1-201. Article 2, which is the principal part of the Code addressed in most contracts courses, deals with transactions involving the sale of goods. The sales article has remained largely unchanged since the 1962 version of the Code, but preliminary work is now underway for what promises to be a major revision of Article 2. Article 2A deals with various aspects of leases of personal property, including formation of lease contracts, performance, and default. "Commercial paper" — checks, notes, and drafts — is the focus of Article 3; the processing of such instruments through the banking system is the subject of Article 4; fund transfers are the topic of Article 4A. Article 5 deals with the rights and liabilities of parties to "letters of credit." Article 6 establishes rules for "bulk sales," transactions in which the owner of a certain type of business sells substantially all of the assets of that business. Article 7 governs "documents of title," such as bills of lading issued by carriers of goods, or warehouse receipts issued by companies that are involved in the storage of goods. Article 8 regulates the ownership and transfer of investment securities. Finally, Article 9 provides for the creation and protection of security interests in personal property.

Unlike the Restatements, which have only persuasive weight, the UCC is a statute, having the force of law. It is important to remember, however, that in each state the "law" is not the official text of the Code promulgated by the ALI and the National Conference of Commissioners, but that state's own enacted version of the Official Code. Most states have made nonuniform changes in certain provisions of the Official Text. To take one example, the South Carolina legislature has enacted nonuniform versions of UCC §§2-316 (disclaimers of warranties) and 2-318 (privity of contract).

Each section of the Official Text of the Code is followed by an Official Comment, which includes reference to prior law, discussion of the purposes of the section, and definitional cross references. What weight should be given to the discussion in the official comments? Since the state legislatures have not enacted the comments, they do not have the force of law. Do they have at least the persuasive status of "legislative history"? Two well-known commentators on the Code have made the following observations:

> Certainly the comments are not entitled to as much weight as ordinary legislative history. In some states the comments were not placed before the enacting body prior to adoption of the Code. Indeed, some of the present comments were not even in existence at the time the section to which they are now appended was adopted. Furthermore, much of the Code is highly technical "lawyer's" law. If the average legislator did not understand the intricacies of Article Four or Article Nine at the time of enactment, it is likely that he did not grasp the relevant comments either.

James J. White & Robert S. Summers, Uniform Commercial Code 13-14 (3d ed. 1988). Nonetheless, court opinions frequently have given the comments substantial weight. Indeed, White and Summers suggest that the courts have taken to use of the comments "like ducks to water." Id. at 12.

This Supplement includes the text of a number of sections from Article 2 of the Code, along with a few provisions from Articles 1, 3, and 9. Official Comments for the most significant sections are included as well. Text and comments are taken from the 1990 Official Text. The editors are grateful to the Permanent Editorial Board for the Uniform Commercial Code for permission to reprint this material. (UCC Comments) — Copyright 1991 by the American Law Institute and the National Conference of Commissioners on Uniform State Laws.

ARTICLE 1. GENERAL PROVISIONS

Part 1. Short Title, Construction, Application and Subject Matter of the Act

Part 2. General Definitions and Principles of Interpretation

ARTICLE 2. SALES

Part 1. Short Title, General Construction and Subject Matter

Part 2. Form, Formation and Readjustment of Contract

Part 7. Remedies

ARTICLE 3. NEGOTIABLE INSTRUMENTS

Part 1. General Provisions and Definitions

Part 3. Enforcement of Instruments

ARTICLE 1.   GENERAL PROVISIONS

Part 1.   *Short Title, Construction, Application and Subject Matter of the Act*

§1-102.   Purposes; Rules of Construction; Variation by Agreement

(1) This Act shall be liberally construed and applied to promote its underlying purposes and policies.

(2) Underlying purposes and policies of this Act are

    (a) to simplify, clarify and modernize the law governing commercial transactions;

    (b) to permit the continued expansion of commercial practices through custom, usage and agreement of the parties;

    (c) to make uniform the law among the various jurisdictions.

(3) The effect of provisions of this Act may be varied by agreement, except as otherwise provided in this Act and except that the obligations of good faith, diligence, reasonableness and care prescribed by this Act may not be disclaimed by agreement but the parties may by agreement determine the standards by which the performance of such obligations is to be measured if such standards are not manifestly unreasonable.

(4) The presence in certain provisions of this Act of the words "unless otherwise agreed" or words of similar import does not imply that the effect of other provisions may not be varied by agreement under subsection (3).

(5) In this Act unless the context otherwise requires

(a) words in the singular number include the plural, and in the plural include the singular;

(b) words of the masculine gender include the feminine and the neuter, and when the sense so indicates words of the neuter gender may refer to any gender.

§1-103. Supplementary General Principles of Law Applicable

Unless displaced by the particular provisions of this Act, the principles of law and equity, including the law merchant and the law relative to capacity to contract, principal and agent, estoppel, fraud, misrepresentation, duress, coercion, mistake, bankruptcy, or other validating or invalidating cause shall supplement its provisions.

§1-105. Territorial Application of the Act; Parties' Power to Choose Applicable Law

(1) Except as provided hereafter in this section, when a transaction bears a reasonable relation to this state and also to another state or nation the parties may agree that the law either of this state or of such other state or nation shall govern their rights and duties. Failing such agreement this Act applies to transactions bearing an appropriate relation to this state.

(2) . . .

§1-106. Remedies to Be Liberally Administered

(1) The remedies provided by this Act shall be liberally administered to the end that the aggrieved party may be put in as good a position as if the other party had fully performed but neither consequential or special nor penal damages may be had except as specifically provided in this Act or by other rule of law.

(2) Any right or obligation declared by this Act is enforceable by action unless the provision declaring it specifies a different and limited effect.

§1-107. Waiver or Renunciation of Claim or Right After Breach

Any claim or right arising out of an alleged breach can be discharged in whole or in part without consideration by a written waiver or renunciation signed and delivered by the aggrieved party.

Part 2. *General Definitions and Principles of Interpretation*

§1-201. General Definitions

Subject to additional definitions contained in the subsequent Articles of this Act which are applicable to specific Articles or Parts thereof, and unless the context otherwise requires, in this Act:

(1) "Action" in the sense of a judicial proceeding includes recoupment, counterclaim, set-off, suit in equity and any other proceedings in which rights are determined.

(2) "Aggrieved party" means a party entitled to resort to a remedy.

(3) "Agreement" means the bargain of the parties in fact as found in their language or by implication from other circumstances including course of dealing or usage of trade or course of performance as provided in this Act (Sections 1-205 and 2-208). Whether an agreement has legal consequences is determined by the provisions of this Act, if applicable; otherwise by the law of contracts (Section 1-103). (Compare "Contract.")

(4) "Bank" means any person engaged in the business of banking.

(5) "Bearer" means the person in possession of an instrument, document of title, or certificated security payable to bearer or indorsed in blank.

(6) "Bill of lading" means a document evidencing the receipt of goods for shipment issued by a person engaged in the business of transporting or forwarding goods, and includes an airbill. "Airbill" means a document serving for air transportation as a bill of lading does for marine or rail transportation, and includes an air consignment note or air waybill.

(7) "Branch" includes a separately incorporated foreign branch of a bank.

(8) "Burden of establishing" a fact means the burden of persuading the triers of fact that the existence of the fact is more probable than its non-existence.

(9) "Buyer in ordinary course of business" means a person who in good faith and without knowledge that the sale to him is in violation of the ownership rights or security interest of a third party in the goods buys in ordinary course from a person in the business of selling goods of that kind but does not include a pawnbroker. All persons who sell minerals or the like (including oil and gas) at wellhead or minehead shall be deemed to be persons in the business of selling goods of that kind. "Buying" may be for cash or by exchange of other property or on secured or unsecured credit and includes receiving goods or documents of title under a pre-existing contract for sale but does not include a transfer in bulk or as security for or in total or partial satisfaction of a money debt.

(10) "Conspicuous": A term or clause is conspicuous when it is so written that a reasonable person against whom it is to operate ought to have noticed it. A printed heading in capitals (as: NON-NEGOTIABLE BILL OF LADING) is conspicuous. Language in the body of a form is "conspicuous" if it is in larger or other contrasting type or color. But in a telegram any stated term

is "conspicuous." Whether a term or clause is "conspicuous" or not is for decision by the court.

(11) "Contract" means the total legal obligation which results from the parties' agreement as affected by this Act and any other applicable rules of law. (Compare "Agreement.")

(12) "Creditor" includes a general creditor, a secured creditor, a lien creditor and any representative of creditors, including an assignee for the benefit of creditors, a trustee in bankruptcy, a receiver in equity and an executor or administrator of an insolvent debtor's or assignor's estate.

(13) "Defendant" includes a person in the position of defendant in a cross-action or counterclaim.

(14) "Delivery" with respect to instruments, documents of title, chattel paper, or certificated securities means voluntary transfer of possession.

(15) "Document of title" includes bill of lading, dock warrant, dock receipt, warehouse receipt or order for the delivery of goods, and also any other document which in the regular course of business or financing is treated as adequately evidencing that the person in possession of it is entitled to receive, hold and dispose of the document and the goods it covers. To be a document of title a document must purport to be issued by or addressed to a bailee and purport to cover goods in the bailee's possession which are either identified or are fungible portions of an identified mass.

(16) "Fault" means wrongful act, omission or breach.

(17) "Fungible" with respect to goods or securities means goods or securities of which any unit is, by nature or usage of trade, the equivalent of any other like unit. Goods which are not fungible shall be deemed fungible for the purposes of this Act to the extent that under a particular agreement or document unlike units are treated as equivalents.

(18) "Genuine" means free of forgery or counterfeiting.

(19) "Good faith" means honesty in fact in the conduct or transaction concerned.

(20) "Holder," with respect to a negotiable instrument, means the person in possession if the instrument is payable to bearer or, in the case of an instrument payable to an identified person, if the identified person is in possession. "Holder" with respect to a document of title means the person in possession if the goods are deliverable to bearer or to the order of the person in possession.

(21) To "honor" is to pay or to accept and pay, or where a credit so engages to purchase or discount a draft complying with the terms of the credit.

(22) "Insolvency proceedings" includes any assignment for the benefit of creditors or other proceedings intended to liquidate or rehabilitate the estate of the person involved.

(23) A person is "insolvent" who either has ceased to pay his debts in the ordinary course of business or cannot pay his debts as they become due or is insolvent within the meaning of the federal bankruptcy law.

(24) "Money" means a medium of exchange authorized or adopted by a domestic or foreign government and includes a monetary unit of account

established by an intergovernmental organization or by agreement between two or more nations.

(25) A person has "notice" of a fact when

(a) he has actual knowledge of it; or

(b) he has received a notice or notification of it; or

(c) from all the facts and circumstances known to him at the time in question he has reason to know that it exists.

A person "knows" or has "knowledge" of a fact when he has actual knowledge of it. "Discover" or "learn" or a word or phrase of similar import refers to knowledge rather than to reason to know. The time and circumstances under which a notice or notification may cease to be effective are not determined by this Act.

(26) A person "notifies" or "gives" a notice or notification to another by taking such steps as may be reasonably required to inform the other in ordinary course whether or not such other actually comes to know of it. A person "receives" a notice or notification when

(a) it comes to his attention; or

(b) it is duly delivered at the place of business through which the contract was made or at any other place held out by him as the place for receipt of such communications.

(27) Notice, knowledge or a notice or notification received by an organization is effective for a particular transaction from the time when it is brought to the attention of the individual conducting that transaction, and in any event from the time when it would have been brought to his attention if the organization had exercised due diligence. An organization exercises due diligence if it maintains reasonable routines for communicating significant information to the person conducting the transaction and there is reasonable compliance with the routines. Due diligence does not require an individual acting for the organization to communicate information unless such communication is part of his regular duties or unless he has reason to know of the transaction and that the transaction would be materially affected by the information.

(28) "Organization" includes a corporation, government or governmental subdivision or agency, business trust, estate, trust, partnership or association, two or more persons having a joint or common interest, or any other legal or commercial entity.

(29) "Party," as distinct from "third party," means a person who has engaged in a transaction or made an agreement within this Act.

(30) "Person" includes an individual or an organization (See Section 1-102).

(31) "Presumption" or "presumed" means that the trier of fact must find the existence of the fact presumed unless and until evidence is introduced which would support a finding of its non-existence.

(32) "Purchase" includes taking by sale, discount, negotiation, mortgage, pledge, lien, issue or re-issue, gift or any other voluntary transaction creating an interest in property.

(33) "Purchaser" means a person who takes by purchase.

(34) "Remedy" means any remedial right to which an aggrieved party is entitled with or without resort to a tribunal.

(35) "Representative" includes an agent, an officer of a corporation or association, and a trustee, executor or administrator of an estate, or any other person empowered to act for another.

(36) "Rights" includes remedies.

(37) "Security interest" means an interest in personal property or fixtures which secures payment or performance of an obligation. The retention or reservation of title by a seller of goods notwithstanding shipment or delivery to the buyer (Section 2-401) is limited in effect to a reservation of a "security interest." The term also includes any interest of a buyer of accounts or chattel paper which is subject to Article 9. The special property interest of a buyer of goods on identification of those goods to a contract for sale under Section 2-401 is not a "security interest," but a buyer may also acquire a "security interest" by complying with Article 9. Unless a consignment is intended as security, reservation of title thereunder is not a "security interest" but a consignment in any event is subject to the provisions on consignment sales (Section 2-326).

Whether a transaction creates a lease or security is to be determined by the facts of each case. [Detailed provisions on when a lease amounts to a security interest have been omitted.]

(38) "Send" in connection with any writing or notice means to deposit in the mail or deliver for transmission by any other usual means of communication with postage or cost of transmission provided for and properly addressed and in the case of an instrument to an address specified thereon or otherwise agreed, or if there be none to any address reasonable under the circumstances. The receipt of any writing or notice within the time at which it would have arrived if properly sent has the effect of a proper sending.

(39) "Signed" includes any symbol executed or adopted by a party with present intention to authenticate a writing.

(40) "Surety" includes guarantor.

(41) "Telegram" includes a message transmitted by radio, teletype, cable, any mechanical method of transmission, or the like.

(42) "Term" means that portion of an agreement which relates to a particular matter.

(43) "Unauthorized" signature means one made without actual, implied or apparent authority and includes a forgery.

(44) "Value." Except as otherwise provided with respect to negotiable instruments and bank collections (Sections 3-303, 4-208 and 4-209) a person gives "value" for rights if he acquires them

(a) in return for a binding commitment to extend credit or for the extension of immediately available credit whether or not drawn upon and whether or not a chargeback is provided for in the event of difficulties in collection; or

(b) as security for or in total or partial satisfaction of a pre-existing claim; or

(c) by accepting delivery pursuant to a pre-existing contract for purchase; or

(d) generally, in return for any consideration sufficient to support a simple contract.

(45) "Warehouse receipt" means a receipt issued by a person engaged in the business of storing goods for hire.

(46) "Written" or "writing" includes printing, typewriting or any other intentional reduction to tangible form.

§1-203. Obligation of Good Faith

Every contract or duty within this Act imposes an obligation of good faith in its performance or enforcement. *applies to all of ucc*

Official Comment

Prior Uniform Statutory Provision: None.

Purposes:

This section sets forth a basic principle running throughout this Act. The principle involved is that in commercial transactions good faith is required in the performance and enforcement of all agreements or duties. Particular applications of this general principle appear in specific provisions of the Act such as the option to accelerate at will (Section 1-208), the right to cure a defective delivery of goods (Section 2-508), the duty of a merchant buyer who has rejected goods to effect salvage operations (Section 2-603), substituted performance (Section 2-614), and failure of presupposed conditions (Section 2-615). The concept, however, is broader than any of these illustrations and applies generally, as stated in this section, to the performance or enforcement of every contract or duty within this Act. It is further implemented by Section 1-205 on course of dealing and usage of trade.

It is to be noted that under the Sales Article definition of good faith (Section 2-103), contracts made by a merchant have incorporated in them the explicit standard not only of honesty in fact (Section 1-201), but also of observance by the merchant of reasonable commercial standards of fair dealing in the trade.

Cross References:

Sections 1-201; 1-205; 1-208; 2-103; 2-508; 2-603; 2-614; 2-615.

Definitional Cross References:

"Contract." Section 1-201.

"Good faith." Section 1-201; 2-103.

§1-204. Time; Reasonable Time; "Seasonably"

(1) Whenever this Act requires any action to be taken within a reasonable time, any time which is not manifestly unreasonable may be fixed by agreement.

(2) What is a reasonable time for taking any action depends on the nature, purpose and circumstances of such action.

(3) An action is taken "seasonably" when it is taken at or within the time agreed or if no time is agreed at or within a reasonable time.

§1-205. Course of Dealing and Usage of Trade

(1) A course of dealing is a sequence of previous conduct between the parties to a particular transaction which is fairly to be regarded as establishing a common basis of understanding for interpreting their expressions and other conduct.

(2) A usage of trade is any practice or method of dealing having such regularity of observance in a place, vocation or trade as to justify an expectation that it will be observed with respect to the transaction in question. The existence and scope of such a usage are to be proved as facts. If it is established that such a usage is embodied in a written trade code or similar writing the interpretation of the writing is for the court.

(3) A course of dealing between parties and any usage of trade in the vocation or trade in which they are engaged or of which they are or should be aware give particular meaning to and supplement or qualify terms of an agreement.

(4) The express terms of an agreement and an applicable course of dealing or usage of trade shall be construed wherever reasonable as consistent with each other; but when such construction is unreasonable express terms control both course of dealing and usage of trade and course of dealing controls usage of trade.

(5) An applicable usage of trade in the place where any part of performance is to occur shall be used in interpreting the agreement as to that part of the performance.

(6) Evidence of a relevant usage of trade offered by one party is not admissible unless and until he has given the other party such notice as the court finds sufficient to prevent unfair surprise to the latter.

Official Comment

Prior Uniform Statutory Provision: No such general provision but see Sections 9(1), 15(5), 18(2), and 71, Uniform Sales Act.

Purposes: This section makes it clear that:

1. This Act rejects both the "lay-dictionary" and the "conveyancer's" reading of a commercial agreement. Instead the meaning of the agreement of the parties is to be determined by the language used by them and by their action, read and interpreted in the light of commercial practices and other surrounding circumstances. The measure and background for interpretation are set by the commercial context, which may explain and supplement even the language of a formal or final writing.

2. Course of dealing under subsection (1) is restricted, literally, to a sequence of conduct between the parties previous to the agreement. However, the provisions of the Act on course of performance make it clear that a sequence of conduct after or under the agreement may have equivalent meaning. (Section 2-208.)

3. "Course of dealing" may enter the agreement either by explicit provisions of the agreement or by tacit recognition.

4. This Act deals with "usage of trade" as a factor in reaching the commercial meaning of the agreement which the parties have made. The language used is to be interpreted as meaning what it may fairly be expected to mean to parties involved in the particular commercial transaction in a given locality or in a given vocation or trade. By adopting in this context the term "usage of trade" this Act expresses its intent to reject those cases which see evidence of "custom" as representing an effort to displace or negate "established rules of law." A distinction is to be drawn between mandatory rules of law such as the Statute of Frauds provisions of Article 2 on Sales whose very office is to control and restrict the actions of the parties, and which cannot be abrogated by agreement, or by a usage of trade, and those rules of law (such as those in Part 3 of Article 2 on Sales) which fill in points which the parties have not considered and in fact agreed upon. The latter rules hold "unless otherwise agreed" but yield to the contrary agreement of the parties. Part of the agreement of the parties to which such rules yield is to be sought for in the usages of trade which furnish the background and give particular meaning to the language used, and are the framework of common understanding controlling any general rules of law which hold only when there is no such understanding.

5. A usage of trade under subsection (2) must have the "regularity of observance" specified. The ancient English tests for "custom" are abandoned in this connection. Therefore, it is not required that a usage of trade be "ancient or immemorial," "universal" or the like. Under the requirement of subsection (2) full recognition is thus available for new usages and for usages currently observed by the great majority of decent dealers, even though dissidents ready to cut corners do not agree. There is room also for proper recognition of usage agreed upon by merchants in trade codes.

6. The policy of this Act controlling explicit unconscionable contracts and clauses (Sections 1-203, 2-302) applies to implicit clauses which rest

on usage of trade and carries forward the policy underlying the ancient requirement that a custom or usage must be "reasonable." However, the emphasis is shifted. The very fact of commercial acceptance makes out a prima facie case that the usage is reasonable, and the burden is no longer on the usage to establish itself as being reasonable. But the anciently established policing of usage by the courts is continued to the extent necessary to cope with the situation arising if an unconscionable or dishonest practice should become standard.

7. Subsection (3), giving the prescribed effect to usages of which the parties "are or should be aware," reinforces the provision of subsection (2) requiring not universality but only the described "regularity of observance" of the practice or method. This subsection also reinforces the point of subsection (2) that such usages may be either general to trade or particular to a special branch of trade.

8. Although the terms in which this Act defines "agreement" include the elements of course of dealing and usage of trade, the fact that express reference is made in some sections to those elements is not to be construed as carrying a contrary intent or implication elsewhere. Compare Section 1-102(4).

9. In cases of a well established line of usage varying from the general rules of this Act where the precise amount of the variation has not been worked out into a single standard, the party relying on the usage is entitled, in any event, to the minimum variation demonstrated. The whole is not to be disregarded because no particular line of detail has been established. In case a dominant pattern has been fairly evidenced, the party relying on the usage is entitled under this section to go to the trier of fact on the question of whether such dominant pattern has been incorporated into the agreement.

10. Subsection (6) is intended to insure that this Act's liberal recognition of the needs of commerce in regard to usage of trade shall not be made into an instrument of abuse.

Cross References:
   Point 1: Sections 1-203, 2-104 and 2-202.
   Point 2: Section 2-208.
   Point 4: Section 2-201 and Part 3 of Article 2.
   Point 6: Sections 1-203 and 2-302.
   Point 8: Sections 1-102 and 1-201.
   Point 9: Section 2-204(3).

Definitional Cross References:
   "Agreement." Section 1-201.
   "Contract." Section 1-201.
   "Party." Section 1-201.
   "Term." Section 1-201.

§1-206. Statute of Frauds for Kinds of Personal Property Not Otherwise Covered

(1) Except in the cases described in subsection (2) of this section a contract for the sale of personal property is not enforceable by way of action or defense beyond five thousand dollars in amount or value of remedy unless there is some writing which indicates that a contract for sale has been made between the parties at a defined or stated price, reasonably identifies the subject matter, and is signed by the party against whom enforcement is sought or by his authorized agent.

(2) Subsection (1) of this section does not apply to contracts for the sale of goods (Section 2-201) nor of securities (Section 8-319) nor to security agreements (Section 9-203).

§1-207. Performance or Acceptance Under Reservation of Rights

(1) A party who with explicit reservation of rights performs or promises performance or assents to performance in a manner demanded or offered by the other party does not thereby prejudice the rights reserved. Such words as "without prejudice," "under protest" or the like are sufficient.

(2) Subsection (1) does not apply to an accord and satisfaction.

§1-208. Option to Accelerate at Will

A term providing that one party or his successor in interest may accelerate payment or performance or require collateral or additional collateral "at will" or "when he deems himself insecure" or in words of similar import shall be construed to mean that he shall have power to do so only if he in good faith believes that the prospect of payment or performance is impaired. The burden of establishing lack of good faith is on the party against whom the power has been exercised.

ARTICLE 2. SALES

Part 1. Short Title, General Construction and Subject Matter

§2-102. Scope; Certain Security and Other Transactions Excluded From This Article

Unless the context otherwise requires, this Article applies to transactions in goods; it does not apply to any transaction which although in the form of an unconditional contract to sell or present sale is intended to operate only as a security transaction nor does this Article impair or repeal any statute regulating sales to consumers, farmers or other specified classes of buyers.

§2-103. Definitions and Index of Definitions

(1) In this Article unless the context otherwise requires
  (a) "Buyer" means a person who buys or contracts to buy goods.
  (b) "Good faith" in the case of a merchant means honesty in fact and the observance of reasonable commercial standards of fair dealing in the trade.
  (c) "Receipt" of goods means taking physical possession of them.
  (d) "Seller" means a person who sells or contracts to sell goods.
(2) Other definitions applying to this Article or to specified Parts thereof, and the sections in which they appear are:

"Acceptance." Section 2-606.
"Banker's credit." Section 2-325.
"Between merchants." Section 2-104.
"Cancellation." Section 2-106(4).
"Commercial unit." Section 2-105.
"Confirmed credit." Section 2-325.
"Conforming to contract." Section 2-106.
"Contract for sale." Section 2-106.
"Cover." Section 2-712.
"Entrusting." Section 2-403.
"Financing agency." Section 2-104.
"Future goods." Section 2-105.
"Goods." Section 2-105.
"Identification." Section 2-501.
"Installment contract." Section 2-612.
"Letter of Credit." Section 2-325.
"Lot." Section 2-105.
"Merchant." Section 2-104.
"Overseas." Section 2-323.
"Person in position of seller." Section 2-707.

"Present sale." Section 2-106.
"Sale." Section 2-106.
"Sale on approval." Section 2-326.
"Sale or return." Section 2-326.
"Termination." Section 2-106.

(3) The following definitions in other Articles apply to this Article:

"Check." Section 3-104.
"Consignee." Section 7-102.
"Consignor." Section 7-102.
"Consumer goods." Section 9-109.
"Dishonor." Section 3-507.
"Draft." Section 3-104.

(4) In addition Article 1 contains general definitions and principles of construction and interpretation applicable throughout this Article.

§2-104. Definitions: "Merchant"; "Between Merchants"; "Financing Agency"

(1) "Merchant" means a person who deals in goods of the kind or otherwise by his occupation holds himself out as having knowledge or skill peculiar to the practices or goods involved in the transaction or to whom such knowledge or skill may be attributed by his employment of an agent or broker or other intermediary who by his occupation holds himself out as having such knowledge or skill.

(2) "Financing agency" means a bank, finance company or other person who in the ordinary course of business makes advances against goods or documents of title or who by arrangement with either the seller or the buyer intervenes in ordinary course to make or collect payment due or claimed under the contract for sale, as by purchasing or paying the seller's draft or making advances against it or by merely taking it for collection whether or not documents of title accompany the draft. "Financing agency" includes also a bank or other person who similarly intervenes between persons who are in the position of seller and buyer in respect to the goods (Section 2-707).

(3) "Between merchants" means in any transaction with respect to which both parties are chargeable with the knowledge or skill of merchants.

§2-105. Definitions: Transferability; "Goods"; "Future" Goods; "Lot"; "Commercial Unit"

(1) "Goods" means all things (including specially manufactured goods) which are movable at the time of identification to the contract for sale other

than the money in which the price is to be paid, investment securities (Article 8) and things in action. "Goods" also includes the unborn young of animals and growing crops and other identified things attached to realty as described in the section on goods to be severed from realty (Section 2-107).

(2) Goods must be both existing and identified before any interest in them can pass. Goods which are not both existing and identified are "future" goods. A purported present sale of future goods or of any interest therein operates as a contract to sell.

(3) There may be a sale of a part interest in existing identified goods.

(4) An undivided share in an identified bulk of fungible goods is sufficiently identified to be sold although the quantity of the bulk is not determined. Any agreed proportion of such a bulk or any quantity thereof agreed upon by number, weight or other measure may to the extent of the seller's interest in the bulk be sold to the buyer who then becomes an owner in common.

(5) "Lot" means a parcel or a single article which is the subject matter of a separate sale or delivery, whether or not it is sufficient to perform the contract.

(6) "Commercial unit" means such a unit of goods as by commercial usage is a single whole for purposes of sale and division of which materially impairs its character or value on the market or in use. A commercial unit may be a single article (as a machine) or a set of articles (as a suite of furniture or an assortment of sizes) or a quantity (as a bale, gross, or carload) or any other unit treated in use or in the relevant market as a single whole.

§2-106. Definitions: "Contract"; "Agreement"; "Contract for Sale"; "Sale"; "Present Sale"; "Conforming" to Contract; "Termination"; "Cancellation"

(1) In this Article unless the context otherwise requires "contract" and "agreement" are limited to those relating to the present or future sale of goods. "Contract for sale" includes both a present sale of goods and a contract to sell goods at a future time. A "sale" consists in the passing of title from the seller to the buyer for a price (Section 2-401). A "present sale" means a sale which is accomplished by the making of the contract.

(2) Goods or conduct including any part of a performance are "conforming" or conform to the contract when they are in accordance with the obligations under the contract.

(3) "Termination" occurs when either party pursuant to a power created by agreement or law puts an end to the contract otherwise than for its breach. On "termination" all obligations which are still executory on both sides are discharged but any right based on prior breach or performance survives.

(4) "Cancellation" occurs when either party puts an end to the contract for breach by the other and its effect is the same as that of "termination" except that the cancelling party also retains any remedy for breach of the whole contract or any unperformed balance.

Part 2. Form, Formation and Readjustment of Contract

§2-201. Formal Requirements; Statute of Frauds

(1) Except as otherwise provided in this section a contract for the sale of goods for the price of $500 or more is not enforceable by way of action or defense unless there is some writing sufficient to indicate that a contract for sale has been made between the parties and signed by the party against whom enforcement is sought or by his authorized agent or broker. A writing is not insufficient because it omits or incorrectly states a term agreed upon but the contract is not enforceable under this paragraph beyond the quantity of goods shown in such writing.

(2) Between merchants if within a reasonable time a writing in confirmation of the contract and sufficient against the sender is received and the party receiving it has reason to know its contents, it satisfies the requirements of subsection (1) against such party unless written notice of objection to its contents is given within 10 days after it is received.

(3) A contract which does not satisfy the requirements of subsection (1) but which is valid in other respects is enforceable

(a) if the goods are to be specially manufactured for the buyer and are not suitable for sale to others in the ordinary course of the seller's business and the seller, before notice of repudiation is received and under circumstances which reasonably indicate that the goods are for the buyer, has made either a substantial beginning of their manufacture or commitments for their procurement; or

(b) if the party against whom enforcement is sought admits in his pleading, testimony or otherwise in court that a contract for sale was made, but the contract is not enforceable under this provision beyond the quantity of goods admitted; or

(c) with respect to goods for which payment has been made and accepted or which have been received and accepted (Sec. 2-606).

Official Comment

Prior Uniform Statutory Provision: Section 4, Uniform Sales Act (which was based on Section 17 of the Statute of 29 Charles II).

Changes: Completely rephrased; restricted to sale of goods. See also Sections 1-206, 8-319 and 9-203.

Purposes of Changes: The changed phraseology of this section is intended to make it clear that:

1. The required writing need not contain all the material terms of the contract and such material terms as are stated need not be precisely stated.

All that is required is that the writing afford a basis for believing that the offered oral evidence rests on a real transaction. It may be written in lead pencil on a scratch pad. It need not indicate which party is the buyer and which the seller. The only term which must appear is the quantity term which need not be accurately stated but recovery is limited to the amount stated. The price, time and place of payment or delivery, the general quality of the goods, or any particular warranties may all be omitted.

Special emphasis must be placed on the permissibility of omitting the price term in view of the insistence of some courts on the express inclusion of this term even where the parties have contracted on the basis of a published price list. In many valid contracts for sale the parties do not mention the price in express terms, the buyer being bound to pay and the seller to accept a reasonable price which the trier of the fact may well be trusted to determine. Again, frequently the price is not mentioned since the parties have based their agreement on a price list or catalogue known to both of them and this list serves as an efficient safeguard against perjury. Finally, "market" prices and valuations that are current in the vicinity constitute a similar check. Thus if the price is not stated in the memorandum it can normally be supplied without danger of fraud. Of course if the "price" consists of goods rather than money the quantity of goods must be stated.

Only three definite and invariable requirements as to the memorandum are made by this subsection. First, it must evidence a contract for the sale of goods; second, it must be "signed," a word which includes any authentication which identifies the party to be charged; and third, it must specify a quantity.

2. "Partial performance" as a substitute for the required memorandum can validate the contract only for the goods which have been accepted or for which payment has been made and accepted.

Receipt and acceptance either of goods or of the price constitutes an unambiguous overt admission by both parties that a contract actually exists. If the court can make a just apportionment, therefore, the agreed price of any goods actually delivered can be recovered without a writing or, if the price has been paid, the seller can be forced to deliver an apportionable part of the goods. The overt actions of the parties make admissible evidence of the other terms of the contract necessary to a just apportionment. This is true even though the actions of the parties are not in themselves inconsistent with a different transaction such as a consignment for resale or a mere loan of money.

Part performance by the buyer requires the delivery of something by him that is accepted by the seller as such performance. Thus, part payment may be made by money or check, accepted by the seller. If the agreed price consists of goods or services, then they must also have been delivered and accepted.

3. Between merchants, failure to answer a written confirmation of a contract within ten days of receipt is tantamount to a writing under

subsection (2) and is sufficient against both parties under subsection (1). The only effect, however, is to take away from the party who fails to answer the defense of the Statute of Frauds; the burden of persuading the trier of fact that a contract was in fact made orally prior to the written confirmation is unaffected. Compare the effect of a failure to reply under Section 2-207.

4. Failure to satisfy the requirements of this section does not render the contract void for all purposes, but merely prevents it from being judicially enforced in favor of a party to the contract. For example, a buyer who takes possession of goods as provided in an oral contract which the seller has not meanwhile repudiated, is not a trespasser. Nor would the Statute of Frauds provisions of this section be a defense to a third person who wrongfully induces a party to refuse to perform an oral contract, even though the injured party cannot maintain an action for damages against the party so refusing to perform.

5. The requirement of "signing" is discussed in the comment to Section 1-201.

6. It is not necessary that the writing be delivered to anybody. It need not be signed or authenticated by both parties but it is, of course, not sufficient against one who has not signed it. Prior to a dispute no one can determine which party's signing of the memorandum may be necessary but from the time of contracting each party should be aware that to him it is signing by the other which is important.

7. If the making of a contract is admitted in court, either in a written pleading, by stipulation or by oral statement before the court, no additional writing is necessary for protection against fraud. Under this section it is no longer possible to admit the contract in court and still treat the Statute as a defense. However, the contract is not thus conclusively established. The admission so made by a party is itself evidential against him of the truth of the facts so admitted and of nothing more; as against the other party, it is not evidential at all.

Cross References:
See Sections 1-201, 2-202, 2-207, 2-209 and 2-304.

Definitional Cross References:
"Action." Section 1-201.
"Between merchants." Section 2-104.
"Buyer." Section 2-103.
"Contract." Section 1-201.
"Contract for sale." Section 2-106.
"Goods." Section 2-105.
"Notice." Section 1-201.
"Party." Section 1-201.
"Reasonable time." Section 1-204.
"Sale." Section 2-106.
"Seller." Section 2-103.

§2-202. Final Written Expression: Parol or Extrinsic Evidence

Terms with respect to which the confirmatory memoranda of the parties agree or which are otherwise set forth in a writing intended by the parties as a final expression of their agreement with respect to such terms as are included therein may not be contradicted by evidence of any prior agreement or of a contemporaneous oral agreement but may be explained or supplemented

(a) by course of dealing or usage of trade (Section 1-205) or by course of performance (Section 2-208); and

(b) by evidence of consistent additional terms unless the court finds the writing to have been intended also as a complete and exclusive statement of the terms of the agreement.

Official Comment

Prior Uniform Statutory Provision: None.

Purposes:

1. This section definitely rejects:

(a) Any assumption that because a writing has been worked out which is final on some matters, it is to be taken as including all the matters agreed upon;

(b) The premise that the language used has the meaning attributable to such language by rules of construction existing in the law rather than the meaning which arises out of the commercial context in which it was used; and

(c) The requirement that a condition precedent to the admissibility of the type of evidence specified in paragraph (a) is an original determination by the court that the language used is ambiguous.

2. Paragraph (a) makes admissible evidence of course of dealing, usage of trade and course of performance to explain or supplement the terms of any writing stating the agreement of the parties in order that the true understanding of the parties as to the agreement may be reached. Such writings are to be read on the assumption that the course of prior dealings between the parties and the usages of trade were taken for granted when the document was phrased. Unless carefully negated they have become an element of the meaning of the words used. Similarly, the course of actual performance by the parties is considered the best indication of what they intended the writing to mean.

3. Under paragraph (b) consistent additional terms, not reduced to writing, may be proved unless the court finds that the writing was intended by both parties as a complete and exclusive statement of all the terms. If the additional terms are such that, if agreed upon, they would certainly have been included in the document in the view of the court, then evidence of their alleged making must be kept from the trier of fact.

Cross References:
Point 3: Sections 1-205, 2-207, 2-302 and 2-316.

Definitional Cross References:
"Agreed" and "agreement." Section 1-201.
"Course of dealing." Section 1-205.
"Parties." Section 1-201.
"Term." Section 1-201.
"Usage of trade." Section 1-205.
"Written" and "writing." Section 1-201.

§2-203. Seals Inoperative

The affixing of a seal to a writing evidencing a contract for sale or an offer to buy or sell goods does not constitute the writing a sealed instrument and the law with respect to sealed instruments does not apply to such a contract or offer.

§2-204. Formation in General

(1) A contract for sale of goods may be made in any manner sufficient to show agreement, including conduct by both parties which recognizes the existence of such a contract.

(2) An agreement sufficient to constitute a contract for sale may be found even though the moment of its making is undetermined.

(3) Even though one or more terms are left open a contract for sale does not fail for indefiniteness if the parties have intended to make a contract and there is a reasonably certain basis for giving an appropriate remedy.

Official Comment

Prior Uniform Statutory Provision: Sections 1 and 3, Uniform Sales Act.

Changes: Completely rewritten by this and other sections of this Article.

Purposes of Changes:
Subsection (1) continues without change the basic policy of recognizing any manner of expression of agreement, oral, written or otherwise. The legal effect of such an agreement is, of course, qualified by other provisions of this Article.

Under subsection (1) appropriate conduct by the parties may be sufficient to establish an agreement. Subsection (2) is directed primarily to the situation where the interchanged correspondence does not disclose the exact point at which the deal was closed, but the actions of the parties indicate that a binding obligation has been undertaken.

Subsection (3) states the principle as to "open terms" underlying later sections of the Article. If the parties intend to enter into a binding agreement, this subsection recognizes that agreement as valid in law, despite missing terms, if there is any reasonably certain basis for granting a remedy. The test is not certainty as to what the parties were to do nor as to the exact amount of damages due the plaintiff. Nor is the fact that one or more terms are left to be agreed upon enough of itself to defeat an otherwise adequate agreement. Rather, commercial standards on the point of "indefiniteness" are intended to be applied, this Act making provision elsewhere for missing terms needed for performance, open price, remedies and the like.

The more terms the parties leave open, the less likely it is that they have intended to conclude a binding agreement, but their actions may be frequently conclusive on the matter despite the omissions.

Cross References:
Subsection (1): Sections 1-103, 2-201 and 2-302.
Subsection (2): Sections 2-205 through 2-209.
Subsection (3): See Part 3.

Definitional Cross References:
"Agreement." Section 1-201.
"Contract." Section 1-201.
"Contract for sale." Section 2-106.
"Goods." Section 2-105.
"Party." Section 1-201.
"Remedy." Section 1-201.
"Term." Section 1-201.

§2-205. Firm Offers

An offer by a merchant to buy or sell goods in a signed writing which by its terms gives assurance that it will be held open is not revocable, for lack of consideration, during the time stated or if no time is stated for a reasonable time, but in no event may such period of irrevocability exceed three months; but any such term of assurance on a form supplied by the offeree must be separately signed by the offeror.

Official Comment

Prior Uniform Statutory Provision: Sections 1 and 3, Uniform Sales Act.

Changes: Completely rewritten by this and other sections of this Article.

Purposes of Changes:
1. This section is intended to modify the former rule which required that "firm offers" be sustained by consideration in order to bind, and to

require instead that they must merely be characterized as such and expressed in signed writings.

2. The primary purpose of this section is to give effect to the deliberate intention of a merchant to make a current firm offer binding. The deliberation is shown in the case of an individualized document by the merchant's signature to the offer, and in the case of an offer included on a form supplied by the other party to the transaction by the separate signing of the particular clause which contains the offer. "Signed" here also includes authentication but the reasonableness of the authentication herein allowed must be determined in the light of the purpose of the section. The circumstances surrounding the signing may justify something less than a formal signature or initialing but typically the kind of authentication involved here would consist of a minimum of initialing of the clause involved. A handwritten memorandum on the writer's letterhead purporting in its terms to "confirm" a firm offer already made would be enough to satisfy this section, although not subscribed, since under the circumstances it could not be considered a memorandum of mere negotiation and it would adequately show its own authenticity. Similarly, an authorized telegram will suffice, and this is true even though the original draft contained only a typewritten signature. However, despite settled courses of dealing or usages of the trade whereby firm offers are made by oral communication and relied upon without more evidence, such offers remain revocable under this Article since authentication by a writing is the essence of this section.

3. This section is intended to apply to current "firm" offers and not to long term options, and an outside time limit of three months during which such offers remain irrevocable has been set. The three month period during which firm offers remain irrevocable under this section need not be stated by days or by date. If the offer states that it is "guaranteed" or "firm" until the happening of a contingency which will occur within the three month period, it will remain irrevocable until that event. A promise made for a longer period will operate under this section to bind the offeror only for the first three months of the period but may of course be renewed. If supported by consideration it may continue for as long as the parties specify. This section deals only with the offer which is not supported by consideration.

4. Protection is afforded against the inadvertent signing of a firm offer when contained in a form prepared by the offeree by requiring that such a clause be separately authenticated. If the offer clause is called to the offeror's attention and he separately authenticates it, he will be bound; Section 2-302 may operate, however, to prevent an unconscionable result which otherwise would flow from other terms appearing in the form.

5. Safeguards are provided to offer relief in the case of material mistake by virtue of the requirement of good faith and the general law of mistake.

Cross References:
Point 1: Section 1-102.

Point 2: Section 1-102.
Point 3: Section 2-201.
Point 5: Section 2-302.

Definitional Cross References:
"Goods." Section 2-105.
"Merchant." Section 2-104.
"Signed." Section 1-201.
"Writing." Section 1-201.

§2-206. Offer and Acceptance in Formation of Contract

(1) Unless otherwise unambiguously indicated by the language or circumstances

(a) an offer to make a contract shall be construed as inviting acceptance in any manner and by any medium reasonable in the circumstances;

(b) an order or other offer to buy goods for prompt or current shipment shall be construed as inviting acceptance either by a prompt promise to ship or by the prompt or current shipment of conforming or non-conforming goods, but such a shipment of non-conforming goods does not constitute an acceptance if the seller seasonably notifies the buyer that the shipment is offered only as an accommodation to the buyer.

(2) Where the beginning of a requested performance is a reasonable mode of acceptance an offeror who is not notified of acceptance within a reasonable time may treat the offer as having lapsed before acceptance.

§2-207. Additional Terms in Acceptance or Confirmation

(1) A definite and seasonable expression of acceptance or a written confirmation which is sent within a reasonable time operates as an acceptance even though it states terms additional to or different from those offered or agreed upon, unless acceptance is expressly made conditional on assent to the additional or different terms.

(2) The additional terms are to be construed as proposals for addition to the contract. Between merchants such terms become part of the contract unless:

(a) the offer expressly limits acceptance to the terms of the offer;

(b) they materially alter it; or

(c) notification of objection to them has already been given or is given within a reasonable time after notice of them is received.

(3) Conduct by both parties which recognizes the existence of a contract is sufficient to establish a contract for sale although the writings of the parties do not otherwise establish a contract. In such case the terms of the particular

contract consist of those terms on which the writings of the parties agree, together with any supplementary terms incorporated under any other provisions of this Act.

Official Comment

Prior Uniform Statutory Provision: Sections 1 and 3, Uniform Sales Act.

Changes: Completely rewritten by this and other sections of this Article.

Purposes of Changes:
1. This section is intended to deal with two typical situations. The one is the written confirmation, where an agreement has been reached either orally or by informal correspondence between the parties and is followed by one or both of the parties sending formal memoranda embodying the terms so far as agreed upon and adding terms not discussed. The other situation is offer and acceptance, in which a wire or letter expressed and intended as an acceptance or the closing of an agreement adds further minor suggestions or proposals such as "ship by Tuesday," "rush," "ship draft against bill of lading inspection allowed," or the like. A frequent example of the second situation is the exchange of printed purchase order and acceptance (sometimes called "acknowledgment") forms. Because the forms are oriented to the thinking of the respective drafting parties, the terms contained in them often do not correspond. Often the seller's form contains terms different from or additional to those set forth in the buyer's form. Nevertheless, the parties proceed with the transaction.

2. Under this Article a proposed deal which in commercial understanding has in fact been closed is recognized as a contract. Therefore, any additional matter contained in the confirmation or in the acceptance falls within subsection (2) and must be regarded as a proposal for an added term unless the acceptance is made conditional on the acceptance of the additional or different terms.

3. Whether or not additional or different terms will become part of the agreement depends upon the provisions of subsection (2). If they are such as materially to alter the original bargain, they will not be included unless expressly agreed to by the other party. If, however, they are terms which would not so change the bargain they will be incorporated unless notice of objection to them has already been given or is given within a reasonable time.

4. Examples of typical clauses which would normally "materially alter" the contract and so result in surprise or hardship if incorporated without express awareness by the other party are: a clause negating such standard warranties as that of merchantability or fitness for a particular purpose in circumstances in which either warranty normally attaches; a clause requiring a guaranty of 90% or 100% deliveries in a case such as a contract by cannery, where the usage of the trade allows greater quantity leeways; a clause reserving to the seller the power to cancel upon the buyer's failure to meet

any invoice when due; a clause requiring that complaints be made in a time materially shorter than customary or reasonable.

5. Examples of clauses which involve no element of unreasonable surprise and which therefore are to be incorporated in the contract unless notice of objection is seasonably given are: a clause setting forth and perhaps enlarging slightly upon the seller's exemption due to supervening causes beyond his control, similar to those covered by the provision of this Article on merchant's excuse by failure of presupposed conditions or a clause fixing in advance any reasonable formula of proration under such circumstances; a clause fixing a reasonable time for complaints within customary limits, or in the case of a purchase for sub-sale, providing for inspection by the sub-purchaser; a clause providing for interest on overdue invoices or fixing the seller's standard credit terms where they are within the range of trade practice and do not limit any credit bargained for; a clause limiting the right of rejection for defects which fall within the customary trade tolerances for acceptance "with adjustment" or otherwise limiting remedy in a reasonable manner (see Sections 2-718 and 2-719).

6. If no answer is received within a reasonable time after additional terms are proposed, it is both fair and commercially sound to assume that their inclusion has been assented to. Where clauses on confirming forms sent by both parties conflict each party must be assumed to object to a clause of the other conflicting with one on the confirmation sent by himself. As a result the requirement that there be notice of objection which is found in subsection (2) is satisfied and the conflicting terms do not become a part of the contract. The contract then consists of the terms originally expressly agreed to, terms on which the confirmations agree, and terms supplied by this Act, including subsection (2). The written confirmation is also subject to Section 2-201. Under that section a failure to respond permits enforcement of a prior oral agreement; under this section a failure to respond permits additional terms to become part of the agreement.

7. In many cases, as where goods are shipped, accepted and paid for before any dispute arises, there is no question whether a contract has been made. In such cases, where the writings of the parties do not establish a contract, it is not necessary to determine which act or document constituted the offer and which the acceptance. See Section 2-204. The only question is what terms are included in the contract, and subsection (3) furnishes the governing rule.

Cross References:
   See generally Section 2-302.
   Point 5: Sections 2-513, 2-602, 2-607, 2-609, 2-612, 2-614, 2-615, 2-616, 2-718 and 2-719.
   Point 6: Sections 1-102 and 2-104.

Definitional Cross References:
   "Between merchants." Section 2-104.
   "Contract." Section 1-201.

"Notification." Section 1-201.
"Reasonable time." Section 1-204.
"Seasonably." Section 1-204.
"Send." Section 1-201.
"Term." Section 1-201.
"Written." Section 1-201.

§2-208. Course of Performance or Practical Construction

(1) Where the contract for sale involves repeated occasions for performance by either party with knowledge of the nature of the performance and opportunity for objection to it by the other, any course of performance accepted or acquiesced in without objection shall be relevant to determine the meaning of the agreement.

(2) The express terms of the agreement and any such course of performance, as well as any course of dealing and usage of trade, shall be construed whenever reasonable as consistent with each other; but when such construction is unreasonable, express terms shall control course of performance and course of performance shall control both course of dealing and usage of trade (Section 1-205).

(3) Subject to the provisions of the next section on modification and waiver, such course of performance shall be relevant to show a waiver or modification of any term inconsistent with such course of performance.

Official Comment

Prior Uniform Statutory Provision: No such general provision but concept of this section recognized by terms such as "course of dealing," "the circumstances of the case," "the conduct of the parties," etc., in Uniform Sales Act.

Purposes:

1. The parties themselves know best what they have meant by their words of agreement and their action under that agreement is the best indication of what that meaning was. This section thus rounds out the set of factors which determines the meaning of the "agreement" and therefore also of the "unless otherwise agreed" qualification to various provisions of this Article.

2. Under this section a course of performance is always relevant to determine the meaning of the agreement. Express mention of course of performance elsewhere in this Article carries no contrary implication when there is a failure to refer to it in other sections.

3. Where it is difficult to determine whether a particular act merely sheds light on the meaning of the agreement or represents a waiver of a term of the agreement, the preference is in favor of "waiver" whenever such

construction, plus the application of the provisions on the reinstatement of rights waived (see Section 2-209), is needed to preserve the flexible character of commercial contracts and to prevent surprise or other hardship.

4. A single occasion of conduct does not fall within the language of this section but other sections such as the ones on silence after acceptance and failure to specify particular defects can affect the parties' rights on a single occasion (see Sections 2-605 and 2-607).

Cross References:
　　Point 1: Section 1-201.
　　Point 2: Section 2-202.
　　Point 3: Sections 2-209, 2-601 and 2-607.
　　Point 4: Sections 2-605 and 2-607.

§2-209. Modification, Rescission and Waiver

(1) An agreement modifying a contract within this Article needs no consideration to be binding.

(2) A signed agreement which excludes modification or rescission except by a signed writing cannot be otherwise modified or rescinded, but except as between merchants such a requirement on a form supplied by the merchant must be separately signed by the other party.

(3) The requirements of the statute of frauds section of this Article (Section 2-201) must be satisfied if the contract as modified is within its provisions.

(4) Although an attempt at modification or rescission does not satisfy the requirements of subsection (2) or (3) it can operate as a waver.

(5) A party who has made a waiver affecting an executory portion of the contract may retract the waiver by reasonable notification received by the other party that strict performance will be required of any term waived, unless the retraction would be unjust in view of a material change of position in reliance on the waiver.

Official Comment

Prior Uniform Statutory Provision: Subsection (1) — Compare Section 1, Uniform Written Obligations Act; Subsections (2) to (5) — none.

Purposes of Changes and New Matter:
1. This section seeks to protect and make effective all necessary and desirable modifications of sales contracts without regard to the technicalities which at present hamper such adjustments.

2. Subsection (1) provides that an agreement modifying a sales contract needs no consideration to be binding.

However, modifications made thereunder must meet the test of good faith imposed by this Act. The effective use of bad faith to escape performance on the original contract terms is barred, and the extortion of a "modification" without legitimate commercial reason is ineffective as a violation of the duty of good faith. Nor can a mere technical consideration support a modification made in bad faith.

The test of "good faith" between merchants or as against merchants includes "observance of reasonable commercial standards of fair dealing in the trade" (Section 2-103), and may in some situations require an objectively demonstrable reason for seeking a modification. But such matters as a market shift which makes performance come to involve a loss may provide such a reason even though there is no such unforeseen difficulty as would make out a legal excuse from performance under Sections 2-615 and 2-616.

3. Subsections (2) and (3) are intended to protect against false allegations of oral modifications. "Modification or rescission" includes abandonment or other change by mutual consent, contrary to the decision in Green v. Doniger, 300 N.Y. 238, 90 N.E.2d 56 (1949); it does not include unilateral "termination" or "cancellation" as defined in Section 2-106.

The Statute of Frauds provisions of this Article are expressly applied to modifications by subsection (3). Under those provisions the "delivery and acceptance" test is limited to the goods which have been accepted, that is, to the past. "Modification" for the future cannot therefore be conjured up by oral testimony if the price involved is $500.00 or more since such modification must be shown at least by an authenticated memo. And since a memo is limited in its effect to the quantity of goods set forth in it there is safeguard against oral evidence.

Subsection (2) permits the parties in effect to make their own Statute of Frauds as regards any future modification of the contract by giving effect to a clause in a signed agreement which expressly requires any modification to be by signed writing. But note that if a consumer is to be held to such a clause on a form supplied by a merchant it must be separately signed.

4. Subsection (4) is intended, despite the provisions of subsections (2) and (3), to prevent contractual provisions excluding modification except by a signed writing from limiting in other respects the legal effect of the parties' actual later conduct. The effect of such conduct as a waiver is further regulated in subsection (5).

Cross References:
Point 1: Section 1-203.
Point 2: Sections 1-201, 1-203, 2-615 and 2-616.
Point 3: Sections 2-106, 2-201 and 2-202.
Point 4: Sections 2-202 and 2-208.

Definitional Cross References:
"Agreement." Section 1-201.
"Between merchants." Section 2-104.
"Contract." Section 1-201.

"Notification." Section 1-201.
"Signed." Section 1-201.
"Term." Section 1-201.
"Writing." Section 1-201.

§2-210.   Delegation of Performance; Assignment of Rights

(1) A party may perform his duty through a delegate unless otherwise agreed or unless the other party has a substantial interest in having his original promisor perform or control the acts required by the contract. No delegation of performance relieves the party delegating of any duty to perform or any liability for breach.

(2) Unless otherwise agreed all rights of either seller or buyer can be assigned except where the assignment would materially change the duty of the other party, or increase materially the burden or risk imposed on him by his contract, or impair materially his chance of obtaining return performance. A right to damages for breach of the whole contract or a right arising out of the assignor's due performance of his entire obligation can be assigned despite agreement otherwise.

(3) Unless the circumstances indicate the contrary a prohibition of assignment of "the contract" is to be construed as barring only the delegation to the assignee of the assignor's performance.

(4) An assignment of "the contract" or of "all my rights under the contract" or an assignment in similar general terms is an assignment of rights and unless the language or the circumstances (as in an assignment for security) indicate the contrary, it is a delegation of performance of the duties of the assignor and its acceptance by the assignee constitutes a promise by him to perform those duties. This promise is enforceable by either the assignor or the other party to the original contract.

(5) The other party may treat any assignment which delegates performance as creating reasonable grounds for insecurity and may without prejudice to his rights against the assignor demand assurances from the assignee (Section 2-609).

Official Comment

Prior Uniform Statutory Provision: None.

Purposes:

1. Generally, this section recognizes both delegation of performance and assignability as normal and permissible incidents of a contract for the sale of goods.

2. Delegation of performance, either in conjunction with an assignment or otherwise, is provided for by subsection (1) where no substantial reason

can be shown as to why the delegated performance will not be as satisfactory as personal performance.

3. Under subsection (2) rights which are no longer executory such as a right to damages for breach or a right to payment of an "account" as defined in the Article on Secured Transactions (Article 9) may be assigned although the agreement prohibits assignment. In such cases no question of delegation of any performance is involved. The assignment of a "contract right" as defined in the Article on Secured Transactions (Article 9) is not covered by this subsection.

4. The nature of the contract or the circumstances of the case, however, may bar assignment of the contract even where delegation of performance is not involved. This Article and this section are intended to clarify this problem, particularly in cases dealing with output requirement and exclusive dealing contracts. In the first place the section on requirements and exclusive dealing removes from the construction of the original contract most of the "personal discretion" element by substituting the reasonably objective standard of good faith operation of the plant or business to be supplied. Secondly, the section on insecurity and assurances, which is specifically referred to in subsection (5) of this section, frees the other party from the doubts and uncertainty which may afflict him under an assignment of the character in question by permitting him to demand adequate assurance of due performance without which he may suspend his own performance. Subsection (5) is not in any way intended to limit the effect of the section on insecurity and assurances and the word "performance" includes the giving of orders under a requirements contract. Of course, in any case where a material personal discretion is sought to be transferred, effective assignment is barred by subsection (2).

5. Subsection (4) lays down a general rule of construction distinguishing between a normal commercial assignment, which substitutes the assignee for the assignor both as to rights and duties, and a financing assignment in which only the assignor's rights are transferred.

This Article takes no position on the possibility of extending some recognition or power to the original parties to work out normal commercial readjustments of the contract in the case of financing assignments even after the original obligor has been notified of the assignment. This question is dealt with in the Article on Secured Transactions (Article 9).

6. Subsection (5) recognizes that the non-assigning original party has a stake in the reliability of the person with whom he has closed the original contract, and is, therefore, entitled to due assurance that any delegated performance will be properly forthcoming.

7. This section is not intended as a complete statement of the law of delegation and assignment but is limited to clarifying a few points doubtful under the case law. Particularly, neither this section nor this Article touches directly on such questions as the need or effect of notice of the assignment, the rights of successive assignees, or any question of the form of an assignment, either as between the parties or as against any third parties. Some of these questions are dealt with in Article 9.

Cross References:
Point 3: Articles 5 and 9.
Point 4: Sections 2-306 and 2-609.
Point 5: Article 9, Sections 9-317 and 9-318.
Point 7: Article 9.

Definitional Cross References:
"Agreement." Section 1-201.
"Buyer." Section 2-103.
"Contract." Section 1-201.
"Party." Section 1-201.
"Rights." Section 1-201.
"Seller." Section 2-103.
"Term." Section 1-201.

Part 3.   General Obligation and Construction of Contract

§2-301.   General Obligations of Parties

The obligation of the seller is to transfer and deliver and that of the buyer is to accept and pay in accordance with the contract.

§2-302.   Unconscionable Contract or Clause

(1) If the court as a matter of law finds the contract or any clause of the contract to have been unconscionable at the time it was made the court may refuse to enforce the contract, or it may enforce the remainder of the contract without the unconscionable cluase, or it may so limit the application of any unconscionable clause as to avoid any unconscionable result.

(2) When it is claimed or appears to the court that the contract or any clause thereof may be unconscionable the parties shall be afforded a reasonable opportunity to present evidence as to its commercial setting, purpose and effect to aid the court in making the determination.

Official Comment

Prior Uniform Statutory Provision: None.

Purposes:
1. This section is intended to make it possible for the courts to police explicitly against the contracts or clauses which they find to be unconscionable. In the past such policing has been accomplished by adverse

construction of language, by manipulation of the rules of offer and acceptance or by determinations that the clause is contrary to public policy or to the dominant purpose of the contract. This section is intended to allow the court to pass directly on the unconscionability of the contract or particular clause therein and to make a conclusion of law as to its unconscionability. The basic test is whether, in the light of the general commercial background and the commercial needs of the particular trade or case, the clauses involved are so one-sided as to be unconscionable under the circumstances existing at the time of the making of the contract. Subsection (2) makes it clear that it is proper for the court to hear evidence upon these questions. The principle is one of the prevention of oppression and unfair surprise (Cf. Campbell Soup Co. v. Wentz, 172 F.2d 80, 3d Cir. 1948) and not of disturbance of allocation of risks because of superior bargaining power. The underlying basis of this section is illustrated by the results in cases such as the following:

Kansas City Wholesale Grocery Co. v. Weber Packing Corporation, 93 Utah 414, 73 P.2d 1272 (1937), where a clause limiting time for complaints was held inapplicable to latent defects in a shipment of catsup which could be discovered only by microscopic analysis; Hardy v. General Motors Acceptance Corporation, 38 Ga. App. 463, 144 S.E. 327 (1928), holding that a disclaimer of warranty clause applied only to express warranties, thus letting in a fair implied warranty; Andrews Bros. v. Singer & Co. (1934 CA) 1 K.B. 17, holding that where a car with substantial mileage was delivered instead of a "new" car, a disclaimer of warranties, including those "implied," left unaffected an "express obligation" on the description, even though the Sale of Goods Act called such an implied warranty; New Prague Flouring Mill Co. v. G. A. Spears, 194 Iowa 417, 189 N.W. 815 (1922), holding that a clause permitting the seller, upon the buyer's failure to supply shipping instructions, to cancel, ship, or allow delivery date to be indefinitely postponed 30 days at a time by the inaction, does not indefinitely postpone the date of measuring damages for the buyer's breach, to the seller's advantage; and Kansas Flour Mills Co. v. Dirks, 100 Kan. 376, 164 P. 273 (1917), where under a similar clause in a rising market the court permitted the buyer to measure his damages for non-delivery at the end of only one 30 day postponement; Green v. Arcos, Ltd. (1931 CA) 47 T.L.R. 336, where a blanket clause prohibiting rejection of shipments by the buyer was restricted to apply to shipments where discrepancies represented merely mercantile variations; Meyer v. Packard Cleveland Motor Co., 106 Ohio St. 328, 140 N.E. 118 (1922), in which the court held that a "waiver" of all agreements not specified did not preclude implied warranty of fitness of a rebuilt dump truck for ordinary use as a dump truck; Austin Co. v. J. H. Tillman Co., 104 Or. 541, 209 P. 131 (1922), where a clause limiting the buyer's remedy to return was held to be applicable only if the seller had delivered a machine needed for a construction job which reasonably met the contract description; Bekkevold v. Potts, 173 Minn. 87, 216 N.W. 790, 59 A.L.R. 1164 (1927), refusing to allow warranty of fitness for purpose imposed by law to be negated by clause excluding all warranties "made" by the seller; Robert A. Munroe & Co. v. Meyer (1930) 2 K.B. 312, holding that the warranty of description overrides a clause reading "with all faults and defects" where adulterated meat not up to the contract description was delivered.

2. Under this section the court, in its discretion, may refuse to enforce the contract as a whole if it is permeated by the unconscionability, or it may strike any single clause or group of clauses which are so tainted or which are contrary to the essential purpose of the agreement, or it may simply limit unconscionable clauses so as to avoid unconscionable results.

3. The present section is addressed to the court, and the decision is to be made by it. The commercial evidence referred to in subsection (2) is for the court's consideration, not the jury's. Only the agreement which results from the court's action on these matters is to be submitted to the general triers of the facts.

Definitional Cross Reference:
"Contract." Section 1-201.

§2-305. Open Price Term

(1) The parties if they so intend can conclude a contract for sale even though the price is not settled. In such a case the price is a reasonable price at the time for delivery if
    (a) nothing is said as to price; or
    (b) the price is left to be agreed by the parties and they fail to agree; or
    (c) the price is to be fixed in terms of some agreed market or other standard as set or recorded by a third person or agency and it is not so set or recorded.

(2) A price to be fixed by the seller or by the buyer means a price for him to fix in good faith.

(3) When a price left to be fixed otherwise than by agreement of the parties fails to be fixed through fault of one party the other may at his option treat the contract as cancelled or himself fix a reasonable price.

(4) Where, however, the parties intend not to be bound unless the price be fixed or agreed and it is not fixed or agreed there is no contract. In such a case the buyer must return any goods already received or if unable so to do must pay their reasonable value at the time of delivery and the seller must return any portion of the price paid on account.

Official Comment

Prior Uniform Statutory Provision: Sections 9 and 10, Uniform Sales Act.

Changes: Completely rewritten.

Purposes of Changes:

1. This section applies when the price term is left open on the making of an agreement which is nevertheless intended by the parties to be a binding agreement. This Article rejects in these instances the formula that "an agreement to agree is unenforceable" if the case falls within subsection (1) of this section, and rejects also defeating such agreements on the ground of "indefiniteness." Instead this Article recognizes the dominant intention of the parties to have the deal continue to be binding upon both. As to future performance, since this Article recognizes remedies such as cover (Section 2-712), resale (Section 2-706) and specific performance (Section 2-716) which go beyond any mere arithmetic as between contract price and market price, there is usually a "reasonably certain basis for granting an appropriate remedy for breach" so that the contract need not fail for indefiniteness.

2. Under some circumstances the postponement of agreement on price will mean that no deal has really been concluded, and this is made express in the preamble of subsection (1) ("The parties *if they so intend*") and in subsection (4). Whether or not this is so is, in most cases, a question to be determined by the trier of fact.

3. Subsection (2), dealing with the situation where the price is to be fixed by one party rejects the uncommercial idea that an agreement that the seller may fix the price means that he may fix any price he may wish by the express qualification that the price so fixed must be fixed in good faith. Good faith includes observance of reasonable commercial standards of fair dealing in the trade if the party is a merchant. (Section 2-103.) But in the normal case a "posted price" or a future seller's or buyer's "given price," "price in effect," "market price," or the like satisfies the good faith requirement.

4. The section recognizes that there may be cases in which a particular person's judgment is not chosen merely as a barometer or index of a fair price but is an essential condition to the parties' intent to make any contract at all. For example, the case where a known and trusted expert is to "value" a particular painting for which there is no market standard differs sharply from the situation where a named expert is to determine the grade of cotton, and the difference would support a finding that in the one the parties did not intend to make a binding agreement if that expert were unavailable whereas in the other they did so intend. Other circumstances would of course affect the validity of such a finding.

5. Under subsection (3), wrongful interference by one party with any agreed machinery for price fixing in the contract may be treated by the other party as a repudiation justifying cancellation, or merely as a failure to take cooperative action thus shifting to the aggrieved party the reasonable leeway in fixing the price.

6. Throughout the entire section, the purpose is to give effect to the agreement which has been made. That effect, however, is always conditioned by the requirement of good faith action which is made an inherent part of all contracts within this Act. (Section 1-203.)

Cross References:
Point 1: Sections 2-204(3) 2-706, 2-712 and 2-716.
Point 3: Section 2-103.
Point 5: Sections 2-311 and 2-610.
Point 6: Section 1-203.

Definitional Cross References:
"Agreement." Section 1-201.
"Burden of establishing." Section 1-201.
"Buyer." Section 2-103.
"Cancellation." Section 2-106
"Contract." Section 1-201.
"Contract for sale." Section 2-106.
"Fault." Section 1-201.
"Goods." Section 2-105.
"Party." Section 1-201.
"Receipt of goods." Section 2-103.
"Seller." Section 2-103.
"Term." Section 1-201.

§2-306. Output, Requirements and Exclusive Dealings

(1) A term which measures the quantity by the output of the seller or the requirements of the buyer means such actual output or requirements as may occur in good faith, except that no quantity unreasonably disproportionate to any stated estimate or in the absence of a stated estimate to any normal or otherwise comparable prior output or requirements may be tendered or demanded.

(2) A lawful agreement by either the seller or the buyer for exclusive dealing in the kind of goods concerned imposes unless otherwise agreed an obligation by the seller to use best efforts to supply the goods and by the buyer to use best efforts to promote their sale.

Official Comment

Prior Uniform Statutory Provision: None.

Purposes:
1. Subsection (1) of this section, in regard to output and requirements, applies to this specific problem the general approach of this Act which requires the reading of commercial background and intent into the language of any agreement and demands good faith in the performance of that agreement. It applies to such contracts of nonproducing establishments such as dealers or distributors as well as to manufacturing concerns.

2. Under this Article, a contract for output or requirements is not too indefinite since it is held to mean the actual good faith output or requirements of the particular party. Nor does such a contract lack mutuality of obligation since, under this section, the party who will determine quantity is required to operate his plant or conduct his business in good faith and according to commercial standards of fair dealing in the trade so that his output or requirements will approximate a reasonably foreseeable figure. Reasonable elasticity in the requirements is expressly envisaged by this section and good faith variations from prior requirements are permitted even when the variation may be such as to result in discontinuance. A shut-down by a requirements buyer for lack of orders might be permissible when a shut-down merely to curtail losses would not. The essential test is whether the party is acting in good faith. Similarly, a sudden expansion of the plant by which requirements are to be measured would not be included within the scope of the contract as made but normal expansion undertaken in good faith would be within the scope of this section. One of the factors in an expansion situation would be whether the market price had risen greatly in a case in which the requirements contract contained a fixed price. Reasonable variation of an extreme sort is exemplified in Southwest Natural Gas Co. v. Oklahoma Portland Cement Co., 102 F.2d 630 (C.C.A. 10, 1939). This Article takes no position as to whether a requirements contract is a provable claim in bankruptcy.

3. If an estimate of output or requirements is included in the agreement, no quantity unreasonably disproportionate to it may be tendered or demanded. Any minimum or maximum set by the agreement shows a clear limit on the intended elasticity. In similar fashion, the agreed estimate is to be regarded as a center around which the parties intend the variation to occur.

4. When an enterprise is sold, the question may arise whether the buyer is bound by an existing output or requirements contract. That question is outside the scope of this Article, and is to be determined on other principles of law. Assuming that the contract continues, the output or requirements in the hands of the new owner continue to be measured by the actual good faith output or requirements under the normal operation of the enterprise prior to sale. The sale itself is not grounds for sudden expansion or decrease.

5. Subsection (2), on exclusive dealing, makes explicit the commercial rule embodied in this Act under which the parties to such contracts are held to have impliedly, even when not expressly, bound themselves to use reasonable diligence as well as good faith in their performance of the contract. Under such contracts the exclusive agent is required, although no express commitment has been made, to use reasonable effort and due diligence in the expansion of the market or the promotion of the product, as the case may be. The principal is expected under such a contract to refrain from supplying any other dealer or agent within the exclusive territory. An exclusive dealing agreement brings into play all of the good faith aspects of the output and requirement problems of subsection (1). It

also raises questions of insecurity and right to adequate assurance under this Article.

Cross References:
    Point 4: Section 2-210.
    Point 5: Sections 1-203 and 2-609.

Definitional Cross References:
    "Agreement." Section 1-201.
    "Buyer." Section 2-103.
    "Contract for sale." Section 2-106.
    "Good faith." Section 1-201.
    "Goods." Section 2-105.
    "Party." Section 1-201.
    "Term." Section 1-203.
    "Seller." Section 2-101.

§2-307. Delivery in Single Lot or Several Lots

Unless otherwise agreed all goods called for by a contract for sale must be tendered in a single delivery and payment is due only on such tender but where the circumstances give either party the right to make or demand delivery in lots the price if it can be apportioned may be demanded for each lot.

§2-308. Absence of Specified Place for Delivery

Unless otherwise agreed
    (a) the place for delivery of goods is the seller's place of business or if he has none his residence; but
    (b) in a contract for sale of identified goods which to the knowledge of the parties at the time of contracting are in some other place, that place is the place for their delivery; and
    (c) documents of title may be delivered through customary banking channels.

§2-309. Absence of Specific Time Provisions; Notice of Termination

(1) The time for shipment or delivery or any other action under a contract if not provided in this Article or agreed upon shall be a reasonable time.

(2) Where the contract provides for successive performances but is indefinite in duration it is valid for a reasonable time but unless otherwise agreed may be terminated at any time by either party.

(3) Termination of a contract by one party except on the happening of an agreed event requires that reasonable notification be received by the other party and an agreement dispensing with notification is invalid if its operation would be unconscionable.

Official Comment

Prior Uniform Statutory Provision: Subsection (1) — see Sections 43(2), 45(2), 47(1) and 48, Uniform Sales Act, for policy continued under this Article; Section (2) — none; Subsection (3) — none.

Changes: Completely different in scope.

Purposes of Changes and New Matter:

1. Subsection (1) requires that all actions taken under a sales contract must be taken within a reasonable time where no time has been agreed upon. The reasonable time under this provision turns on the criteria as to "reasonable time" and on good faith and commercial standards set forth in Sections 1-203, 1-204 and 2-103. It thus depends upon what constitutes acceptable commercial conduct in view of the nature, purpose and circumstances of the action to be taken. Agreement as to a definite time, however, may be found in a term implied from the contractual circumstances, usage of trade or course of dealing or performance as well as in an express term. Such cases fall outside of this subsection since in them the time for action is "agreed" by usage.

2. The time for payment, where not agreed upon, is related to the time for delivery; the particular problems which arise in connection with determining the appropriate time of payment and the time for any inspection before payment which is both allowed by law and demanded by the buyer are covered in Section 2-513.

3. The facts in regard to shipment and delivery differ so widely as to make detailed provision for them in the text of this Article impracticable. The applicable principles, however, make it clear that surprise is to be avoided, good faith judgment is to be protected, and notice or negotiation to reduce the uncertainty to certainty is to be favored.

4. When the time for delivery is left open, unreasonably early offers of or demands for delivery are intended to be read under this Article as expressions of desire or intention, requesting the assent or acquiescence of the other party, not as final positions which may amount without more to breach or to create breach by the other side. See Sections 2-207 and 2-609.

5. The obligation of good faith under this Act requires reasonable notification before a contract may be treated as breached because a reasonable time for delivery or demand has expired. This operates both in the case of a contract originally indefinite as to time and of one subsequently made indefinite by waiver.

When both parties let an originally reasonable time go by in silence, the course of conduct under the contract may be viewed as enlarging the reasonable time for tender or demand of performance. The contract may be terminated by abandonment.

6. Parties to a contract are not required in giving reasonable notification to fix, at peril of breach, a time which is in fact reasonable in the unforeseeable judgment of a later trier of fact. Effective communication of a proposed time limit calls for a response, so that failure to reply will make out acquiescence. Where objection is made, however, or if the demand is merely for information as to when goods will be delivered or will be ordered out, demand for assurances on the ground of insecurity may be made under this Article pending further negotiations. Only when a party insists on undue delay or on rejection of the other party's reasonable proposal is there a question of flat breach under the present section.

7. Subsection (2) applies a commercially reasonable view to resolve the conflict which has arisen in the cases as to contracts of indefinite duration. The "reasonable time" of duration appropriate to a given arrangement is limited by the circumstances. When the arrangement has been carried on by the parties over the years, the "reasonable time" can continue indefinitely and the contract will not terminate until notice.

8. Subsection (3) recognizes that the application of principles of good faith and sound commercial practice normally call for such notification of the termination of a going contract relationship as will give the other party reasonable time to seek a substitute arrangement. An agreement dispensing with notification or limiting the time for the seeking of a substitute arrangement is, of course, valid under this subsection unless the results of putting it into operation would be the creation of an unconscionable state of affairs.

9. Justifiable cancellation for breach is a remedy for breach and is not the kind of termination covered by the present subsection.

10. The requirement of notification is dispensed with where the contract provides for termination on the happening of an "agreed event." "Event" is a term chosen here to contrast with "option" or the like.

Cross References:
 Point 1: Sections 1-203, 1-204 and 2-103.
 Point 2: Sections 2-320, 2-321, 2-504, and 2-511 through 2-514.
 Point 5: Section 1-203.
 Point 6: Section 2-609.
 Point 7: Section 2-204.
 Point 9: Sections 2-106, 2-318, 2-610 and 2-703.

Definitional Cross References:
 "Agreement." Section 1-201.
 "Contract." Section 1-201.
 "Notification." Section 1-201.
 "Party." Section 1-201.

"Reasonable time." Section 1-204.
"Termination." Section 2-106.

§2-311. Options and Cooperation Respecting Performance

(1) An agreement for sale which is otherwise sufficiently definite (subsection (3) of Section 2-204) to be a contract is not made invalid by the fact that it leaves particulars of performance to be specified by one of the parties. Any such specification must be made in good faith and within limits set by commercial reasonableness.

(2) Unless otherwise agreed specifications relating to assortment of the goods are at the buyer's option and except as otherwise provided in subsections (1)(c) and (3) of Section 2-319 specifications or arrangements relating to shipment are at the seller's option.

(3) Where such specification would materially affect the other party's performance but it not seasonably made or where one party's cooperation is necessary to the agreed performance of the other but is not seasonably forthcoming, the other party in addition to all other remedies

(a) is excused for any resulting delay in his own performance; and

(b) may also either proceed to perform in any reasonable manner or after the time for a material part of his own performance treat the failure to specify or to cooperate as a breach by failure to deliver or accept the goods.

§2-312. Warranty of Title and Against Infringement; Buyer's Obligation Against Infringement

(1) Subject to subsection (2) there is in a contract for sale a warranty by the seller that

(a) the title conveyed shall be good, and its transfer rightful; and

(b) the goods shall be delivered free from any security interest or other lien or encumbrance of which the buyer at the time of contracting has no knowledge.

(2) A warranty under subsection (1) will be excluded or modified only by specific language or by circumstances which give the buyer reason to know that the person selling does not claim title in himself or that he is purporting to sell only such right or title as he or a third person may have.

(3) Unless otherwise agreed a seller who is a merchant regularly dealing in goods of the kind warrants that the goods shall be delivered free of the rightful claim of any third person by way of infringement or the like but a buyer who furnishes specifications to the seller must hold the seller harmless against any such claim which arises out of compliance with the specifications.

§2-313. Express Warranties by Affirmation, Promise, Description, Sample

(1) Express warranties by the seller are created as follows:

(a) Any affirmation of fact or promise made by the seller to the buyer which relates to the goods and becomes part of the basis of the bargain creates an express warranty that the goods shall conform to the affirmation or promise.

(b) Any description of the goods which is made part of the basis of the bargain creates an express warranty that the goods shall conform to the description.

(c) Any sample or model which is made part of the basis of the bargain creates an express warranty that the whole of the goods shall conform to the sample or model

(2) It is not necessary to the creation of an express warranty that the seller use formal words such as "warrant" or "guarantee" or that he have a specific intention to make a warranty, but an affirmation merely of the value of the goods or a statement purporting to be merely the seller's opinion or commendation of the goods does not create a warranty.

Official Comment

Prior Uniform Statutory Provision: Sections 12, 14 and 16, Uniform Sales Act.

Changes: Rewritten.

Purposes of Changes: To consolidate and systematize basic principles with the result that:

1. "Express" warranties rest on "dickered" aspects of the individual bargain, and go so clearly to the essence of that bargain that words of disclaimer in a form are repugnant to the basic dickered terms. "Implied" warranties rest so clearly on a common factual situation or set of conditions that no particular language or action is necessary to evidence them and they will arise in such a situation unless unmistakably negated.

This section reverts to the older case law insofar as the warranties of description and sample are designated "express" rather than "implied."

2. Although this section is limited in its scope and direct purpose to warranties made by the seller to the buyer as part of a contract for sale, the warranty sections of this Article are not designed in any way to disturb those lines of case law growth which have recognized that warranties need not be confined either to sales contracts or to the direct parties to such a contract. They may arise in other appropriate circumstances such as in the case of bailments for hire, whether such bailment is itself the main contract or is merely a supplying of containers under a contract for the sale of their contents. The provisions of Section 2-318 on third party beneficiaries

expressly recognize this case law development within one particular area. Beyond that, the matter is left to the case law with the intention that the policies of this Act may offer useful guidance in dealing with further cases as they arise.

3. The present section deals with affirmations of fact by the seller, descriptions of the goods or exhibitions of samples, exactly as any other part of a negotiation which ends in a contract is dealt with. No specific intention to make a warranty is necessary if any of these factors is made part of the basis of the bargain. In actual practice affirmations of fact made by the seller about the goods during a bargain are regarded as part of the description of those goods; hence no particular reliance on such statements need be shown in order to weave them into the fabric of the agreement. Rather, any fact which is to take such affirmations, once made, out of the agreement requires clear affirmative proof. The issue normally is one of fact.

4. In view of the principle that the whole purpose of the law of warranty is to determine what it is that the seller has in essence agreed to sell, the policy is adopted of those cases which refuse except in unusual circumstances to recognize a material deletion of the seller's obligation. Thus, a contract is normally a contract for a sale of something describable and described. A clause generally disclaiming "all warranties, express or implied" cannot reduce the seller's obligation with respect to such description and therefore cannot be given literal effect under Section 2-316.

This is not intended to mean that the parties, if they consciously desire, cannot make their own bargain as they wish. But in determining what they have agreed upon good faith is a factor and consideration should be given to the fact that the probability is small that a real price is intended to be exchanged for a pseudo-obligation.

5. Paragraph (1)(b) makes specific some of the principles set forth above when a description of the goods is given by the seller.

A description need not be by words. Technical specifications, blueprints and the like can afford more exact description than mere language and if made part of the basis of the bargain goods must conform with them. Past deliveries may set the description of quality, either expressly or impliedly by course of dealing. Of course, all descriptions by merchants must be read against the applicable trade usages with the general rules as to merchantability resolving any doubts.

6. The basic situation as to statements affecting the true essence of the bargain is no different when a sample or model is involved in the transaction. This section includes both a "sample" actually drawn from the bulk of goods which is the subject matter of the sale, and a "model" which is offered for inspection when the subject matter is not at hand and which has not been drawn from the bulk of the goods.

Although the underlying principles are unchanged, the facts are often ambiguous when something is shown as illustrative, rather than as a straight sample. In general, the presumption is that any sample or model just as any affirmation of fact is intended to become a basis of the bargain. But there is no escape from the question of fact. When the seller exhibits a sample purporting to be drawn from an existing bulk, good faith of course requires that the sample be fairly drawn. But in mercantile experience the mere exhibition of a "sample" does not of itself show whether it is merely intended to "suggest" or to "be" the character of the subject-matter of the contract. The question is whether the seller has so acted with reference to the sample as to make him responsible that the whole shall have at least the values shown by it. The circumstances aid in answering this question. If the sample has been drawn from an existing bulk, it must be regarded as describing values of the goods contracted for unless it is accompanied by an unmistakable denial of such responsibility. If, on the other hand, a model of merchandise not on hand is offered, the mercantile presumption that it has become a literal description of the subject matter is not so strong, and particularly so if modification on the buyer's initiative impairs any feature of the model.

7. The precise time when words of description or affirmation are made or samples are shown is not material. The sole question is whether the language or samples or models are fairly to be regarded as part of the contract. If language is used after the closing of the deal (as when the buyer when taking delivery asks and receives an additional assurance), the warranty becomes a modification, and need not be supported by consideration if it is otherwise reasonable and in order (Section 2-209).

8. Concerning affirmations of value or a seller's opinion or commendation under subsection (2), the basic question remains the same: What statements of the seller have in the circumstances and in objective judgment become part of the basis of the bargain? As indicated above, all of the statements of the seller do so unless good reason is shown to the contrary. The provisions of subsection (2) are included, however, since common experience discloses that some statements or predictions cannot fairly be viewed as entering into the bargain. Even as to false statements of value, however, the possibility is left open that a remedy may be provided by the law relating to fraud or misrepresentation.

Cross References:
   Point 1: Section 2-316.
   Point 2: Sections 1-102(3) and 2-318.
   Point 3: Section 2-316(2)(b).
   Point 4: Section 2-316.
   Point 5: Sections 1-205(4) and 2-314.
   Point 6: Section 2-316.
   Point 7: Section 2-209.
   Point 8: Section 1-103.

Definitional Cross References:
   "Buyer." Section 2-103.
   "Conforming." Section 2-106.

"Goods." Section 2-105.
"Seller." Section 2-103.

§2-314. Implied Warranty: Merchantability; Usage of Trade

(1) Unless excluded or modified (Section 2-316), a warranty that the goods shall be merchantable is implied in a contract for their sale if the seller is a merchant with respect to goods of that kind. Under this section the serving for value of food or drink to be consumed either on the premises or elsewhere is a sale.

(2) Goods to be merchantable must be at least such as
(a) pass without objection in the trade under the contract description; and
(b) in the case of fungible goods, are of fair average quality within the description; and
(c) are fit for the ordinary purposes for which such goods are used; and
(d) run, within the variations permitted by the agreement, of even kind, quality and quantity within each unit and among all units involved; and
(e) are adequately contained, packaged, and labeled as the agreement may require; and
(f) conform to the promises or affirmations of fact made on the container or label if any.

(3) Unless excluded or modified (Section 2-316) other implied warranties may arise from course of dealing or usage of trade.

Official Comment

Prior Uniform Statutory Provision: Section 15(2), Uniform Sales Act.

Changes: Completely rewritten.

Purposes of Changes: This section, drawn in view of the steadily developing case law on the subject, is intended to make it clear that:

1. The seller's obligation applies to present sales as well as to contracts to sell subject to the effects of any examination of specific goods. (Subsection (2) of Section 2-316). Also, the warranty of merchantability applies to sales for use as well as to sales for resale.

2. The question when the warranty is imposed turns basically on the meaning of the terms of the agreement as recognized in the trade. Goods delivered under an agreement made by a merchant in a given line of trade must be of a quality comparable to that generally acceptable in that line of trade under the description or other designation of the goods used in the agreement. The responsibility imposed rests on any merchant-seller, and the absence of the words "grower or manufacturer or not" which appeared in Section 15(2) of the Uniform Sales Act does not restrict the applicability of this section.

3. A specific designation of goods by the buyer does not exclude the seller's obligation that they be fit for the general purposes appropriate to such goods. A contract for the sale of second-hand goods, however, involves only such obligation as is appropriate to such goods for that is their contract description. A person making an isolated sale of goods is not a "merchant" within the meaning of the full scope of this section and, thus, no warranty of merchantability would apply. His knowledge of any defects not apparent on inspection would, however, without need for express agreement and in keeping with the underlying reason of the present section and the provisions on good faith, impose an obligation that known material but hidden defects be fully disclosed.

4. Although a seller may not be a "merchant" as to the goods in question, if he states generally that they are "guaranteed" the provisions of this section may furnish a guide to the content of the resulting express warranty. This has particular significance in the case of second-hand sales, and has further significance in limiting the effect of fine-print disclaimer clauses where their effect would be inconsistent with large-print assertions of "guarantee."

5. The second sentence of subsection (1) covers the warranty with respect to food and drink. Serving food or drink for value is a sale, whether to be consumed on the premises or elsewhere. Cases to the contrary are rejected. The principal warranty is that stated in subsections (1) and (2)(c) of this section.

6. Subsection (2) does not purport to exhaust the meaning of "merchantable" nor to negate any of its attributes not specifically mentioned in the text of the statute, but arising by usage of trade or through case law. The language used is "must be at least such as . . . ," and the intention is to leave open other possible attributes of merchantability.

7. Paragraphs (a) and (b) of subsection (2) are to be read together. Both refer, as indicated above, to the standards of that line of the trade which fits the transaction and the seller's business. "Fair average" is a term directly appropriate to agricultural bulk products and means goods centering around the middle belt of quality, not the least or the worst that can be understood in the particular trade by the designation, but such as can pass "without objection." Of course a fair percentage of the least is permissible but the goods are not "fair average" if they are all of the least or worst quality possible under the description. In cases of doubt as to what quality is intended, the price at which a merchant closes a contract is an excellent index of the nature and scope of his obligation under the present section.

8. Fitness for the ordinary purposes for which goods of the type are used is a fundamental concept of the present section and is covered in paragraph (c). As stated above, merchantability is also a part of the obligation owing to the purchaser for use. Correspondingly, protection, under this aspect of the warranty, of the person buying for resale to the ultimate consumer is equally necessary, and merchantable goods must therefore be "honestly" resalable in the normal course of business because they are what they purport to be.

9. Paragraph (d) on evenness of kind, quality and quantity follows case

law. But precautionary language has been added as a reminder of the frequent usages of trade which permit substantial variations both with and without an allowance or an obligation to replace the varying units.

10. Paragraph (e) applies only where the nature of the goods and of the transaction require a certain type of container, package or label. Paragraph (f) applies, on the other hand, wherever there is a label or container on which representations are made, even though the original contract, either by express terms or usage of trade, may not have required either the labelling or the representation. This follows from the general obligation of good faith which requires that a buyer should not be placed in the position of reselling or using goods delivered under false representations appearing on the package or container. No problem of extra consideration arises in this connection since, under this Article, an obligation is imposed by the original contract not to deliver mislabeled articles, and the obligation is imposed where mercantile good faith so requires and without reference to the doctrine of consideration.

11. Exclusion or modification of the warranty of merchantability, or of any part of it, is dealt with in the section to which the text of the present section makes explicit precautionary references. That section must be read with particular reference to its subsection (4) on limitation of remedies. The warranty of merchantability, wherever it is normal, is so commonly taken for granted that its exclusion from the contract is a matter threatening surprise and therefore requiring special precaution.

12. Subsection (3) is to make explicit that usage of trade and course of dealing can create warranties and that they are implied rather than express warranties and thus subject to exclusion or modification under Section 2-316. A typical instance would be the obligation to provide predigree papers to evidence conformity of the animal to the contract in the case of a pedigreed dog or blooded bull.

13. In an action based on breach of warranty, it is of course necessary to show not only the existence of the warranty but the fact that the warranty was broken and that the breach of the warranty was the proximate cause of the loss sustained. In such an action an affirmative showing by the seller that the loss resulted from some action or event following his own delivery of the goods can operate as a defense. Equally, evidence indicating that the seller exercised care in the manufacture, processing or selection of the goods is relevant to the issue of whether the warranty was in fact broken. Action by the buyer following an examination of the goods which ought to have indicated the defect complained of can be shown as matter bearing on whether the breach itself was the cause of the injury.

Cross References:
    Point 1: Section 2-316.
    Point 3: Sections 1-203 and 2-104.
    Point 5: Section 2-315.
    Point 11: Section 2-316.
    Point 12: Sections 1-201, 1-205 and 2-316.

Definitional Cross References:
  "Agreement." Section 1-201.
  "Contract." Section 1-201.
  "Contract for sale." Section 2-106.
  "Goods." Section 2-105.
  "Merchant." Section 2-104.
  "Seller." Section 2-103.

§2-315. Implied Warranty: Fitness for Particular Purpose

Where the seller at the time of contracting has reason to know any particular purpose for which the goods are required and that the buyer is relying on the seller's skill or judgment to select or furnish suitable goods, there is unless excluded or modified under the next section an implied warranty that the goods shall be fit for such purpose.

Official Comment

Prior Uniform Statutory Provision: Section 15(1), (4), (5), Uniform Sales Act.

Changes: Rewritten.

Purposes of Changes:
  1. Whether or not this warranty arises in any individual case is basically a question of fact to be determined by the circumstances of the contracting. Under this section the buyer need not bring home to the seller actual knowledge of the particular purpose for which the goods are intended or of his reliance on the seller's skill and judgment, if the circumstances are such that the seller has reason to realize the purpose, intended or that the reliance exists. The buyer, of course, must actually be relying on the seller.
  2. A "particular purpose" differs from the ordinary purpose for which the goods are used in that it envisages a specific use by the buyer which is peculiar to the nature of his business whereas the ordinary purposes for which goods are used are those envisaged in the concept of merchantability and go to uses which are customarily made of the goods in question. For example, shoes are generally used for the purpose of walking upon ordinary ground, but a seller may know that a particular pair was selected to be used for climbing mountains.
  A contract may of course include both a warranty of merchantability and one of fitness for a particular purpose.

The provisions of this Article on the cumulation and conflict of express and implied warranties must be considered on the question of inconsistency between or among warranties. In such a case any question of fact as to which warranty was intended by the parties to apply must be resolved in favor of the warranty of fitness for particular purpose as against all other warranties except where the buyer has taken upon himself the responsibility of furnishing the technical specifications.

3. In connection with the warranty of fitness for a particular purpose the provisions of this Article on the allocation or division of risks are particularly applicable in any transaction in which the purpose for which the goods are to be used combines requirements both as to the quality of the goods themselves and compliance with certain laws or regulations. How the risks are divided is a question of fact to be determined, where not expressly contained in the agreement, from the circumstances of contracting, usage of trade, course of performance and the like, matters which may constitute the "otherwise agreement" of the parties by which they may divide the risk or burden.

4. The absence from this section of the language used in the Uniform Sales Act in referring to the seller, "whether he be the grower or manufacturer or not," is not intended to impose any requirement that the seller be a grower or manufacturer. Although normally the warranty will arise only where the seller is a merchant with the appropriate "skill or judgment," it can arise as to nonmerchants where this is justified by the particular circumstances.

5. The elimination of the "patent or other trade name" exception constitutes the major extension of the warranty of fitness which has been made by the cases and continued in this Article. Under the present section the existence of a patent or other trade name and the designation of the article by that name, or indeed in any other definite manner, is only one of the facts to be considered on the question of whether the buyer actually relied on the seller, but it is not of itself decisive of the issue. If the buyer himself is insisting on a particular brand he is not relying on the seller's skill and judgment and so no warranty results. But the mere fact that the article purchased has a particular patent or trade name is not sufficient to indicate nonreliance if the article has been recommended by the seller as adequate for the buyer's purposes.

6. The specific reference forward in the present section to the following section on exclusion or modification of warranties is to call attention to the possibility of eliminating the warranty in any given case. However it must be noted that under the following section the warranty of fitness for a particular purpose must be excluded or modified by a conspicuous writing.

Cross References:
Point 2: Sections 2-314 and 2-317.
Point 3: Section 2-303.
Point 6: Section 2-316.

Definitional Cross References:
"Buyer." Section 2-103.
"Goods." Section 2-105.
"Seller." Section 2-103.

§2-316.   Exclusion or Modification of Warranties

(1) Words or conduct relevant to the creation of an express warranty and words or conduct tending to negate or limit warranty shall be construed wherever reasonable as consistent with each other; but subject to the provisions of this Article on parol or extrinsic evidence (Section 2-202) negation or limitation is inoperative to the extent that such construction is unreasonable.

(2) Subject to subsection (3), to exclude or modify the implied warranty of merchantability or any part of it the language must mention merchantability and in case of a writing must be conspicuous, and to exclude or modify any implied warranty of fitness the exclusion must be by a writing and conspicuous. Language to exclude all implied warranties of fitness is sufficient if it states, for example, that "There are no warranties which extend beyond the description on the face hereof."

(3) Notwithstanding subsection (2)

(a) unless the circumstances indicate otherwise, all implied warranties are excluded by expressions like "as is," "with all faults" or other language which in common understanding calls the buyer's attention to the exclusion of warranties and makes plain that there is no implied warranty; and

(b) when the buyer before entering into the contract has examined the goods or the sample or model as fully as he desired or has refused to examine the goods there is no implied warranty with regard to defects which an examination ought in the circumstances to have revealed to him; and

(c) an implied warranty can also be excluded or modified by course of dealing or course of performance or usage of trade.

(4) Remedies for breach of warranty can be limited in accordance with the provisions of this Article on liquidation or limitation of damages and on contractual modification of remedy (Sections 2-718 and 2-719).

Official Comment

Prior Uniform Statutory Provision: None. See sections 15 and 71, Uniform Sales Act.

Purposes:
1. This section is designed principally to deal with those frequent clauses in sales contracts which seek to exclude "all warranties, express or implied." It seeks to protect a buyer from unexpected and unbargained language of disclaimer by denying effect to such language when inconsistent with

language of express warranty and permitting the exclusion of implied warranties only by conspicuous language or other circumstances which protect the buyer from surprise.

2. The seller is protected under this Article against false allegations of oral warranties by its provisions on parol and extrinsic evidence and against unauthorized representations by the customary "lack of authority" clauses. This Article treats the limitation or avoidance of consequential damages as a matter of limiting remedies for breach, separate from the matter of creation of liability under a warranty. If no warranty exists, there is of course no problem of limiting remedies for breach of warranty. Under subsection (4) the question of limitation of remedy is governed by the sections referred to rather than by this section.

3. Disclaimer of the implied warranty of merchantability is permitted under subsection (2), but with the safeguard that such disclaimers must mention merchantability and in case of a writing must be conspicuous.

4. Unlike the implied warranty of merchantability, implied warranties of fitness for a particular purpose may be excluded by general language, but only if it is in writing and conspicuous.

5. Subsection (2) presupposes that the implied warranty in question exists unless excluded or modified. Whether or not language of disclaimer satisfies the requirements of this section, such language may be relevant under other sections to the question whether the warranty was ever in fact created. Thus, unless the provisions of this Article on parol and extrinsic evidence prevent, oral language of disclaimer may raise issues of fact as to whether reliance by the buyer occurred and whether the seller had "reason to know" under the section on implied warranty of fitness for a particular purpose.

6. The exceptions to the general rule set forth in paragraphs (a), (b) and (c) of subsection (3) are common factual situations in which the circumstances surrounding the transaction are in themselves sufficient to call the buyer's attention to the fact that no implied warranties are made or that a certain implied warranty is being excluded.

7. Paragraph (a) of subsection (3) deals with general terms such as "as is," "as they stand," "with all faults," and the like. Such terms in ordinary commercial usage are understood to mean that the buyer takes the entire risk as to the quality of the goods involved. The terms covered by paragraph (a) are in fact merely a particularization of paragraph (c) which provides for exclusion or modification of implied warranties by usage of trade.

8. Under paragraph (b) of subsection (3) warranties may be excluded or modified by the circumstances where the buyer examines the goods or a sample or model of them before entering into the contract. "Examination" as used in this paragraph is not synonymous with inspection before acceptance or at any other time after the contract has been made. It goes rather to the nature of the responsibility assumed by the seller at the time of the making of the contract. Of course if the buyer discovers the defect and uses the goods anyway, or if he unreasonably fails to examine the goods before he uses them, resulting injuries may be found to result from

his own action rather than proximately from a breach of warranty. See Sections 2-314 and 2-715 and comments thereto.

In order to bring the transaction within the scope of "refused to examine" in paragraph (b), it is not sufficient that the goods are available for inspection. There must in addition be a demand by the seller that the buyer examine the goods fully. The seller by the demand puts the buyer on notice that he is assuming the risk of defects which the examination ought to reveal. The language "refused to examine" in this paragraph is intended to make clear the necessity for such demand.

Application of the doctrine of "caveat emptor" in all cases where the buyer examines the goods regardless of statements made by the seller is, however, rejected by this Article. Thus, if the offer of examination is accompanied by words as to their merchantability or specific attributes and the buyer indicates clearly that he is relying on those words rather than on his examination, they give rise to an "express" warranty. In such cases the question is one of fact as to whether a warranty of merchantability has been expressly incorporated in the agreement. Disclaimer of such an express warranty is governed by subsection (1) of the present section.

The particular buyer's skill and the normal method of examining goods in the circumstances determine what defects are excluded by the examination. A failure to notice defects which are obvious cannot excuse the buyer. However, an examination under circumstances which do not permit chemical or other testing of the goods would not exclude defects which could be ascertained only by such testing. Nor can latent defects be excluded by a simple examination. A professional buyer examining a product in his field will be held to have assumed the risk as to all defects which a professional in the field ought to observe, while a nonprofessional buyer will be held to have assumed the risk only for such defects as a layman might be expected to observe.

9. The situation in which the buyer gives precise and complete specifications to the seller is not explicitly covered in this section, but this is a frequent circumstance by which the implied warranties may be excluded. The warranty of fitness for a particular purpose would not normally arise since in such a situation there is usually no reliance on the seller by the buyer. The warranty of merchantability in such a transaction, however, must be considered in connection with the next section on the cumulation and conflict of warranties. Under paragraph (c) of that section in case of such an inconsistency the implied warranty of merchantability is displaced by the express warranty that the goods will comply with the specifications. Thus, where the buyer gives detailed specifications as to the goods, neither of the implied warranties as to quality will normally apply to the transaction unless consistent with the specifications.

Cross References:
Point 2: Sections 2-202, 2-718 and 2-719.
Point 7: Sections 1-205 and 2-208.

Definitional Cross References:
"Agreement." Section 1-201.
"Buyer." Section 2-103.
"Contract." Section 1-201.
"Course of dealing." Section 1-205.
"Goods." Section 2-105.
"Remedy." Section 1-201.
"Seller." Section 2-103.
"Usage of trade." Section 1-205.

§2-317. Cumulation and Conflict of Warranties Express or Implied

Warranties whether express or implied shall be construed as consistent with each other and as cumulative, but if such construction is unreasonable the intention of the parties shall determine which warranty is dominant. In ascertaining that intention the following rules apply:

(a) Exact or technical specifications displace an inconsistent sample or model or general language of description.

(b) A sample from an existing bulk displaces inconsistent general language of description.

(c) Express warranties displace inconsistent implied warranties other than an implied warranty of fitness for a particular purpose.

§2-318. Third Party Beneficiaries of Warranties Express or Implied

Note: *If this Act is introduced in the Congress of the United States this section should be omitted. (States to select one alternative.)*

ALTERNATIVE A

A seller's warranty whether express or implied extends to any natural person who is in the family or household of his buyer or who is a guest in his home if it is reasonable to expect that such person may use, consume or be affected by the goods and who is injured in person by breach of the warranty. A seller may not exclude or limit the operation of this section.

ALTERNATIVE B

A seller's warranty whether express or implied extends to any natural person who may reasonably be expected to use, consume or be affected by the goods and who is injured in person by breach of the warranty. A seller may not exclude or limit the operation of this section.

ALTERNATIVE C

A seller's warranty whether express or implied extends to any person who may reasonably be expected to use, consume or be affected by the goods and who is injured by breach of the warranty. A seller may not exclude or limit the operation of this section with respect to injury to the person of an individual to whom the warranty extends.

§2-319. F.O.B. and F.A.S. Terms

(1) Unless otherwise agreed the term F.O.B. (which means "free on board") at a named place, even though used only in connection with the stated price, is a delivery term under which

    (a) when the term is F.O.B. the place of shipment, the seller must at that place ship the goods in the manner provided in this Article (Section 2-504) and bear the expense and risk of putting them into the possession of the carrier; or

    (b) when the term is F.O.B. the place of destination, the seller must at his own expense and risk transport the goods to that place and there tender delivery of them in the manner provided in this Article (Section 2-503);

    (c) when under either (a) or (b) the term is also F.O.B. vessel, car or other vehicle, the seller must in addition at his own expense and risk load the goods on board. If the term is F.O.B. vessel the buyer must name the vessel and in an appropriate case the seller must comply with the provisions of this Article on the form of bill of lading (Section 2-323).

(2) Unless otherwise agreed the term F.A.S. vessel (which means "free alongside") at a named port, even though used only in connection with the stated price, is a delivery term under which the seller must

    (a) at his own expense and risk deliver the goods alongside the vessel in the manner usual in that port or on a dock designated and provided by the buyer; and

    (b) obtain and tender a receipt for the goods in exchange for which the carrier is under a duty to issue a bill of lading.

(3) Unless otherwise agreed in any case falling within subsection (1) (a) or (c) or subsection (2) the buyer must seasonably give any needed instructions for making delivery, including when the term is F.A.S. or F.O.B. the loading berth of the vessel and in an appropriate case its name and sailing date. The seller may treat the failure of needed instructions as a failure of cooperation under this Article (Section 2-311). He may also at his option move the goods in any reasonable manner preparatory to delivery or shipment.

(4) Under the term F.O.B. vessel or F.A.S. unless otherwise agreed the buyer must make payment against tender of the required documents and the seller may not tender nor the buyer demand delivery of the goods in substitution for the documents.

§2-326. Sale on Approval and Sale or Return; Consignment Sales and Rights of Creditors

(1) Unless otherwise agreed, if delivered goods may be returned by the buyer even though they conform to the contract, the transaction is

    (a) a "sale on approval" if the goods are delivered primarily for use, and

    (b) a "sale or return" if the goods are delivered primarily for resale.

(2) Except as provided in subsection (3), goods held on approval are not subject to the claims of the buyer's creditors until acceptance; goods held on sale or return are subject to such claims while in the buyer's possession.

(3) Where goods are delivered to a person for sale and such person maintains a place of business at which he deals in goods of the kind involved, under a name other than the name of the person making delivery, then with respect to claims of creditors of the person conducting the business the goods are deemed to be on sale or return. The provisions of this subsection are applicable even though an agreement purports to reserve title to the person making delivery until payment or resale or uses such words as "on consignment" or "on memorandum." However, this subsection is not applicable if the person making delivery

    (a) complies with an applicable law providing for a consignor's interest or the like to be evidenced by a sign, or

    (b) establishes that the person conducting the business is generally known by his creditors to be substantially engaged in selling the goods of others, or

    (c) complies with the filing provisions of the Article on Secured Transactions (Article 9).

(4) Any "or return" term of a contract for sale is to be treated as a separate contract for sale within the statute of frauds section of this Article (Section 2-201) and as contradicting the sale aspect of the contract within the provisions of this Article on parol or extrinsic evidence (Section 2-202).

§2-327. Special Incidents of Sale on Approval and Sale or Return

(1) Under a sale on approval unless otherwise agreed

    (a) although the goods are identified to the contract the risk of loss and the title do not pass to the buyer until acceptance; and

    (b) use of the goods consistent with the purpose of trial is not acceptance but failure seasonably to notify the seller of election to return the goods is acceptance, and if the goods conform to the contract acceptance of any part is acceptance of the whole; and

    (c) after due notification of election to return, the return is at the seller's risk and expense but a merchant buyer must follow any reasonable instructions.

(2) Under a sale or return unless otherwise agreed

(a) the option to return extends to the whole or any commercial unit of the goods while in substantially their original condition, but must be exercised seasonably; and

(b) the return is at the buyer's risk and expense.

§2-328. Sale by Auction

(1) In a sale by auction if goods are put up in lots each lot is the subject of a separate sale.

(2) A sale by auction is complete when the auctioneer so announces by the fall of the hammer or in other customary manner. Where a bid is made while the hammer is falling in acceptance of a prior bid the auctioneer may in his discretion reopen the bidding or declare the goods sold under the bid on which the hammer was falling.

(3) Such a sale is with reserve unless the goods are in explicit terms put up without reserve. In an auction with reserve the auctioneer may withdraw the goods at any time until he announces completion of the sale. In an auction without reserve, after the auctioneer calls for bids on an article or lot, that article or lot cannot be withdrawn unless no bid is made within a reasonable time. In either case a bidder may retract his bid until the auctioneer's announcement of completion of the sale, but a bidder's retraction does not revive any previous bid.

(4) If the auctioneer knowingly receives a bid on the seller's behalf or the seller makes or procures such a bid, and notice has not been given that liberty for such bidding is reserved, the buyer may at his option avoid the sale or take the goods at the price of the last good faith bid prior to the completion of the sale. This subsection shall not apply to any bid at a forced sale.

Part 4.   Title, Creditors and Good Faith Purchasers

§2-401. Passing of Title; Reservation for Security; Limited Application of This Section

Each provision of this Article with regard to the rights, obligations and remedies of the seller, the buyer, purchasers or other third parties applies irrespective of title to the goods except where the provision refers to such title. Insofar as situations are not covered by the other provisions of this Article and matters concerning title become material the following rules apply:

(1) Title to goods cannot pass under a contract for sale prior to their identification to the contract (Section 2-501), and unless otherwise explicitly

agreed the buyer acquires by their identification a special property as limited by this Act. Any retention or reservation by the seller of the title (property) in goods shipped or delivered to the buyer is limited in effect to a reservation of a security interest. Subject to these provisions and to the provisions of the Article on Secured Transactions (Article 9), title to goods passes from the seller to the buyer in any manner and on any conditions explicitly agreed on by the parties.

(2) Unless otherwise explicitly agreed title passes to the buyer at the time and place at which the seller completes his performance with reference to the physical delivery of the goods, despite any reservation of a security interest and even though a document of title is to be delivered at a different time or place; and in particular and despite any reservation of a security interest by the bill of lading

(a) if the contract requires or authorizes the seller to send the goods to the buyer but does not require him to deliver them at destination, title passes to the buyer at the time and place of shipment; but

(b) if the contract requires delivery at destination, title passes on tender there.

(3) Unless otherwise explicitly agreed where delivery is to be made without moving the goods,

(a) if the seller is to deliver a document of title, title passes at the time when and the place where he delivers such documents; or

(b) if the goods are at the time of contracting already identified and no documents are to be delivered, title passes at the time and place of contracting.

(4) A rejection or other refusal by the buyer to receive or retain the goods, whether or not justified, or a justified revocation of acceptance revests title to the goods in the seller. Such revesting occurs by operation of law and is not a "sale."

§2-402. Rights of Seller's Creditors Against Sold Goods

(1) Except as provided in subsections (2) and (3), rights of unsecured creditors of the seller with respect to goods which have been identified to a contract for sale are subject to the buyer's rights to recover the goods under this Article (Sections 2-502 and 2-716).

(2) A creditor of the seller may treat a sale or an identification of goods to a contract for sale as void if as against him a retention of possession by the seller is fraudulent under any rule of law of the state where the goods are situated, except that retention of possession in good faith and current course of trade by a merchant-seller for a commercially reasonable time after a sale or identification is not fraudulent.

(3) Nothing in this Article shall be deemed to impair the rights of creditors of the seller

(a) under the provisions of the Article on Secured Transactions (Article 9); or

(b) where identification to the contract or delivery is made not in current course of trade but in satisfaction of or as security for a pre-existing claim for money, security or the like and is made under circumstances which under any rule of law of the state where the goods are situated would apart from this Article constitute the transaction a fraudulent transfer or voidable preference.

§2-403. Power to Transfer; Good Faith Purchase of Goods; "Entrusting"

(1) A purchaser of goods acquires all title which his transferor had or had power to transfer except that a purchaser of a limited interest acquires rights only to the extent of the interest purchased. A person with voidable title has power to transfer a good title to a good faith purchaser for value. When goods have been delivered under a transaction of purchase the purchaser has such power even though

(a) the transferor was deceived as to the identity of the purchaser, or

(b) the delivery was in exchange for a check which is later dishonored, or

(c) it was agreed that the transaction was to be a "cash sale," or

(d) the delivery was procured through fraud punishable as larcenous under the criminal law.

(2) Any entrusting of possession of goods to a merchant who deals in goods of that kind gives him power to transfer all rights of the entruster to a buyer in ordinary course of business.

(3) "Entrusting" includes any delivery and any acquiescence in retention of possession regardless of any condition expressed between the parties to the delivery or acquiescence and regardless of whether the procurement of the entrusting or the possessor's disposition of the goods have been such as to be larcenous under the criminal law.

(4) The rights of other purchasers of goods and of lien creditors are governed by the Articles on Secured Transactions (Article 9), Bulk Transfers (Article 6) and Documents of Title (Article 7).

Part 5. Performance

§2-501. Insurable Interest in Goods; Manner of Identification of Goods

(1) The buyer obtains a special property and an insurable interest in goods by identification of existing goods as goods to which the contract refers even

though the goods so identified are non-conforming and he has an option to return or reject them. Such identification can be made at any time and in any manner explicitly agreed to by the parties. In the absence of explicit agreement identification occurs

(a) when the contract is made if it is for the sale of goods already existing and identified;

(b) if the contract is for the sale of future goods other than those described in paragraph (c), when goods are shipped, marked or otherwise designated by the seller as goods to which the contract refers;

(c) when the crops are planted or otherwise become growing crops or the young are conceived if the contract is for the sale of unborn young to be born within twelve months after contracting or for the sale of crops to be harvested within twelve months or the next normal harvest season after contracting whichever is longer.

(2) The seller retains an insurable interest in goods so long as title to or any security interest in the goods remains in him and where the identification is by the seller alone he may until default or insolvency or notification to the buyer that the identification is final substitute other goods for those identified.

(3) Nothing in this section impairs any insurable interest recognized under any other statute or rule of law.

§2-502. Buyer's Right to Goods on Seller's Insolvency

(1) Subject to subsection (2) and even though the goods have not been shipped a buyer who has paid a part or all of the price of goods in which he has a special property under the provisions of the immediately preceding section may on making and keeping good a tender of any unpaid portion of their price recover them from the seller if the seller becomes insolvent within ten days after receipt of the first installment on their price.

(2) If the identification creating his special property has been made by the buyer he acquires the right to recover the goods only if they conform to the contract for sale.

§2-503. Manner of Seller's Tender of Delivery

(1) Tender of delivery requires that the seller put and hold conforming goods at the buyer's disposition and give the buyer any notification reasonably necessary to enable him to take delivery. The manner, time and place for tender are determined by the agreement and this Article, and in particular

(a) tender must be at a reasonable hour, and if it is of goods they must be kept available for the period reasonably necessary to enable the buyer to take possession; but

(b) unless otherwise agreed the buyer must furnish facilities reasonably suited to the receipt of the goods.

(2) Where the case is within the next section respecting shipment tender requires that the seller comply with its provisions.

(3) Where the seller is required to deliver at a particular destination tender requires that he comply with subsection (1) and also in any appropriate case tender documents as described in subsections (4) and (5) of this section.

(4) Where goods are in the possession of a bailee and are to be delivered without being moved

(a) tender requires that the seller either tender a negotiable document of title covering such goods or procure acknowledgment by the bailee of the buyer's right to possession of the goods; but

(b) tender to the buyer of a non-negotiable document of title or of a written direction to the bailee to deliver is sufficient tender unless the buyer seasonably objects, and receipt by the bailee of notification of the buyer's rights fixes those rights as against the bailee and all third persons; but risk of loss of the goods and of any failure by the bailee to honor the non-negotiable document of title or to obey the direction remains on the seller until the buyer has had a reasonable time to present the document or direction, and a refusal by the bailee to honor the document or to obey the direction defeats the tender.

(5) Where the contract requires the seller to deliver documents

(a) he must tender all such documents in correct form, except as provided in this Article with respect to bills of lading in a set (subsection (2) of Section 2-323); and

(b) tender through customary banking channels is sufficient and dishonor of a draft accompanying the documents constitutes non-acceptance or rejection.

§2-504. Shipment by Seller

Where the seller is required or authorized to send the goods to the buyer and the contract does not require him to deliver them at a particular destination, then unless otherwise agreed he must

(a) put the goods in the possession of such a carrier and make such a contract for their transportation as may be reasonable having regard to the nature of the goods and other circumstances of the case; and

(b) obtain and promptly deliver or tender in due form any document necessary to enable the buyer to obtain possession of the goods or otherwise required by the agreement or by usage of trade; and

(c) promptly notify the buyer of the shipment.

Failure to notify the buyer under paragraph (c) or to make a proper contract under paragraph (a) is a ground for rejection only if material delay or loss ensues.

§2-507. Effect of Seller's Tender; Delivery on Condition

(1) Tender of delivery is a condition to the buyer's duty to accept the goods and, unless otherwise agreed, to his duty to pay for them. Tender entitles the seller to acceptance of the goods and to payment according to the contract.

(2) Where payment is due and demanded on the delivery to the buyer of goods or documents of title, his right as against the seller to retain or dispose of them is conditional upon his making the payment due.

§2-508. Cure by Seller of Improper Tender or Delivery; Replacement

(1) Where any tender or delivery by the seller is rejected because non-conforming and the time for performance has not yet expired, the seller may seasonably notify the buyer of his intention to cure and may then within the contract time make a conforming delivery.

(2) Where the buyer rejects a non-conforming tender which the seller had reasonable grounds to believe would be acceptable with or without money allowance the seller may if he seasonably notifies the buyer have a further reasonable time to substitute a conforming tender.

Official Comment

Prior Uniform Statutory Provision: None

Purposes:

1. Subsection (1) permits a seller who has made a non-conforming tender in any case to make a conforming delivery within the contract time upon seasonable notification to the buyer. It applies even where the seller has taken back the non-conforming goods and refunded the purchase price. He may still make a good tender within the contract period. The closer, however, it is to the contract date, the greater is the necessity for extreme promptness on the seller's part in notifying of his intention to cure, if such notification is to be "seasonable" under this subsection.

The rule of this subsection, moreover, is qualified by its underlying reasons. Thus if, after contracting for June delivery, a buyer later makes known to the seller his need for shipment early in the month and the seller ships accordingly, the "contract time" has been cut down by the supervening modification and the time for cure of tender must be referred to this modified time term.

2. Subsection (2) seeks to avoid injustice to the seller by reason of a surprise rejection by the buyer. However, the seller is not protected unless he had "reasonable grounds to believe" that the tender would be acceptable.

Such reasonable grounds can lie in prior course of dealing, course of performance or usage of trade as well as in the particular circumstances surrounding the making of the contract. The seller is charged with commercial knowledge of any factors in a particular sales situation which require him to comply strictly with his obligations under the contract as, for example, strict conformity of documents in an overseas shipment or the sale of precision parts or chemicals for use in manufacture. Further, if the buyer gives notice either implicitly, as by a prior course of dealing involving rigorous inspections, or expressly, as by the deliberate inclusion of a "no replacement" clause in the contract, the seller is to be held to rigid compliance. If the clause appears in a "form" contract evidence that it is out of line with trade usage or the prior course of dealing and was not called to the seller's attention may be sufficient to show that the seller had reasonable grounds to believe that the tender would be acceptable.

3. The words "a further reasonable time to substitute a conforming tender" are intended as words of limitation to protect the buyer. What is a "reasonable time" depends upon the attending circumstances. Compare Section 2-511 on the comparable case of a seller's surprise demand for legal tender.

4. Existing trade usages permitting variations without rejection but with price allowance enter into the agreement itself as contractual limitations of remedy and are not covered by this section.

Cross References:
Point 2: Section 2-302.
Point 3: Section 2-511.
Point 4: Sections 1-205 and 2-721.

Definitional Cross References:
"Buyer." Section 2-103.
"Conforming." Section 2-106.
"Contract." Section 1-201.
"Money." Section 1-201.
"Notifies." Section 1-201.
"Reasonable time." Section 1-204.
"Seasonably." Section 1-204.
"Seller." Section 2-103.

§2-509.   Risk of Loss in the Absence of Breach

(1) Where the contract requires or authorizes the seller to ship the goods by carrier

(a) if it does not require him to deliver them at a particular destination, the risk of loss passes to the buyer when the goods are duly delivered to the carrier even though the shipment is under reservation (Section 2-505); but

(b) if it does require him to deliver them at a particular destination and the goods are there duly tendered while in the possession of the carrier, the risk of loss passes to the buyer when the goods are there duly so tendered as to enable the buyer to take delivery.

(2) Where the goods are held by a bailee to be delivered without being moved, the risk of loss passes to the buyer

(a) on his receipt of a negotiable document of title covering the goods; or

(b) on acknowledgment by the bailee of the buyer's right to possession of the goods; or

(c) after his receipt of a non-negotiable document of title or other written direction to deliver, as provided in subsection (4)(b) of Section 2-503.

(3) In any case not within subsection (1) or (2), the risk of loss passes to the buyer on his receipt of the goods if the seller is a merchant; otherwise the risk passes to the buyer on tender of delivery.

(4) The provisions of this section are subject to contrary agreement of the parties and to the provisions of this Article on sale on approval (Section 2-327) and on effect of breach on risk of loss (Section 2-510).

§2-510. Effect of Breach on Risk of Loss

(1) Where a tender or delivery of goods so fails to conform to the contract as to give a right of rejection the risk of their loss remains on the seller until cure or acceptance.

(2) Where the buyer rightfully revokes acceptance he may to the extent of any deficiency in his effective insurance coverage treat the risk of loss as having rested on the seller from the beginning.

(3) Where the buyer as to conforming goods already identified to the contract for sale repudiates or is otherwise in breach before risk of their loss has passed to him, the seller may to the extent of any deficiency in his effective insurance coverage treat the risk of loss as resting on the buyer for a commercially reasonable time.

§2-511. Tender of Payment by Buyer; Payment by Check

(1) Unless otherwise agreed tender of payment is a condition to the seller's duty to tender and complete any delivery.

(2) Tender of payment is sufficient when made by any means or in any manner current in the ordinary course of business unless the seller demands payment in legal tender and gives any extension of time reasonably necessary to procure it.

(3) Subject to the provisions of this Act on the effect of an instrument on

an obligation (Section 3-802), payment by check is conditional and is defeated as between the parties by dishonor of the check on due presentment.

§2-512.   Payment by Buyer Before Inspection

(1) Where the contract requires payment before inspection non-conformity of goods does not excuse the buyer from so making payment unless

(a) the non-conformity appears without inspection; or

(b) despite tender of the required documents the circumstances would justify injunction against honor under the provisions of this Act (Section 5-114).

(2) Payment pursuant to subsection (1) does not constitute an acceptance of goods or impair the buyer's right to inspect or any of his remedies.

§2-513.   Buyer's Right to Inspection of Goods

(1) Unless otherwise agreed and subject to subsection (3), where goods are tendered or delivered or identified to the contract for sale, the buyer has a right before payment or acceptance to inspect them at any reasonable place and time and in any reasonable manner. When the seller is required or authorized to send the goods to the buyer, the inspection may be after their arrival.

(2) Expenses of inspection must be borne by the buyer but may be recovered from the seller if the goods do not conform and are rejected.

(3) Unless otherwise agreed and subject to the provisions of this Article on C.I.F. contracts (subsection (3) of Section 2-321), the buyer is not entitled to inspect the goods before payment of the price when the contract provides

(a) for delivery "C.O.D." or on other like terms; or

(b) for payment against documents of title, except where such payment is due only after the goods are to become available for inspection.

(4) A place or method of inspection fixed by the parties is presumed to be exclusive but unless otherwise expressly agreed it does not postpone identification or shift the place for delivery or for passing the risk of loss. If compliance becomes impossible, inspection shall be as provided in this section unless the place or method fixed was clearly intended as an indispensable condition failure of which avoids the contract.

Part 6.   Breach, Repudiation and Excuse

§2-601.   Buyer's Rights on Improper Delivery

Subject to the provisions of this Article on breach in installment contracts (Section 2-612) and unless otherwise agreed under the sections on contractual limitations of remedy (Sections 2-718 and 2-719), if the goods or the tender of delivery fail in any respect to conform to the contract, the buyer may

    (a) reject the whole; or

    (b) accept the whole; or

    (c) accept any commercial unit or units and reject the rest.

§2-602. Manner and Effect of Rightful Rejection

(1) Rejection of goods must be within a reasonable time after their delivery or tender. It is ineffective unless the buyer seasonably notifies the seller.

(2) Subject to the provisions of the two following sections on rejected goods (Sections 2-603 and 2-604),

    (a) after rejection any exercise of ownership by the buyer with respect to any commercial unit is wrongful as against the seller; and

    (b) if the buyer has before rejection taken physical possession of goods in which he does not have a security interest under the provisions of this Article (subsection (3) of Section 2-711), he is under a duty after rejection to hold them with reasonable care at the seller's disposition for a time sufficient to permit the seller to remove them; but

    (c) the buyer has no further obligations with regard to goods rightfully rejected.

(3) The seller's rights with respect to goods wrongfully rejected are governed by the provisions of this Article on Seller's remedies in general (Section 2-703).

§2-603. Merchant Buyer's Duties as to Rightfully Rejected Goods

(1) Subject to any security interest in the buyer (subsection (3) of Section 2-711), when the seller has no agent or place of business at the market of rejection a merchant buyer is under a duty after rejection of goods in his possession or control to follow any reasonable instructions received from the seller with respect to the goods and in the absence of such instructions to make reasonable efforts to sell them for the seller's account if they are perishable or threaten to decline in value speedily. Instructions are not reasonable if on demand indemnity for expenses is not forthcoming.

(2) When the buyer sells goods under subsection (1), he is entitled to reimbursement from the seller or out of the proceeds for reasonable expenses of caring for and selling them, and if the expenses include no selling commission then to such commission as is usual in the trade or if there is none to a reasonable sum not exceeding ten per cent on the gross proceeds.

(3) In complying with this section the buyer is held only to good faith and good faith conduct hereunder is neither acceptance nor conversion nor the basis of an action for damages.

§2-604. Buyer's Options as to Salvage of Rightfully Rejected Goods

Subject to the provisions of the immediately preceding section on perishables if the seller gives no instructions within a reasonable time after notification of rejection the buyer may store the rejected goods for the seller's account or reship them to him or resell them for the seller's account with reimbursement as provided in the preceding section. Such action is not acceptance or conversion.

§2-605. Waiver of Buyer's Objections by Failure to Particularize

(1) The buyer's failure to state in connection with rejection a particular defect which is ascertainable by reasonable inspection precludes him from relying on the unstated defect to justify rejection or to establish breach

    (a) where the seller could have cured it if stated seasonably; or

    (b) between merchants when the seller has after rejection made a request in writing for a full and final written statement of all defects on which the buyer proposes to rely.

(2) Payment against documents made without reservation of rights precludes recovery of the payment for defects apparent on the face of the documents.

§2-606. What Constitutes Acceptance of Goods

(1) Acceptance of goods occurs when the buyer

    (a) after a reasonable opportunity to inspect the goods signifies to the seller that the goods are conforming or that he will take or retain them in spite of their non-conformity; or

    (b) fails to make an effective rejection (subsection (1) of Section 2-602), but such acceptance does not occur until the buyer has had a reasonable opportunity to inspect them; or

    (c) does any act inconsistent with the seller's ownership; but if such act is wrongful as against the seller it is an acceptance only if ratified by him.

(2) Acceptance of a part of any commercial unit is acceptance of that entire unit.

§2-607. Effect of Acceptance; Notice of Breach; Burden of Establishing Breach After Acceptance; Notice of Claim or Litigation to Person Answerable Over

(1) The buyer must pay at the contract rate for any goods accepted.

(2) Acceptance of goods by the buyer precludes rejection of the goods

accepted and if made with knowledge of a non-conformity cannot be revoked because of it unless the acceptance was on the reasonable assumption that the non-conformity would be seasonably cured but acceptance does not of itself impair any other remedy provided by this Article for non-conformity.

(3) Where a tender has been accepted

(a) the buyer must within a reasonable time after he discovers or should have discovered any breach notify the seller of breach or be barred from any remedy; and

(b) if the claim is one for infringement or the like (subsection (3) of Section 2-312) and the buyer is sued as a result of such a breach he must so notify the seller within a reasonable time after he receives notice of the litigation or be barred from any remedy over for liability established by the litigation.

(4) The burden is on the buyer to establish any breach with respect to the goods accepted.

(5) Where the buyer is sued for breach of a warranty or other obligation for which his seller is answerable over

(a) he may give his seller written notice of the litigation. If the notice states that the seller may come in and defend and that if the seller does not do so he will be bound in any action against him by his buyer by any determination of fact common to the two litigations, then unless the seller after seasonable receipt of the notice does come in and defend he is so bound.

(b) if the claim is one for infringement or the like (subsection (3) of Section 2-312) the original seller may demand in writing that his buyer turn over to him control of the litigation including settlement or else be barred from any remedy over and if he also agrees to bear all expense and to satisfy any adverse judgment, then unless the buyer after seasonable receipt of the demand does turn over control the buyer is so barred.

(6) The provisions of subsections (3), (4) and (5) apply to any obligation of a buyer to hold the seller harmless against infringement or the like (subsection (3) of Section 2-312).

§2-608. Revocation of Acceptance in Whole or in Part

(1) The buyer may revoke his acceptance of a lot or commercial unit whose non-conformity substantially impairs its value to him if he has accepted it

(a) on the reasonable assumption that its non-conformity would be cured and it has not been seasonably cured; or

(b) without discovery of such non-conformity if his acceptance was reasonably induced either by the difficulty of discovery before acceptance or by the seller's assurances.

(2) Revocation of acceptance must occur within a reasonable time after the buyer discovers or should have discovered the ground for it and before any

substantial change in condition of the goods which is not caused by their own defects. It is not effective until the buyer notifies the seller of it.

(3) A buyer who so revokes has the same rights and duties with regard to the goods involved as if he had rejected them.

§2-609. Right to Adequate Assurance of Performance

(1) A contract for sale imposes an obligation on each party that the other's expectation of receiving due performance will not be impaired. When reasonable grounds for insecurity arise with respect to the performance of either party the other may in writing demand adequate assurance of due performance and until he receives such assurance may if commercially reasonable suspend any performance for which he has not already received the agreed return.

(2) Between merchants the reasonableness of grounds for insecurity and the adequacy of any assurance offered shall be determined according to commercial standards.

(3) Acceptance of any improper delivery or payment does not prejudice the aggrieved party's right to demand adequate assurance of future performance.

(4) After receipt of a justified demand failure to provide within a reasonable time not exceeding thirty days such assurance of due performance as is adequate under the circumstances of the particular case is a repudiation of the contract.

Official Comment

Prior Uniform Statutory Provision: See Sections 53, 54(1)(b), 55 and 63(2), Uniform Sales Act.

Purposes:

1. The section rests on the recognition of the fact that the essential purpose of a contract between commercial men is actual performance and they do not bargain merely for a promise, or for a promise plus the right to win a lawsuit and that a continuing sense of reliance and security that the promised performance will be forthcoming when due, is an important feature of the bargain. If either the willingness or the ability of a party to perform declines materially between the time of contracting and the time for performance, the other party is threatened with the loss of a substantial part of what he has bargained for. A seller needs protection not merely against having to deliver on credit to a shaky buyer, but also against having to procure and manufacture the goods, perhaps turning down other customers. Once he has been given reason to believe that the buyer's

performance has become uncertain, it is an undue hardship to force him to continue his own performance. Similarly, a buyer who believes that the seller's deliveries have become uncertain cannot safely wait for the due date of performance when he has been buying to assure himself of materials for his current manufacturing or to replenish his stock of merchandise.

2. Three measures have been adopted to meet the needs of commercial men in such situations. First, the aggrieved party is permitted to suspend his own performance and any preparation therefor, with excuse for any resulting necessary delay, until the situation has been clarified. "Suspend performance" under this section means to hold up performance pending the outcome of the demand, and includes also the holding up of any preparatory action. This is the same principle which governs the ancient law of stoppage and seller's lien, and also of excuse of a buyer from prepayment if the seller's actions manifest that he cannot or will not perform. (Original Act, Section 63(2).)

Secondly, the aggrieved party is given the right to require adequate assurance that the other party's performance will be duly forthcoming. This principle is reflected in the familiar clauses permitting the seller to curtail deliveries if the buyer's credit becomes impaired, which when held within the limits of reasonableness and good faith actually express no more than the fair business meaning of any commercial contract.

Third, and finally, this section provides the means by which the aggrieved party may treat the contract as broken if his reasonable grounds for insecurity are not cleared up within a reasonable time. This is the principle underlying the law of anticipatory breach, whether by way of defective part performance or by repudiation. The present section merges these three principles of law and commercial practice into a single theory of general application to all sales agreements looking to future performance.

3. Subsection (2) of the present section requires that "reasonable" grounds and "adequate" assurance as used in subsection (1) be defined by commercial rather than legal standards. The express reference to commercial standards carries no connotation that the obligation of good faith is not equally applicable here.

Under commercial standards and in accord with commercial practice, a ground for insecurity need not arise from or be directly related to the contract in question. The law as to "dependence" or "independence" of promises within a single contract does not control the application of the present section.

Thus a buyer who falls behind in "his account" with the seller, even though the items involved have to do with separate and legally distinct contracts, impairs the seller's expectation of due performance. Again, under the same test, a buyer who requires precision parts which he intends to use immediately upon delivery, may have reasonable grounds for insecurity if he discovers that his seller is making defective deliveries of such parts to other buyers with similar needs. Thus, too, in a situation such as arose in Jay Dreher Corporation v. Delco Appliance Corporation, 93 F.2d 275

(C.C.A.2, 1937), where a manufacturer gave a dealer an exclusive franchise for the sale of his product but on two or three occasions breached the exclusive dealing clause, although there was no default in orders, deliveries or payments under the separate sales contract between the parties, the aggrieved dealer would be entitled to suspend his performance of the contract for sale under the present section and to demand assurance that the exclusive dealing contract would be lived up to. There is no need for an explicit clause tying the exclusive franchise into the contract for the sale of goods since the situation itself ties the agreements together.

The nature of the sales contract enters also into the question of reasonableness. For example, a report from an apparently trustworthy source that the seller had shipped defective goods or was planning to ship them would normally give the buyer reasonable grounds for insecurity. But when the buyer has assumed the risk of payment before inspection of the goods, as in a sales contract on C.I.F. or similar cash against documents terms, that risk is not to be evaded by a demand for assurance. Therefore no ground for insecurity would exist under this section unless the report went to a ground which would excuse payment by the buyer.

4. What constitutes "adequate" assurance of due performance is subject to the same test of factual conditions. For example, where the buyer can make use of a defective delivery, a mere promise by a seller of good repute that he is giving the matter his attention and that the defect will not be repeated, is normally sufficient. Under the same circumstances, however, a similar statement by a known corner-cutter might well be considered insufficient without the posting of a guaranty or, if so demanded by the buyer, a speedy replacement of the delivery involved. By the same token where a delivery has defects, even though easily curable, which interfere with easy use by the buyer, no verbal assurance can be deemed adequate which is not accompanied by replacement, repair, money-allowance, or other commercially reasonable cure.

A fact situation such as arose in Corn Products Refining Co. v. Fasola, 94 N.J.L. 181, 109 A. 505 (1920) offers illustration both of reasonable grounds for insecurity and "adequate" assurance. In that case a contract for the sale of oils on 30 days' credit, 2% off for payment within 10 days, provided that credit was to be extended to the buyer only if his financial responsibility was satisfactory to the seller. The buyer had been in the habit of taking advantage of the discount but at the same time that he failed to make his customary 10 day payment, the seller heard rumors, in fact false, that the buyer's financial condition was shaky. Thereupon, the seller demanded cash before shipment or security satisfactory to him. The buyer sent a good credit report from his banker, expressed willingness to make payments when due on the 30 day terms and insisted on further deliveries under the contract. Under this Article the rumors, although false, were enough to make the buyer's financial condition "unsatisfactory" to the seller under the contract clause. Moreover, the buyer's practice of taking the cash discounts is enough, apart from the contract clause, to lay a commercial foundation for suspicion when the practice is suddenly stopped. These matters, however, go only to the justification of the seller's demand for security, or his "reasonable grounds for insecurity."

The adequacy of the assurance given is not measured as in the type of "satisfaction" situation affected with intangibles, such as in personal service cases, cases involving a third party's judgment as final, or cases in which the whole contract is dependent on one party's satisfaction, as in a sale on approval. Here, the seller must exercise good faith and observe commercial standards. This Article thus approves the statement of the court in James B. Berry's Sons Co. of Illinois v. Monark Gasoline & Oil Co., Inc., 32 F.2d 74 (C.C.A.8, 1929), that the seller's satisfaction under such a clause must be based upon reason and must not be arbitrary or capricious; and rejects the purely personal "good faith" test of the Corn Products Refining Co. case, which held that in the seller's sole judgment, if for *any* reason he was dissatisfied, he was entitled to revoke the credit. In the absence of the buyer's failure to take the 2% discount as was his custom, the banker's report given in that case would have been "adequate" assurance under this Act, regardless of the language of the "satisfaction" clause. However, the seller is reasonably entitled to feel insecure at a sudden expansion of the buyer's use of a credit term, and should be entitled either to security or to a satisfactory explanation.

The entire foregoing discussion as to adequacy of assurance by way of explanation is subject to qualification when repeated occasions for the application of this section arise. This Act recognizes that repeated delinquencies must be viewed as cumulative. On the other hand, commercial sense also requires that if repeated claims for assurance are made under this section, the basis for these claims must be increasingly obvious.

5. A failure to provide adequate assurance of performance and thereby to re-establish the security of expectation, results in a breach only "by repudiation" under subsection (4). Therefore, the possibility is continued of retraction of the repudiation under the section dealing with that problem, unless the aggrieved party has acted on the breach in some manner.

The thirty day limit on the time to provide assurance is laid down to free the question of reasonable time from uncertainty in later litigation.

6. Clauses seeking to give the protected party exceedingly wide powers to cancel or readjust the contract when ground for insecurity arises must be read against the fact that good faith is a part of the obligation of the contract and not subject to modification by agreement and includes, in the case of a merchant, the reasonable observance of commercial standards of fair dealing in the trade. Such clauses can thus be effective to enlarge the protection given by the present section to a certain extent, to fix the reasonable time within which requested assurance must be given, or to define adequacy of the assurance in any commercially reasonable fashion. But any clause seeking to set up arbitrary standards for action is ineffective

under this Article. Acceleration clauses are treated similarly in the Articles on Commercial Paper and Secured Transactions.

Cross References:
  Point 3: Section 1-203.
  Point 5: Section 2-611.
  Point 6: Sections 1-203 and 1-208 and Articles 3 and 9.

Definitional Cross References:
  "Aggrieved party." Section 1-201.
  "Between merchants." Section 2-104.
  "Contract." Section 1-201.
  "Contract for sale." Section 2-106.
  "Party." Section 1-201.
  "Reasonable time." Section 1-204.
  "Rights." Section 1-201.
  "Writing." Section 1-201

§2-610. Anticipatory Repudiation

When either party repudiates the contract with respect to a performance not yet due the loss of which will substantially impair the value of the contract to the other, the aggrieved party may

  (a) for a commercially reasonable time await performance by the repudiating party; or

  (b) resort to any remedy for breach (Section 2-703 or Section 2-711), even though he has notified the repudiating party that he would await the latter's performance and has urged retraction; and

  (c) in either case suspend his own performance or proceed in accordance with the provisions of this Article on the seller's right to identify goods to the contract notwithstanding breach or to salvage unfinished goods (Section 2-704).

Official Comment

Prior Uniform Statutory Provision: See Sections 63(2) and 65, Uniform Sales Act.

Purposes: To make it clear that:

1. With the problem of insecurity taken care of by the preceding section and with provision being made in this Article as to the effect of a defective delivery under an installment contract, anticipatory repudiation centers upon an overt communication of intention or an action which renders

performance impossible or demonstrates a clear determination not to continue with performance.

Under the present section when such a repudiation substantially impairs the value of the contract, the aggrieved party may at any time resort to his remedies for breach, or he may suspend his own performance while he negotiates with, or awaits performance by, the other party. But if he awaits performance beyond a commercially reasonable time he cannot recover resulting damages which he should have avoided.

2. It is not necessary for repudiation that performance be made literally and utterly impossible. Repudiation can result from action which reasonably indicates a rejection of the continuing obligation. And, a repudiation automatically results under the preceding section on insecurity when a party fails to provide adequate assurance of due future performance within thirty days after a justifiable demand therefor has been made. Under the language of this section, a demand by one or both parties for more than the contract calls for in the way of counter-performance is not in itself a repudiation nor does it invalidate a plain expression of desire for future performance. However, when under a fair reading it amounts to a statement of intention not to perform except on conditions which go beyond the contract, it becomes a repudiation.

3. The test chosen to justify an aggrieved party's action under this section is the same as that in the section on breach in installment contracts — namely the substantial value of the contract. The most useful test of substantial value is to determine whether material inconvenience or injustice will result if the aggrieved party is forced to wait and receive an ultimate tender minus the part or aspect repudiated.

4. After repudiation, the aggrieved party may immediately resort to any remedy he chooses provided he moves in good faith (see Section 1-203). Inaction and silence by the aggrieved party may leave the matter open but it cannot be regarded as misleading the repudiating party. Therefore the aggrieved party is left free to proceed at any time with his options under this section, unless he has taken some positive action which in good faith requires notification to the other party before the remedy is pursued.

Cross References:
    Point 1: Sections 2-609 and 2-612.
    Point 2: Section 2-609.
    Point 3: Section 2-612.
    Point 4: Section 1-203.

Definitional Cross References:
    "Aggrieved party." Section 1-201.
    "Contract." Section 1-201.
    "Party." Section 1-201.
    "Remedy." Section 1-201.

§2-611.   Retraction of Anticipatory Repudiation

(1) Until the repudiating party's next performance is due he can retract his repudiation unless the aggrieved party has since the repudiation cancelled or materially changed his position or otherwise indicated that he considers the repudiation final.

(2) Retraction may be by any method which clearly indicates to the aggrieved party that the repudiating party intends to perform, but must include any assurance justifiably demanded under the provisions of this Article (Section 2-609).

(3) Retraction reinstates the repudiating party's rights under the contract with due excuse and allowance to the aggrieved party for any delay occasioned by the repudiation.

§2-612.   "Installment Contract"; Breach

(1) An "installment contract" is one which requires or authorizes the delivery of goods in separate lots to be separately accepted, even though the contract contains a clause "each delivery is a separate contract" or its equivalent.

(2) The buyer may reject any installment which is non-conforming if the non-conformity substantially impairs the value of that installment and cannot be cured or if the non-conformity is a defect in the required documents; but if the non-conformity does not fall within subsection (3) and the seller gives adequate assurance of its cure the buyer must accept that installment.

(3) Whenever non-conformity or default with respect to one or more install-ments substantially impairs the value of the whole contract there is a breach of the whole. But the aggrieved party reinstates the contract if he accepts a non-conforming installment without seasonably notifying of cancellation or if he brings an action with respect only to past installments or demands perfor-mance as to future installments.

§2-613.   Casualty to Identified Goods

Where the contract requires for its performance goods identified when the contract is made, and the goods suffer casualty without fault of either party before the risk of loss passes to the buyer, or in a proper case under a "no arrival, no sale" term (Section 2-324) then

  (a) if the loss is total the contract is avoided; and

  (b) if the loss is partial or the goods have so deteriorated as no longer to conform to the contract the buyer may nevertheless demand inspection and at his option either treat the contract as avoided or accept the goods with due allowance from the contract price for the deterioration or the deficiency in quantity but without further right against the seller.

§2-614. Substituted Performance

(1) Where without fault of either party the agreed berthing, loading, or unloading facilities fail or an agreed type of carrier becomes unavailable or the agreed manner of delivery otherwise becomes commercially impracticable but a commercially reasonable substitute is available, such substitute performance must be tendered and accepted.

(2) If the agreed means or manner of payment fails because of domestic or foreign governmental regulation, the seller may withhold or stop delivery unless the buyer provides a means or manner of payment which is commercially a substantial equivalent. If delivery has already been taken, payment by the means or in the manner provided by the regulation discharges the buyer's obligation unless the regulation is discriminatory, oppressive or predatory.

§2-615. Excuse by Failure of Presupposed Conditions

Except so far as a seller may have assumed a greater obligation and subject to the preceding section on substituted performance:

(a) Delay in delivery or non-delivery in whole or in part by a seller who complies with paragraphs (b) and (c) is not a breach of his duty under a contract for sale if performance as agreed has been made impracticable by the occurrence of a contingency the non-occurrence of which was a basic assumption on which the contract was made or by compliance in good faith with any applicable foreign or domestic governmental regulation or order whether or not it later proves to be invalid.

(b) Where the causes mentioned in paragraph (a) affect only a part of the seller's capacity to perform, he must allocate production and deliveries among his customers but may at his option include regular customers not then under contract as well as his own requirements for further manufacture. He may so allocate in any manner which is fair and reasonable.

(c) The seller must notify the buyer seasonably that there will be delay or non-delivery and, when allocation is required under paragraph (b), of the estimated quota thus made available for the buyer.

Official Comment

Prior Uniform Statutory Provision: None.

Purposes:
1. This section excuses a seller from timely delivery of goods contracted for, where his performance has become commercially impracticable because of unforeseen supervening circumstances not within the contemplation of the parties at the time of contracting. The destruction of specific goods

and the problem of the use of substituted performance on points other than delay or quantity, treated elsewhere in this Article, must be distinguished from the matter covered by this section.

2. The present section deliberately refrains from any effort at an exhaustive expression of contingencies and is to be interpreted in all cases sought to be brought within its scope in terms of its underlying reason and purpose.

3. The first test for excuse under this Article in terms of basic assumption is a familiar one. The additional test of commercial impracticability (as contrasted with "impossibility," "frustration of performance" or "frustration of the venture") has been adopted in order to call attention to the commercial character of the criterion chosen by this Article.

4. Increased cost alone does not excuse performance unless the rise in cost is due to some unforeseen contingency which alters the essential nature of the performance. Neither is a rise or a collapse in the market in itself a justification, for that is exactly the type of business risk which business contracts made at fixed prices are intended to cover. But a severe shortage of raw materials or of supplies due to a contingency such as war, embargo, local crop failure, unforeseen shutdown of major sources of supply or the like, which either causes a marked increase in cost or altogether prevents the seller from securing supplies necessary to his performance, is within the contemplation of this section. (See Ford & Sons, Ltd. v. Henry Leetham & Sons, Ltd., 21 Com. Cas. 55 (1915, K.B.D.).)

5. Where a particular source of supply is exclusive under the agreement and fails through casualty, the present section applies rather than the provision on destruction or deterioration of specific goods. The same holds true where a particular source of supply is shown by the circumstances to have been contemplated or assumed by the parties at the time of contracting. (See Davis Co. v. Hoffmann-LaRoche Chemical Works, 178 App. Div. 855, 166 N.Y.S. 179 (1917) and International Paper Co. v. Rockefeller, 161 App. Div. 180, 146 N.Y.S. 371 (1914).) There is no excuse under this section, however, unless the seller has employed all due measures to assure himself that his source will not fail. (See Canadian Industrial Alcohol Co., Ltd. v. Dunbar Molasses Co., 258 N.Y. 194, 179 N.E. 383, 80 A.L.R. 1173 (1932) and Washington Mfg. Co. v. Midland Lumber Co., 113 Wash. 593, 194 P. 777 (1921).)

In the case of failure of production by an agreed source for causes beyond the seller's control, the seller should, if possible, be excused since production by an agreed source is without more a basic assumption of the contract. Such excuse should not result in relieving the defaulting supplier from liability nor in dropping into the seller's lap an unearned bonus of damages over. The flexible adjustment machinery of this Article provides the solution under the provision on the obligation of good faith. A condition to his making good the claim of excuse is the turning over to the buyer of his rights against the defaulting source of supply to the extent of the buyer's contract in relation to which excuse is being claimed.

6. In situations in which neither sense nor justice is served by either answer when the issue is posed in flat terms of "excuse" or "no excuse," adjustment under the various provisions of this Article is necessary, especially the sections on good faith, on insecurity and assurance and on the reading of all provisions in the light of their purposes, and the general policy of this Act to use equitable principles in furtherance of commercial standards and good faith.

7. The failure of conditions which go to convenience or collateral values rather than to the commercial practicability of the main performance does not amount to a complete excuse. However, good faith and the reason of the present section and of the preceding one may properly be held to justify and even to require any needed delay involved in a good faith inquiry seeking a readjustment of the contract terms to meet the new conditions.

8. The provisions of this section are made subject to assumption of greater liability by agreement and such agreement is to be found not only in the expressed terms of the contract but in the circumstances surrounding the contracting, in trade usage and the like. Thus the exemptions of this section do not apply when the contingency in question is sufficiently foreshadowed at the time of contracting to be included among the business risks which are fairly to be regarded as part of the dickered terms, either consciously or as a matter of reasonable, commercial interpretation from the circumstances. (See Madeirense Do Brasil, S. A. v. Stulman-Emrick Lumber Co., 147 F.2d 399 (C.C.A., 2 Cir., 1945).) The exemption otherwise present through usage of trade under the present section may also be expressly negated by the language of the agreement. Generally, express agreements as to exemptions designed to enlarge upon or supplant the provisions of this section are to be read in the light of mercantile sense and reason, for this section itself sets up the commercial standard for normal and reasonable interpretation and provides a minimum beyond which agreement may not go.

Agreement can also be made in regard to the consequences of exemption as laid down in paragraphs (b) and (c) and the next section on procedure on notice claiming excuse.

9. The case of a farmer who has contracted to sell crops to be grown on designated land may be regarded as falling either within the section on casualty to identified goods or this section, and he may be excused, when there is a failure of the specific crop, either on the basis of the destruction of identified goods or because of the failure of a basic assumption of the contract.

Exemption of the buyer in the case of a "requirements" contract is covered by the "Output and Requirements" section both as to assumption and allocation of the relevant risks. But when a contract by a manufacturer to buy fuel or raw material makes no specific reference to a particular venture and no such reference may be drawn from the circumstances, commercial understanding views it as a general deal in the general market and not conditioned on any assumption of the continuing operation of the buyer's plant. Even when notice is given by the buyer that the supplies are needed to fill a specific contract of a normal commercial kind, commercial understanding does not see such a supply contract as conditioned on the continuance of the buyer's further contract for outlet. On the other hand, where the buyer's contract is in reasonable commercial understanding conditioned on a definite and specific venture or assumption as, for instance, a war procurement subcontract known to be based on a prime contract which is subject to termination, or a supply contract for a particular construction venture, the reason of the present section may well apply and entitle the buyer to the exemption.

10. Following its basic policy of using commercial practicability as a test for excuse, this section recognizes as of equal significance either a foreign or domestic regulation and disregards any technical distinctions between "law," "regulation," "order" and the like. Nor does it make the present action of the seller depend upon the eventual judicial determination of the legality of the particular governmental action. The seller's good faith belief in the validity of the regulation is the test under this Article and the best evidence of his good faith is the general commercial acceptance of the regulation. However, governmental intereference cannot excuse unless it truly "supervenes" in such a manner as to be beyond the seller's assumption of risk. And any action by the party claiming excuse which causes or colludes in inducing the governmental action preventing his performance would be in breach of good faith and would destroy his exemption.

11. An excused seller must fulfill his contract to the extent which the supervening contingency permits, and if the situation is such that his customers are generally affected he must take account of all in supplying one. Subsections (a) and (b), therefore, explicitly permit in any proration a fair and reasonable attention to the needs of regular customers who are probably relying on spot orders for supplies. Customers at different stages of the manufacturing process may be fairly treated by including the seller's manufacturing requirements. A fortiori, the seller may also take account of contracts later in date than the one in question. The fact that such spot orders may be closed at an advanced price causes no difficulty, since any allocation which exceeds normal past requirements will not be reasonable. However, good faith requires, when prices have advanced, that the seller exercise real care in making his allocations, and in case of doubt his contract customers should be favored and supplies prorated evenly among them regardless of price. Save for the extra care thus required by changes in the market, this section seeks to leave every reasonable business leeway to the seller.

Cross References:
Point 1: Sections 2-613 and 2-614.
Point 2: Section 1-102.
Point 5: Sections 1-203 and 2-613.
Point 6: Sections 1-102, 1-203 and 2-609.

Point 7: Section 2-614.
Point 8: Sections 1-201, 2-302 and 2-616.
Point 9: Sections 1-102, 2-306 and 2-613.

Definitional Cross References:
"Between merchants." Section 2-104.
"Buyer." Section 2-103.
"Contract." Section 1-201.
"Contract for sale." Section 2-106.
"Good faith." Section 1-201.
"Merchant." Section 2-104.
"Notifies." Section 1-201.
"Seasonably." Section 1-204.
"Seller." Section 2-103.

§2-616.   Procedure on Notice Claiming Excuse

(1) Where the buyer receives notification of a material or indefinite delay or an allocation justified under the preceding section he may by written notification to the seller as to any delivery concerned, and where the prospective deficiency substantially impairs the value of the whole contract under the provisions of this Article relating to breach of installment contracts (Section 2-612), then also as to the whole,

(a) terminate and thereby discharge any unexecuted portion of the contract; or

(b) modify the contract by agreeing to take his available quota in substitution.

(2) If after receipt of such notification from the seller the buyer fails so to modify the contract within a reasonable time not exceeding thirty days the contract lapses with respect to any deliveries affected.

(3) The provisions of this section may not be negated by agreement except in so far as the seller has assumed a greater obligation under the preceding section.

Part 7.   Remedies

§2-702.   Seller's Remedies on Discovery of Buyer's Insolvency

(1) Where the seller discovers the buyer to be insolvent he may refuse delivery except for cash including payment for all goods theretofore delivered under the contract, and stop delivery under this Article (Section 2-705).

(2) Where the seller discovers that the buyer has received goods on credit while insolvent he may reclaim the goods upon demand made within ten days after the receipt, but if misrepresentation of solvency has been made to the particular seller in writing within three months before delivery the ten day limitation does not apply. Except as provided in this subsection the seller may not base a right to reclaim goods on the buyer's fraudulent or innocent misrepresentation of solvency or of intent to pay.

(3) The seller's right to reclaim under subsection (2) is subject to the rights of a buyer in ordinary course or other good faith purchaser under this Article (Section 2-403). Successful reclamation of goods excludes all other remedies with respect to them.

§2-703.   Seller's Remedies in General

Where the buyer wrongfully rejects or revokes acceptance of goods or fails to make a payment due on or before delivery or repudiates with respect to a part or the whole, then with respect to any goods directly affected and, if the breach is of the whole contract (Section 2-612), then also with respect to the whole undelivered balance, the aggrieved seller may

(a) withhold delivery of such goods;

(b) stop delivery by any bailee as hereafter provided (Section 2-705);

(c) proceed under the next section respecting goods still unidentified to the contract;

(d) resell and recover damages as hereafter provided (Section 2-706);

(e) recover damages for non-acceptance (Section 2-708) or in a proper case the price (Section 2-709);

(f) cancel.

§2-704.   Seller's Right to Identify Goods to the Contract Notwithstanding Breach or to Salvage Unfinished Goods

(1) An aggrieved seller under the preceding section may

(a) identify to the contract conforming goods not already identified if at the time he learned of the breach they are in his possession or control;

(b) treat as the subject of resale goods which have demonstrably been intended for the particular contract even though those goods are unfinished.

(2) Where the goods are unfinished an aggrieved seller may in the exercise of reasonable commercial judgment for the purposes of avoiding loss and of effective realization either complete the manufacture and wholly identify the

goods to the contract or cease manufacture and resell for scrap or salvage value or proceed in any other reasonable manner.

§2-705. Seller's Stoppage of Delivery in Transit or Otherwise

(1) The seller may stop delivery of goods in the possession of a carrier or other bailee when he discovers the buyer to be insolvent (Section 2-702) and may stop delivery of carload, truckload, planeload or larger shipments of express or freight when the buyer repudiates or fails to make a payment due before delivery or if for any other reason the seller has a right to withhold or reclaim the goods.

(2) As against such buyer the seller may stop delivery until

(a) receipt of the goods by the buyer; or

(b) acknowledgment to the buyer by any bailee of the goods except a carrier that the bailee holds the goods for the buyer; or

(c) such acknowledgment to the buyer by a carrier by reshipment or as warehouseman; or

(d) negotiation to the buyer of any negotiable document of title covering the goods.

(3) (a) To stop delivery the seller must so notify as to enable the bailee by reasonable diligence to prevent delivery of the goods.

(b) After such notification the bailee must hold and deliver the goods according to the directions of the seller but the seller is liable to the bailee for any ensuing charges or damages.

(c) If a negotiable document of title has been issued for goods the bailee is not obliged to obey a notification to stop until surrender of the document.

(d) A carrier who has issued a non-negotiable bill of lading is not obliged to obey a notification to stop received from a person other than the consignor.

§2-706. Seller's Resale Including Contract for Resale

(1) Under the conditions stated in Section 2-703 on seller's remedies, the seller may resell the goods concerned or the undelivered balance thereof. Where the resale is made in good faith and in a commercially reasonable manner the seller may recover the difference between the resale price and the contract price together with any incidental damages allowed under the provisions of this Article (Section 2-710), but less expenses saved in consequence of the buyer's breach.

(2) Except as otherwise provided in subsection (3) or unless otherwise agreed

resale may be at public or private sale including sale by way of one or more contracts to sell or of identification to an existing contract of the seller. Sale may be as a unit or in parcels and at any time and place and on any terms but every aspect of the sale including the method, manner, time, place and terms must be commercially reasonable. The resale must be reasonably identified as referring to the broken contract, but it is not necessary that the goods be in existence or that any or all of them have been identified to the contract before the breach.

(3) Where the resale is at private sale the seller must give the buyer reasonable notification of his intention to resell.

(4) Where the resale is at public sale

(a) only identified goods can be sold except where there is a recognized market for a public sale of futures in goods of the kind; and

(b) it must be made at a usual place or market for public sale if one is reasonably available and except in the case of goods which are perishable or threaten to decline in value speedily the seller must give the buyer reasonable notice of the time and place of the resale; and

(c) if the goods are not to be within the view of those attending the sale the notification of sale must state the place where the goods are located and provide for their reasonable inspection by prospective bidders; and

(d) the seller may buy.

(5) A purchaser who buys in good faith at a resale takes the goods free of any rights of the original buyer even though the seller fails to comply with one or more of the requirements of this section.

(6) The seller is not accountable to the buyer for any profit made on any resale. A person in the position of a seller (Section 2-707) or a buyer who has rightfully rejected or justifiably revoked acceptance must account for any excess over the amount of his security interest, as hereinafter defined (subsection (3) of Section 2-711).

§2-708. Seller's Damages for Non-acceptance or Repudiation

(1) Subject to subsection (2) and to the provisions of this Article with respect to proof of market price (Section 2-723), the measure of damages for non-acceptance or repudiation by the buyer is the difference between the market price at the time and place for tender and the unpaid contract price together with any incidental damages provided in this Article (Section 2-710), but less expenses saved in consequence of the buyer's breach.

(2) If the measure of damages provided in subsection (1) is inadequate to put the seller in as good a position as performance would have done then the measure of damages is the profit (including reasonable overhead) which the seller would have made from full performance by the buyer, together with any incidental damages provided in this Article (Section

2-710), due allowance for costs reasonably incurred and due credit for payments or proceeds of resale.

§2-709.   Action for the Price

(1) When the buyer fails to pay the price as it becomes due the seller may recover, together with any incidental damages under the next section, the price
   (a) of goods accepted or of conforming goods lost or damaged within a commercially reasonable time after risk of their loss has passed to the buyer; and
   (b) of goods identified to the contract if the seller is unable after reasonable effort to resell them at a reasonable price or the circumstances reasonably indicate that such effort will be unavailing.

(2) Where the seller sues for the price he must hold for the buyer any goods which have been identified to the contract and are still in his control except that if resale becomes possible he may resell them at any time prior to the collection of the judgment. The net proceeds of any such resale must be credited to the buyer and payment of the judgment entitles him to any goods not resold.

(3) After the buyer has wrongfully rejected or revoked acceptance of the goods or has failed to make a payment due or has repudiated (Section 2-610), a seller who is held not entitled to the price under this section shall nevertheless be awarded damages for non-acceptance under the preceding section.

§2-710.   Seller's Incidental Damages

Incidental damages to an aggrieved seller include any commercially reasonable charges, expenses or commissions incurred in stopping delivery, in the transportation, care and custody of goods after the buyer's breach, in connection with return or resale of the goods or otherwise resulting from the breach.

§2-711.   Buyer's Remedies in General; Buyer's Security Interest in Rejected Goods

(1) Where the seller fails to make delivery or repudiates or the buyer rightfully rejects or justifiably revokes acceptance then with respect to any goods involved, and with respect to the whole if the breach goes to the whole contract (Section 2-612), the buyer may cancel and whether or not he has done so may in addition to recovering so much of the price as has been paid
   (a) "cover" and have damages under the next section as to all the goods affected whether or not they have been identified to the contract; or

(b) recover damages for non-delivery as provided in this Article (Section 2-713).

(2) Where the seller fails to deliver or repudiates the buyer may also

(a) if the goods have been identified recover them as provided in this Article (Section 2-502); or

(b) in a proper case obtain specific performance or replevy the goods as provided in this Article (Section 2-716).

(3) On rightful rejection or justifiable revocation of acceptance a buyer has a security interest in goods in his possession or control for any payments made on their price and any expenses reasonably incurred in their inspection, receipt, transportation, care and custody and may hold such goods and resell them in like manner as an aggrieved seller (Section 2-706).

§2-712. "Cover"; Buyer's Procurement of Substitute Goods

(1) After a breach within the preceding section the buyer may "cover" by making in good faith and without unreasonable delay any reasonable purchase of or contract to purchase goods in substitution for those due from the seller.

(2) The buyer may recover from the seller as damages the difference between the cost of cover and the contract price together with any incidental or consequential damages as hereinafter defined (Section 2-715), but less expenses saved in consequence of the seller's breach.

(3) Failure of the buyer to effect cover within this section does not bar him from any other remedy.

§2-713. Buyer's Damages for Non-Delivery or Repudiation

(1) Subject to the provisions of this Article with respect to proof of market price (Section 2-723), the measure of damages for non-delivery or repudiation by the seller is the difference between the market price at the time when the buyer learned of the breach and the contract price together with any incidental and consequential damages provided in this Article (Section 2-715), but less expenses saved in consequence of the seller's breach.

(2) Market price is to be determined as of the place for tender or, in cases of rejection after arrival or revocation of acceptance, as of the place of arrival.

§2-714. Buyer's Damages for Breach in Regard to Accepted Goods

(1) Where the buyer has accepted goods and given notification (subsection (3) of Section 2-607) he may recover as damages for any non-conformity of

tender the loss resulting in the ordinary course of events from the seller's breach as determined in any manner which is reasonable.

(2) The measure of damages for breach of warranty is the difference at the time and place of acceptance between the value of the goods accepted and the value they would have had if they had been as warranted, unless special circumstances show proximate damages of a different amount.

(3) In a proper case any incidental and consequential damages under the next section may also be recovered.

§2-715. Buyer's Incidental and Consequential Damages

(1) Incidental damages resulting from the seller's breach include expenses reasonably incurred in inspection, receipt, transportation and care and custody of goods rightfully rejected, any commercially reasonable charges, expenses or commissions in connection with effecting cover and any other reasonable expense incident to the delay or other breach.

(2) Consequential damages resulting from the seller's breach include

(a) any loss resulting from general or particular requirements and needs of which the seller at the time of contracting had reason to know and which could not reasonably be prevented by cover or otherwise; and

(b) injury to person or property proximately resulting from any breach of warranty.

§2-716. Buyer's Right to Specific Performance or Replevin

(1) Specific performance may be decreed where the goods are unique or in other proper circumstances.

(2) The decree for specific performance may include such terms and conditions as to payment of the price, damages, or other relief as the court may deem just.

(3) The buyer has a right of replevin for goods identified to the contract if after reasonable effort he is unable to effect cover for such goods or the circumstances reasonably indicate that such effort will be unavailing or if the goods have been shipped under reservation and satisfaction of the security interest in them has been made or tendered.

§2-717. Deduction of Damages From the Price

The buyer on notifying the seller of his intention to do so may deduct all or any part of the damages resulting from any breach of the contract from any part of the price still due under the same contract.

§2-718. Liquidation or Limitation of Damages; Deposits

(1) Damages for breach by either party may be liquidated in the agreement but only at an amount which is reasonable in the light of the anticipated or actual harm caused by the breach, the difficulties of proof of loss, and the inconvenience or nonfeasibility of otherwise obtaining an adequate remedy. A term fixing unreasonably large liquidated damages is void as a penalty.

(2) Where the seller justifiably withholds delivery of goods because of the buyer's breach, the buyer is entitled to restitution of any amount by which the sum of his payments exceeds

(a) the amount to which the seller is entitled by virtue of terms liquidating the seller's damages in accordance with subsection (1), or

(b) in the absence of such terms, twenty per cent of the value of the total performance for which the buyer is obligated under the contract or $500, whichever is smaller.

(3) The buyer's right to restitution under subsection (2) is subject to offset to the extent that the seller establishes

(a) a right to recover damages under the provisions of this Article other than subsection (1), and

(b) the amount or value of any benefits received by the buyer directly or indirectly by reason of the contract.

(4) Where a seller has received payment in goods their reasonable value or the proceeds of their resale shall be treated as payments for the purposes of subsection (2); but if the seller has notice of the buyer's breach before reselling goods received in part performance, his resale is subject to the conditions laid down in this Article on resale by an aggrieved seller (Section 2-706).

§2-719. Contractual Modification or Limitation of Remedy

(1) Subject to the provisions of subsections (2) and (3) of this section and of the preceding section on liquidation and limitation of damages,

(a) the agreement may provide for remedies in addition to or in substitution for those provided in this Article and may limit or alter the measure of damages recoverable under this Article, as by limiting the buyer's remedies to return of the goods and repayment of the price or to repair and replacement of non-conforming goods or parts; and

(b) resort to a remedy as provided is optional unless the remedy is expressly agreed to be exclusive, in which case it is the sole remedy.

(2) Where circumstances cause an exclusive or limited remedy to fail of its essential purpose, remedy may be had as provided in this Act.

(3) Consequential damages may be limited or excluded unless the limitation or exclusion is unconscionable. Limitation of consequential damages for injury

to the person in the case of consumer goods is prima facie unconscionable but limitation of damages where the loss is commercial is not.

§2-721. Remedies for Fraud

Remedies for material misrepresentation or fraud include all remedies available under this Article for non-fraudulent breach. Neither rescission or a claim for rescission of the contract for sale nor rejection or return of the goods shall bar or be deemed inconsistent with a claim for damages or other remedy.

§2-723. Proof of Market Price: Time and Place

(1) If an action based on anticipatory repudiation comes to trial before the time for performance with respect to some or all of the goods, any damages based on market price (Section 2-708 or Section 2-713) shall be determined according to the price of such goods prevailing at the time when the aggrieved party learned of the repudiation.

(2) If evidence of a price prevailing at the times or places described in this Article is not readily available the price prevailing within any reasonable time before or after the time described or at any other place which in commercial judgment or under usage of trade would serve as a reasonable substitute for the one described may be used, making any proper allowance for the cost of transporting the goods to or from such other place.

(3) Evidence of a relevant price prevailing at a time or place other than the one described in this Article offered by one party is not admissible unless and until he has given the other party such notice as the court finds sufficient to prevent unfair surprise.

§2-725. Statute of Limitations in Contracts for Sale

(1) An action for breach of any contract for sale must be commenced within four years after the cause of action has accrued. By the original agreement the parties may reduce the period of limitation to not less than one year but may not extend it.

(2) A cause of action accrues when the breach occurs, regardless of the aggrieved party's lack of knowledge of the breach. A breach of warranty occurs when tender of delivery is made, except that where a warranty explicitly extends to future performance of the goods and discovery of the breach must await the time of such performance the cause of action accrues when the breach is or should have been discovered.

(3) Where an action commenced within the time limited by subsection (1) is so terminated as to leave available a remedy by another action for the same breach such other action may be commenced after the expiration of the time limited and within six months after the termination of the first action unless the termination resulted from voluntary discontinuance or from dismissal for failure or neglect to prosecute.

(4) This section does not alter the law on tolling of the statute of limitations nor does it apply to causes of action which have accrued before this Act becomes effective.

ARTICLE 3.   NEGOTIABLE INSTRUMENTS

Part 1.   *General Provisions and Definitions*

§3-104.   Negotiable Instrument

(a) Except as provided in subsections (c) and (d), "negotiable instrument" means an unconditional promise or order to pay a fixed amount of money, with or without interest or other charges described in the promise or order, if it:

(1) is payable to bearer or to order at the time it is issued or first comes into possession of a holder;

(2) is payable on demand or at a definite time; and

(3) does not state any other undertaking or instruction by the person promising or ordering payment to do any act in addition to the payment of money, but the promise or order may contain

(i) an undertaking or power to give, maintain, or protect collateral to secure payment,

(ii) an authorization or power to the holder to confess judgment or realize on or dispose of collateral, or

(iii) a waiver of the benefit of any law intended for the advantage or protection of an obligor.

(b) "Instrument" means a negotiable instrument.

(c) An order that meets all of the requirements of subsection (a), except paragraph (1), and otherwise falls within the definition of "check" in subsection (f) is a negotiable instrument and a check.

(d) A promise or order other than a check is not an instrument if, at the time it is issued or first comes into possession of a holder, it contains a conspicuous statement, however expressed, to the effect that the promise or order is not negotiable or is not an instrument governed by this Article.

(e) An instrument is a "note" if it is a promise and is a "draft" if it is an order. If an instrument falls within the definition of both "note" and "draft," a person entitled to enforce the instrument may treat it as either.

(f) "Check" means (i) a draft, other than a documentary draft, payable on demand and drawn on a bank or (ii) a cashier's check or teller's check. An instrument may be a check even though it is described on its face by another term, such as "money order."

(g) "Cashier's check" means a draft with respect to which the drawer and drawee are the same bank or branches of the same bank.

(h) "Teller's check" means a draft drawn by a bank (i) on another bank, or (ii) payable at or through a bank.

(i) "Traveler's check" means an instrument that (i) is payable on demand, (ii) is drawn on or payable at or through a bank, (iii) is designated by the term "traveler's check" or by a substantially similar term, and (iv) requires, as a condition to payment, a countersignature by a person whose specimen signature appears on the instrument.

(j) "Certificate of deposit" means an instrument containing an acknowledgment by a bank that a sum of money has been received by the bank and a promise by the bank to repay the sum of money. A certificate of deposit is a note of the bank.

Part 3.   Enforcement of Instruments

§3-302.   Holder in Due Course

(a) Subject to subsection (c) and Section 3-106(d), "holder in due course" means the holder of an instrument if:

(1) the instrument when issued or negotiated to the holder does not bear such apparent evidence of forgery or alteration or is not otherwise so irregular or incomplete as to call into question its authenticity; and

(2) the holder took the instrument

(i) for value,

(ii) in good faith,

(iii) without notice that the instrument is overdue or has been dishonored or that there is an uncured default with respect to payment of another instrument issued as part of the same series,

(iv) without notice that the instrument contains an unauthorized signature or has been altered,

(v) without notice of any claim to the instrument described in Section 3-306, and

(vi) without notice that any party has a defense or claim in recoupment described in Section 3-305(a).

(b) Notice of discharge of a party, other than discharge in an insolvency proceeding, is not notice of a defense under subsection (a), but discharge is effective against a person who became a holder in due course with notice of the discharge. Public filing or recording of a document does not of itself constitute notice of a defense, claim in recoupment, or claim to the instrument.

(c) Except to the extent a transferor or predecessor in interest has rights as a holder in due course, a person does not acquire rights of a holder in due course of an instrument taken

   (i) by legal process or by purchase in an execution, bankruptcy, or creditor's sale or similar proceeding,

   (ii) by purchase as part of a bulk transaction not in ordinary course of business of the transferor, or

   (iii) as the successor in interest to an estate or other organization.

(d) If, under Section 3-303(a)(1), the promise of performance that is the consideration for an instrument has been partially performed, the holder may assert rights as a holder in due course of the instrument only to the fraction of the amount payable under the instrument equal to the value of the partial performance divided by the value of the promised performance.

(e) If (i) the person entitled to enforce an instrument has only a security interest in the instrument and (ii) the person obliged to pay the instrument has a defense, claim in recoupment, or claim to the instrument that may be asserted against the person who granted the security interest, the person entitled to enforce the instrument may assert rights as a holder in due course only to an amount payable under the instrument which, at the time of enforcement of the instrument, does not exceed the amount of the unpaid obligation secured.

(f) To be effective, notice must be received at a time and in a manner that gives a reasonable opportunity to act on it.

(g) This section is subject to any law limiting status as a holder in due course in particular classes of transactions.

§3-305. Defenses and Claims in Recoupment

(a) Except as stated in subsection (b), the right to enforce the obligation of a party to pay an instrument is subject to the following:

   (1) a defense of the obligor based on (i) infancy of the obligor to the extent it is a defense to a simple contract, (ii) duress, lack of legal capacity, or illegality of the transaction, which under other law, nullifies the obligation of the obligor, (iii) fraud that induced the obligor to sign the instrument with neither knowledge nor reasonable opportunity to learn of its character or its essential terms, or (iv) discharge of the obligor in insolvency proceedings;

   (2) a defense of the obligor stated in another section of this Article or a defense of the obligor that would be available if the person entitled to enforce the instrument were enforcing a right to payment under a simple contract; and

(3) a claim in recoupment of the obligor against the original payee of the instrument if the claim arose from the transaction that gave rise to the instrument; but the claim of the obligor may be asserted against a transferee of the instrument only to reduce the amount owing on the instrument at the time the action is brought.

(b) The right of a holder in due course to enforce the obligation of a party to pay the instrument is subject to defenses of the obligor stated in subsection (a)(1), but is not subject to defenses of the obligor stated in subsection (a)(2) or claims in recoupment stated in subsection (a)(3) against a person other than the holder.

(c) Except as stated in subsection (d), in an action to enforce the obligation of a party to pay the instrument, the obligor may not assert against the person entitled to enforce the instrument a defense, claim in recoupment, or claim to the instrument (Section 3-306) of another person, but the other person's claim to the instrument may be asserted by the obligor if the other person is joined in the action and personally asserts the claim against the person entitled to enforce the instrument. An obligor is not obliged to pay the instrument if the person seeking enforcement of the instrument does not have rights of a holder in due course and the obligor proves that the instrument is a lost or stolen instrument.

(d) In an action to enforce the obligation of an accommodation party to pay an instrument, the accommodation party may assert against the person entitled to enforce the instrument any defense or claim in recoupment under subsection (a) that the accommodated party could assert against the person entitled to enforce the instrument, except the defenses of discharge in insolvency proceedings, infancy, and lack of legal capacity.

§3-306. Claims to an Instrument

A person taking an instrument, other than a person having rights of a holder in due course, is subject to a claim of a property or possessory right in the instrument or its proceeds, including a claim to rescind a negotiation and to recover the instrument or its proceeds. A person having rights of a holder in due course takes free of the claim to the instrument.

§3-311. Accord and Satisfaction by Use of Instrument

(a) If a person against whom a claim is asserted proves that
    (i) that person in good faith tendered an instrument to the claimant as full satisfaction of the claim,
    (ii) the amount of the claim was unliquidated or subject to a bona fide dispute, and

(iii) the claimant obtained payment of the instrument, the following subsections apply.

(b) Unless subsection (c) applies, the claim is discharged if the person against whom the claim is asserted proves that the instrument or an accompanying written communication contained a conspicuous statement to the effect that the instrument was tendered as full satisfaction of the claim.

(c) Subject to subsection (d), a claim is not discharged under subsection (b) if either of the following applies:

(1) The claimant, if an organization, proves that

(i) within a reasonable time before the tender, the claimant sent a conspicuous statement to the person against whom the claim is asserted that communications concerning disputed debts, including an instrument tendered as full satisfaction of a debt, are to be sent to a designated person, office, or place, and

(ii) the instrument or accompanying communication was not received by that designated person, office, or place.

(2) The claimant, whether or not an organization, proves that within 90 days after payment of the instrument, the claimant tendered repayment of the amount of the instrument to the person against whom the claim is asserted. This paragraph does not apply if the claimant is an organization that sent a statement complying with paragraph (1)(i).

(d) A claim is discharged if the person against whom the claim is asserted proves that within a reasonable time before collection of the instrument was initiated, the claimant, or an agent of the claimant having direct responsibility with respect to the disputed obligation, knew that the instrument was tendered in full satisfaction of the claim.

ARTICLE 9.   SECURED TRANSACTIONS; SALES OF ACCOUNTS AND CHATTEL PAPER

Part 1.   Short Title, Applicability and Definitions

§9-102.   Policy and Subject Matter of Article

(1) Except as otherwise provided in Section 9-104 on excluded transactions, this Article applies

(a) to any transaction (regardless of its form) which is intended to create a security interest in personal property or fixtures including goods, documents, instruments, general intangibles, chattel paper or accounts; and also

(b) to any sale of accounts or chattel paper.

(2) This Article applies to security interests created by contract including pledge, assignment, chattel mortgage, chattel trust, trust deed, factor's lien,

equipment trust, conditional sale, trust receipt, other lien or title retention contract and lease or consignment intended as security. This Article does not apply to statutory liens except as provided in Section 9-310.

(3) The application of this Article to a security interest in a secured obligation is not affected by the fact that the obligation is itself secured by a transaction or interest to which this Article does not apply.

§9-104. Transactions Excluded from Article

This Article does not apply

(a) to a security interest subject to any statute of the United States, to the extent that such statute governs the rights of parties to and third parties affected by transactions in particular types of property; or

(b) to a landlord's lien; or

(c) to a lien given by statute or other rule of law for services or materials except as provided in Section 9-310 on priority of such liens; or

(d) to a transfer of a claim for wages, salary or other compensation of an employee; or

(e) to a transfer by a government or governmental subdivision or agency; or

(f) to a sale of accounts or chattel paper as part of a sale of the business out of which they arose, or an assignment of accounts or chattel paper which is for the purpose of collection only, or a transfer of a right to payment under a contract to an assignee who is also to do the performance under the contract or a transfer of a single account to an assignee in whole or partial satisfaction of a preexisting indebtedness; or

(g) to a transfer of an interest in or claim in or under any policy of insurance, except as provided with respect to proceeds (Section 9-306) and priorities in proceeds (Section 9-312); or

(h) to a right represented by a judgment (other than a judgment taken on a right to payment which was collateral); or

(i) to any right of set-off; or

(j) except to the extent that provision is made for fixtures in Section 9-313, to the creation or transfer of an interest in or lien on real estate, including a lease or rents thereunder; or

(k) to a transfer in whole or in part of any claim arising out of tort; or

(l) to a transfer of an interest in any deposit account (subsection (1) of Section 9-105), except as provided with respect to proceeds (Section 9-306) and priorities in proceeds (Section 9-312).

Part 2. Validity of Security Agreement and Rights of Parties Thereto

§9-206. Agreement Not to Assert Defenses Against Assignee; Modification of Sales Warranties Where Security Agreement Exists

(1) Subject to any statute or decision which establishes a different rule for buyers or lessees of consumer goods, an agreement by a buyer or lessee that he will not assert against an assignee any claim or defense which he may have against the seller or lessor is enforceable by an assignee who takes his assignment for value, in good faith and without notice of a claim or defense, except as to defenses of a type which may be asserted against a holder in due course of a negotiable instrument under the Article on Commercial Paper (Article 3). A buyer who as part of one transaction signs both a negotiable instrument and a security agreement makes such an agreement.

(2) When a seller retains a purchase money security interest in goods the Article on Sales (Article 2) governs the sale and any disclaimer, limitation or modification of the seller's warranties.

Part 3. Rights of Third Parties; Perfected and Unperfected Security Interests; Rules of Priority

§9-318. Defenses Against Assignee; Modification of Contract After Notification of Assignment; Term Prohibiting Assignment Ineffective; Identification and Proof of Assignment

(1) Unless an account debtor has made an enforceable agreement not to assert defenses or claims arising out of a sale as provided in Section 9-206 the rights of an assignee are subject to

(a) all the terms of the contract between the account debtor and assignor and any defense or claim arising therefrom; and

(b) any other defense or claim of the account debtor against the assignor which accrues before the account debtor receives notification of the assignment.

(2) So far as the right to payment or a part thereof under an assigned contract has not been fully earned by performance, and notwithstanding notification of the assignment, any modification of or substitution for the contract made in good faith and in accordance with reasonable commercial

standards is effective against an assignee unless the account debtor has otherwise agreed but the assignee acquires corresponding rights under the modified or substituted contract. The assignment may provide that such modification or substitution is a breach by the assignor.

(3) The account debtor is authorized to pay the assignor until the account debtor receives notification that the amount due or to become due has been assigned and that payment is to be made to the assignee. A notification which does not reasonably identify the rights assigned is ineffective. If requested by the account debtor, the assignee must seasonably furnish reasonable proof that the assignment has been made and unless he does so the account debtor may pay the assignor.

(4) A term in any contract between an account debtor and an assignor is ineffective if it prohibits assignment of an account or prohibits creation of a security interest in a general intangible for money due or to become due or requires the account debtor's consent to such assignment or security interest.

Convention on Contracts for the International Sale of Goods

EDITORS' NOTE

On December 11, 1986, the United States ratified the United Nations Convention on Contracts for the International Sale of Goods (CISG). The Convention, which became effective January 1, 1988, was the product of almost two decades of work by the United Nations Commission on International Trade Law (UNCITRAL). The Commission was itself the outgrowth of earlier efforts to unify the law of international trade, particularly the Hague Convention of 1964, which had approved a uniform law on the international sale of goods. For the history of these developments, see John Honnold, The Uniform Law for the International Sale of Goods: the Hague Convention of 1964, 30 Law & Contemp. Probs. 326 (1965).

Article 1(1) of the Convention provides that the Convention applies to contracts between parties in different countries when the countries are parties to the Convention. A growing number of countries have adopted the Convention, including some of the United States' major trading partners: Canada, Mexico, France, and Germany. Others are expected to follow.

Article 6 of the Convention provides that the parties may exclude the application of the Convention or "derogate from or vary the effect of any of its provisions." If a buyer and seller in different countries that are parties to the Convention agree to a sales contract that is silent about the applicability of the Convention, the Convention would apply and its terms would supersede provisions of the Uniform Commercial Code. Thus, it is important for lawyers to be aware of the applicability of the Convention and to evaluate its substantive provisions to decide whether a contract of sale should exclude the applicability of the Convention entirely or modify any of its provisions.

Convention on Contracts for the International Sale of Goods

PART I.   SPHERE OF APPLICATION AND GENERAL PROVISIONS

Chapter I.   Sphere of Application

Chapter II.   General Provisions

PART II.   FORMATION OF THE CONTRACT

PART III.   SALE OF GOODS

Chapter I.   General Provisions

Chapter II.   Obligations of the Seller

Section I.   Delivery of the Goods and Handing Over of Documents

---

* The titles of articles listed in this table have been prepared by the editors and are not part of the Convention.

Convention on Contracts for the International Sale of Goods

Chapter IV.   Passing of Risk

Chapter V.   Provisions Common to the Obligations of the Seller and of the Buyer

PART IV.   FINAL PROVISIONS

The States Parties to This Convention,

BEARING IN MIND the broad objectives in the resolutions adopted by the sixth special session of the General Assembly of the United Nations on the establishment of a New International Economic Order,

CONSIDERING that the development of international trade on the basis of equality and mutual benefit is an important element in promoting friendly relations among States,

BEING OF THE OPINION that the adoption of uniform rules which govern contracts for the international sale of goods and take into account the different social, economic and legal systems would contribute to the removal of legal barriers in international trade and promote the development of international trade,

Have agreed as follows:

PART I. SPHERE OF APPLICATION AND GENERAL PROVISIONS

Chapter I. Sphere of Application

Article 1

(1) This Convention applies to contracts of sale of goods between parties whose places of business are in different States:

(a) When the States are Contracting States; or

(b) When the rules of private international law lead to the application of the law of a Contracting State.*

(2) The fact that the parties have their places of business in different States is to be disregarded whenever this fact does not appear either from the contract or from any dealings between, or from information disclosed by, the parties at any time before or at the conclusion of the contract.

(3) Neither the nationality of the parties nor the civil or commercial character of the parties or of the contract is to be taken into consideration in determining the application of this Convention.

Article 2

This Convention does not apply to sales:

(a) Of goods bought for personal, family or household use, unless the seller, at any time before or at the conclusion of the contract, neither knew nor ought to have known that the goods were bought for any such use;

(b) By auction;

(c) On execution or otherwise by authority of law;

(d) Of stocks, shares, investment securities, negotiable instruments or money;

---

* The United States has declared a reservation under Article 95 and is not bound by §1(b). — EDS.

(e) Of ships, vessels, hovercraft or aircraft;

(f) Of electricity.

Article 3

(1) Contracts for the supply of goods to be manufactured or produced are to be considered sales unless the party who order[s] the goods undertakes to supply a substantial part of the materials necessary for such manufacture or production.

(2) This Convention does not apply to contracts in which the preponderant part of the obligations of the party who furnishes the goods consists in the supply of labour or other services.

Article 4

This Convention governs only the formation of the contract of sale and the rights and obligations of the seller and the buyer arising from such a contract. In particular, except as otherwise expressly provided in this Convention, it is not concerned with:

(a) The validity of the contract or of any of its provisions or of any usage;

(b) The effect which the contract may have on the property in the goods sold.

Article 5

This Convention does not apply to the liability of the seller for death or personal injury caused by the goods to any person.

Article 6

The parties may exclude the application of this Convention or, subject to article 12, derogate from or vary the effect of any of its provisions.

Chapter II.   General Provisions

Article 7

(1) In the interpretation of this Convention, regard is to be had to its international character and to the need to promote uniformity in its application and the observance of good faith in international trade.

(2) Questions concerning matters governed by this Convention which are not expressly settled in it are to be settled in conformity with the general principles on which it is based or, in the absence of such principles, in conformity with the law applicable by virtue of the rules of private international law.

Article 8

(1) For the purposes of this Convention statements made by and other conduct of a party are to be interpreted according to his intent where the other party knew or could not have been unaware what that intent was.

(2) If the preceding paragraph is not applicable, statements made by and other conduct of a party are to be interpreted according to the understanding that a reasonable person of the same kind as the other party would have had in the same circumstances.

(3) In determining the intent of a party or the understanding a reasonable person would have had, due consideration is to be given to all relevant circumstances of the case including the negotiations, any practices which the parties have established between themselves, usages and any subsequent conduct of the parties.

Article 9

(1) The parties are bound by any usages to which they have agreed and by any practices which they have established between themselves.

(2) The parties are considered, unless otherwise agreed, to have impliedly made applicable to their contract or its formation a usage of which the parties knew or ought to have known and which in international trade is widely known to, and regularly observed by, parties to contracts of the type involved in the particular trade concerned.

Article 10

For the purposes of this Convention:

(a) If a party has more than one place of business, the place of business is that which has the closest relationship to the contract and its performance, having regard to the circumstances known to or contemplated by the parties at any time before or at the conclusion of the contract;

(b) If a party does not have a place of business, reference is to be made to his habitual residence.

Article 11

A contract of sale need not be concluded in or evidenced by writing and is not subject to any other requirement as to form. It may be proved by any means, including witnesses.

Article 12

Any provision of article 11, article 29 or Part II of this Convention that allows a contract of sale or its modification or termination by agreement or any offer, acceptance or other indication of intention to be made in any form other than in writing does not apply where any party has his place of business in a Contracting State which has made a declaration under article 96 of this Convention. The parties may not derogate from or vary the effect of this article.

Article 13

For the purposes of this Convention "writing" includes telegram and telex.

PART II. FORMATION OF
THE CONTRACT

Article 14

(1) A proposal for concluding a contract addressed to one or more specific persons constitutes an offer if it is sufficiently definite and indicates the intention of the offeror to be bound in case of acceptance. A proposal is sufficiently definite if it indicates the goods and expressly or implicitly fixes or makes provision for determining the quantity and the price.

(2) A proposal other than one addressed to one or more specific persons is to be considered merely as an invitation to make offers, unless the contrary is clearly indicated by the person making the proposal.

Article 15

(1) An offer becomes effective when it reaches the offeree.

(2) An offer, even if it is irrevocable, may be withdrawn if the withdrawal reaches the offeree before or at the same time as the offer.

Article 16

(1) Until a contract is concluded an offer may be revoked if the revocation reaches the offeree before he has dispatched an acceptance.

(2) However, an offer cannot be revoked:

(a) If it indicates, whether by stating a fixed time for acceptance or otherwise, that it is irrevocable; or

(b) If it was reasonable for the offeree to rely on the offer as being irrevocable and the offeree has acted in reliance on the offer.

Article 17

An offer, even if it is irrevocable, is terminated when a rejection reaches the offeror.

Article 18

(1) A statement made by or other conduct of the offeree indicating assent to an offer is an acceptance. Silence or inactivity does not in itself amount to acceptance.

(2) An acceptance of an offer becomes effective at the moment the indication of assent reaches the offeror. An acceptance is not effective if the indication

of assent does not reach the offeror within the time he has fixed or, if no time is fixed, within a reasonable time, due account being taken of the circumstances of the transaction, including the rapidity of the means of communication employed by the offeror. An oral offer must be accepted immediately unless the circumstances indicate otherwise.

(3) However, if, by virtue of the offer or as a result of practices which the parties have established between themselves or of usage, the offeree may indicate assent by performing an act, such as one relating to the dispatch of the goods or payment of the price, without notice to the offeror, the acceptance is effective at the moment the act is performed, provided that the act is performed within the period of time laid down in the preceding paragraph.

Article 19

(1) A reply to an offer which purports to be an acceptance but contains additions, limitations or other modifications is a rejection of the offer and constitutes a counter-offer.

(2) However, a reply to an offer which purports to be an acceptance but contains additional or different terms which do not materially alter the terms of the offer constitutes an acceptance, unless the offeror, without undue delay, objects orally to the discrepancy or dispatches a notice to that effect. If he does not so object, the terms of the contract are the terms of the offer with the modifications contained in the acceptance.

(3) Additional or different terms relating, among other things, to the price, payment, quality and quantity of the goods, place and time of delivery, extent of one party's liability to the other or the settlement of disputes are considered to alter the terms of the offer materially.

Article 20

(1) A period of time for acceptance fixed by the offeror in a telegram or a letter begins to run from the moment the telegram is handed in for dispatch or from the date shown on the letter or, if no such date is shown, from the date shown on the envelope. A period of time for acceptance fixed by the offeror by telephone, telex or other means of instantaneous communication, begins to run from the moment that the offer reaches the offeree.

(2) Official holidays or non-business days occurring during the period for acceptance are included in calculating the period. However, if a notice of acceptance cannot be delivered at the address of the offeror on the last day of the period because that day falls on an official holiday or a non-business day at the place of business of the offeror, the period is extended until the first business day which follows.

Article 21

(1) A late acceptance is nevertheless effective as an acceptance if without delay the offeror orally so informs the offeree or dispatches a notice to that effect.

(2) If a letter or other writing containing a late acceptance shows that it has been sent in such circumstances that if its transmission had been normal it would have reached the offeror in due time, the late acceptance is effective as an acceptance unless, without delay, the offeror orally informs the offeree that he considers his offer as having lapsed or dispatches a notice to that effect.

Article 22

An acceptance may be withdrawn if the withdrawal reaches the offeror before or at the same time as the acceptance would have become effective.

Article 23

A contract is concluded at the moment when an acceptance of an offer becomes effective in accordance with the provisions of this Convention.

Article 24

For the purposes of this Part of the Convention, an offer, declaration of acceptance or any other indication of intention "reaches" the addressee when it is made orally to him or delivered by any other means to him personally, to his place of business or mailing address or, if he does not have a place of business or mailing address, to his habitual residence.

PART III.   SALE OF GOODS

Chapter I.   General Provisions

Article 25

A breach of contract committed by one of the parties is fundamental if it results in such detriment to the other party as substantially to deprive him of what he is entitled to expect under the contract, unless the party in breach did not foresee, and a reasonable person of the same kind in the same circumstances would not have foreseen, such a result.

Article 26

A declaration of avoidance of the contract is effective only if made by notice to the other party.

Article 27

Unless otherwise expressly provided in this Part of the Convention, if any notice, request or other communication is given or made by a party in accordance with this Part and by means appropriate in the circumstances, a delay or error in the transmission of the communication or its failure to arrive does not deprive that party of the right to rely on the communication.

Article 28

If, in accordance with the provisions of this Convention, one party is entitled to require performance of any obligation by the other party, a court is not bound to enter a judgement for specific performance unless the court would do so under its own law in respect of similar contracts of sale not governed by this Convention.

Article 29

(1) A contract may be modified or terminated by the mere agreement of the parties.

(2) A contract in writing which contains a provision requiring any modification or termination by agreement to be in writing may not be otherwise modified or terminated by agreement. However, a party may be precluded by his conduct from asserting such a provision to the extent that the other party has relied on that conduct.

Chapter II. Obligations of the Seller

Article 30

The seller must deliver the goods, hand over any documents relating to them and transfer the property in the goods, as required by the contract and this Convention.

Section I. Delivery of the Goods and Handing Over of Documents

Article 31

If the seller is not bound to deliver the goods at any other particular place, his obligation to deliver consists:

(a) If the contract of sale involves carriage of the goods — in handing the goods over to the first carrier for transmission to the buyer;

(b) If, in cases not within the preceding subparagraph, the contract relates to specific goods, or unidentified goods to be drawn from a specific stock or to be manufactured or produced, and at the time of the conclusion of the contract the parties knew that the goods were at, or were to be manufactured or produced at, a particular place — in placing the goods at the buyer's disposal at that place;

(c) In other cases — in placing the goods at the buyer's disposal at the place where the seller had his place of business at the time of the conclusion of the contract.

Article 32

(1) If the seller, in accordance with the contract or this Convention, hands the goods over to a carrier and if the goods are not clearly identified to the contract by markings on the goods, by shipping documents or otherwise, the seller must give the buyer notice of the consignment specifying the goods.

(2) If the seller is bound to arrange for carriage of the goods, he must make such contracts as are necessary for carriage to the place fixed by means of transportation appropriate in the circumstances and according to the usual terms for such transportation.

(3) If the seller is not bound to effect insurance in respect of the carriage of the goods, he must, at the buyer's request, provide him with all available information necessary to enable him to effect such insurance.

Article 33

The seller must deliver the goods:

(a) If a date is fixed by or determinable from the contract, on that date;

(b) If a period of time is fixed by or determinable from the contract, at any time within that period unless circumstances indicate that the buyer is to choose a date; or

(c) In any other case, within a reasonable time after the conclusion of the contract.

Article 34

If the seller is bound to hand over documents relating to the goods, he must hand them over at the time and place and in the form required by the contract. If the seller has handed over documents before that time, he may, up to that time, cure any lack of conformity in the documents, if the exercise of this right does not cause the buyer unreasonable inconvenience or unreasonable expense. However, the buyer retains any right to claim damages as provided for in this Convention.

Section II. Conformity of the Goods and Third Party Claims

Article 35

(1) The seller must deliver goods which are of the quantity, quality and description required by the contract and which are contained or packaged in the manner required by the contract.

(2) Except where the parties have agreed otherwise, the goods do not conform with the contract unless they:

(a) Are fit for the purposes for which goods of the same description would ordinarily be used;

(b) Are fit for any particular purpose expressly or impliedly made known to the seller at the time of the conclusion of the contract, except where the circumstances show that the buyer did not rely, or that it was unreasonable for him to rely, on the seller's skill and judgment;

(c) Possess the qualities of goods which the seller has held out to the buyer as a sample or model;

(d) Are contained or packaged in the manner usual for such goods or, where there is no such manner, in a manner adequate to preserve and protect the goods.

(3) The seller is not liable under subparagraphs (a) to (d) of the preceding paragraph for any lack of conformity of the goods if at the time of the conclusion of the contract the buyer knew or could not have been unaware of such lack of conformity.

Article 36

(1) The seller is liable in accordance with the contract and this Convention for any lack of conformity which exists at the time when the risk passes to the buyer, even though the lack of conformity becomes apparent only after that time.

(2) The seller is also liable for any lack of conformity which occurs after the time indicated in the preceding paragraph and which is due to a breach of any of his obligations, including a breach of any guarantee that for a period of time the goods will remain fit for their ordinary purpose or for some particular purpose or will retain specified qualities or characteristics.

Article 37

If the seller has delivered goods before the date for delivery, he may, up to that date, deliver any missing part or make up any deficiency in the quantity of the goods delivered, or deliver goods in replacement of any nonconforming goods delivered or remedy any lack of conformity in the goods delivered, provided that the exercise of this right does not cause the buyer unreasonable inconvenience or unreasonable expense. However, the buyer retains any right to claim damages as provided for in this Convention.

Article 38

(1) The buyer must examine the goods, or cause them to be examined, within as short a period as is practicable in the circumstances.

(2) If the contract involves carriage of the goods, examination may be deferred until after the goods have arrived at their destination.

(3) If the goods are redirected in transit or redispatched by the buyer without a reasonable opportunity for examination by him and at the time of the conclusion of the contract the seller knew or ought to have known of the possibility of such redirection or redispatch, examination may be deferred until after the goods have arrived at the new destination.

Article 39

(1) The buyer loses the right to rely on a lack of conformity of the goods if he does not give notice to the seller specifying the nature of the lack of conformity within a reasonable time after he has discovered it or ought to have discovered it.

(2) In any event, the buyer loses the right to rely on a lack of conformity of the goods if he does not give the seller notice thereof at the latest within a period of two years from the date on which the goods were actually handed over to the buyer, unless this time-limit is inconsistent with a contractual period of guarantee.

Article 40

The seller is not entitled to rely on the provisions of articles 38 and 39 if the lack of conformity relates to facts of which he knew or could not have been unaware and which he did not disclose to the buyer.

Article 41

The seller must deliver goods which are free from any right or claim of a third party, unless the buyer agreed to take the goods subject to that right or claim. However, if such right or claim is based on industrial property or other intellectual property, the seller's obligation is governed by article 42.

Article 42

(1) The seller must deliver goods which are free from any right or claim of a third party based on industrial property or other intellectual property, of which at the time of the conclusion of the contract the seller knew or could not have been unaware, provided that the right or claim is based on industrial property or other intellectual property:

(a) Under the law of the State where the goods will be resold or otherwise used, if it was contemplated by the parties at the time of the conclusion of the contract that the goods would be resold or otherwise used in that State; or

(b) In any other case, under the law of the State where the buyer has his place of business.

(2) The obligation of the seller under the preceding paragraph does not extend to cases where:

(a) At the time of the conclusion of the contract the buyer knew or could not have been unaware of the right or claim; or

(b) The right or claim results from the seller's compliance with technical drawings, designs, formulæ or other such specifications furnished by the buyer.

Article 43

(1) The buyer loses the right to rely on the provisions of article 41 or article 42 if he does not give notice to the seller specifying the nature of the right

or claim of the third party within a reasonable time after he has become aware or ought to have become aware of the right or claim.

(2) The seller is not entitled to rely on the provisions of the preceding paragraph if he knew of the right or claim of the third party and the nature of it.

Article 44

Notwithstanding the provisions of paragraph (1) of article 39 and paragraph (1) of article 43, the buyer may reduce the price in accordance with article 50 or claim damages, except for loss of profit, if he has a reasonable excuse for his failure to give the required notice.

Section III. Remedies for Breach of Contract by the Seller

Article 45

(1) If the seller fails to perform any of his obligations under the contract or this Convention, the buyer may:

(a) Exercise the rights provided in articles 46 to 52;

(b) Claim damages as provided in articles 74 to 77.

(2) The buyer is not deprived of any right he may have to claim damages by exercising his right to other remedies.

(3) No period of grace may be granted to the seller by a court or arbitral tribunal when the buyer resorts to a remedy for breach of contract.

Article 46

(1) The buyer may require performance by the seller of his obligations unless the buyer has resorted to a remedy which is inconsistent with this requirement.

(2) If the goods do not conform with the contract, the buyer may require delivery of substitute goods only if the lack of conformity constitutes a fundamental breach of contract and a request for substitute goods is made either in conjunction with notice given under article 39 or within a reasonable time thereafter.

(3) If the goods do not conform with the contract, the buyer may require the seller to remedy the lack of conformity by repair, unless this is unreasonable having regard to all the circumstances. A request for repair must be made either in conjunction with notice given under article 39 or within a reasonable time thereafter.

Article 47

(1) The buyer may fix an additional period of time of reasonable length for performance by the seller of his obligations.

(2) Unless the buyer has received notice from the seller that he will not perform within the period so fixed, the buyer may not, during that period, resort to any remedy for breach of contract. However, the buyer is not deprived thereby of any right he may have to claim damages for delay in performance.

Article 48

(1) Subject to article 49, the seller may, even after the date for delivery, remedy at his own expense any failure to perform his obligations, if he can do so without unreasonable delay and without causing the buyer unreasonable inconvenience or uncertainty of reimbursement by the seller of expenses advanced by the buyer. However, the buyer retains any right to claim damages as provided for in this Convention.

(2) If the seller requests the buyer to make known whether he will accept performance and the buyer does not comply with the request within a reasonable time, the seller may perform within the time indicated in his request. The buyer may not, during that period of time, resort to any remedy which is inconsistent with performance by the seller.

(3) A notice by the seller that he will perform within a specified period of time is assumed to include a request, under the preceding paragraph, that the buyer make known his decision.

(4) A request or notice by the seller under paragraph (2) or (3) of this article is not effective unless received by the buyer.

Article 49

(1) The buyer may declare the contract avoided:

(a) If the failure by the seller to perform any of his obligations under the contract or this Convention amounts to a fundamental breach of contract; or

(b) In case of non-delivery, if the seller does not deliver the goods within the additional period of time fixed by the buyer in accordance with paragraph (1) of article 47 or declares that he will not deliver within the period so fixed.

(2) However, in cases where the seller has delivered the goods, the buyer loses the right to declare the contract avoided unless he does so:

(a) In respect of late delivery, within a reasonable time after he has become aware that delivery has been made;

(b) In respect of any breach other than late delivery, within a reasonable time:

(i) After he knew or ought to have known of the breach;

(ii) After the expiration of any additional period of time fixed by the buyer in accordance with paragraph (1) of article 47, or after the seller has declared that he will not perform his obligations within such an additional period; or

(iii) After the expiration of any additional period of time indicated by the seller in accordance with paragraph (2) of article 48, or after the buyer has declared that he will not accept performance.

Article 50

If the goods do not conform with the contract and whether or not the price has already been paid, the buyer may reduce the price in the same proportion as the value that the goods actually delivered had at the time of the delivery bears to the value that conforming goods would have had at that time. However, if the seller remedies any failure to perform his obligations in accordance with article 37 or article 48 or if the buyer refuses to accept performance by the seller in accordance with those articles, the buyer may not reduce the price.

Article 51

(1) If the seller delivers only a part of the goods or if only a part of the goods delivered is in conformity with the contract, articles 46 to 50 apply in respect of the part which is missing or which does not conform.

(2) The buyer may declare the contract avoided in its entirety only if the failure to make delivery completely or in conformity with the contract amounts to a fundamental breach of the contract.

Article 52

(1) If the seller delivers the goods before the date fixed, the buyer may take delivery or refuse to take delivery.

(2) If the seller delivers a quantity of goods greater than that provided for in the contract, the buyer may take delivery or refuse to take delivery of the excess quantity. If the buyer takes delivery of all or part of the excess quantity, he must pay for it at the contract rate.

Chapter III.   Obligations of the Buyer

Article 53

The buyer must pay the price for the goods and take delivery of them as required by the contract and this Convention.

Section I.   Payment of the Price

Article 54

The buyer's obligation to pay the price includes taking such steps and complying with such formalities as may be required under the contract or any laws and regulations to enable payment to be made.

Article 55

Where a contract has been validly concluded but does not expressly or implicitly fix or make provision for determining the price, the parties are considered, in the absence of any indication to the contrary, to have impliedly made reference to the price generally charged at the time of the conclusion of the contract for such goods sold under comparable circumstances in the trade concerned.

Article 56

If the price is fixed according to the weight of the goods, in case of doubt it is to be determined by the net weight.

Article 57

(1) If the buyer is not bound to pay the price at any other particular place, he must pay it to the seller:

(a) At the seller's place of business; or

(b) If the payment is to be made against the handing over of the goods or of documents, at the place where the handing over takes place.

(2) The seller must bear any increase in the expenses incidental to payment which is caused by a change in his place of business subsequent to the conclusion of the contract.

Article 58

(1) If the buyer is not bound to pay the price at any other specific time, he must pay it when the seller places either the goods or documents controlling their disposition at the buyer's disposal in accordance with the contract and this Convention. The seller may make such payment a condition for handing over the goods or documents.

(2) If the contract involves carriage of the goods, the seller may dispatch the goods on terms whereby the goods, or documents controlling their disposition, will not be handed over to the buyer except against payment of the price.

(3) The buyer is not bound to pay the price until he has had an opportunity to examine the goods, unless the procedures for delivery or payment agreed upon by the parties are inconsistent with his having such an opportunity.

Article 59

The buyer must pay the price on the date fixed by or determinable from the contract and this Convention without the need for any request or compliance with any formality on the part of the seller.

Section II.   Taking Delivery

Article 60

The buyer's obligation to take delivery consists:

(a) In doing all the acts which could reasonably be expected of him in order to enable the seller to make delivery; and

(b) In taking over the goods.

Section III.   Remedies for Breach of Contract
by the Buyer

Article 61

(1) If the buyer fails to perform any of his obligations under the contract or this Convention, the seller may:

(a) Exercise the rights provided in articles 62 to 65;

(b) Claim damages as provided in articles 74 to 77.

(2) The seller is not deprived of any right he may have to claim damages by exercising his right to other remedies.

(3) No period of grace may be granted to the buyer by a court or arbitral tribunal when the seller resorts to a remedy for breach of contract.

Article 62

The seller may require the buyer to pay the price, take delivery or perform his other obligations, unless the seller has resorted to a remedy which is inconsistent with this requirement.

Article 63

(1) The seller may fix an additional period of time of reasonable length for performance by the buyer of his obligations.

(2) Unless the seller has received notice from the buyer that he will not perform within the period so fixed, the seller may not, during that period, resort to any remedy for breach of contract. However, the seller is not deprived thereby of any right he may have to claim damages for delay in performance.

Article 64

(1) The seller may declare the contract avoided:

(a) If the failure by the buyer to perform any of his obligations under the contract or this Convention amounts to a fundamental breach of contract; or

(b) If the buyer does not, within the additional period of time fixed by the seller in accordance with paragraph (1) of article 63, perform his obligation to pay the price or take delivery of the goods, or declares that he will not do so within the period so fixed.

(2) However, in cases where the buyer has paid the price, the seller loses the right to declare the contract avoided unless he does so:

(a) In respect of late performance by the buyer, before the seller has become aware that performance has been rendered; or

(b) In respect of any breach other than late performance by the buyer, within a reasonable time:

(i) After the seller knew or ought to have known of the breach; or

(ii) After the expiration of any additional period of time fixed by the seller in accordance with paragraph (1) of article 63, or after the buyer has declared that he will not perform his obligations within such an additional period.

Article 65

(1) If under the contract the buyer is to specify the form, measurement or other features of the goods and he fails to make such specification either on the date agreed upon or within a reasonable time after receipt of a request from the seller, the seller may, without prejudice to any other rights he may have, make the specification himself in accordance with the requirements of the buyer that may be known to him.

(2) If the seller makes the specification himself, he must inform the buyer of the details thereof and must fix a reasonable time within which the buyer may make a different specification. If, after receipt of such a communication, the buyer fails to do so within the time so fixed, the specification made by the seller is binding.

Chapter IV.   Passing of Risk

Article 66

Loss of or damage to the goods after the risk has passed to the buyer does not discharge him from his obligation to pay the price, unless the loss or damage is due to an act or omission of the seller.

Article 67

(1) If the contract of sale involves carriage of the goods and the seller is not bound to hand them over at a particular place, the risk passes to the buyer when the goods are handed over to the first carrier for transmission to the buyer in accordance with the contract of sale. If the seller is bound to hand the goods over to a carrier at a particular place, the risk does not pass to the buyer until the goods are handed over to the carrier at that place. The fact that the seller is authorized to retain documents controlling the disposition of the goods does not affect the passage of the risk.

(2) Nevertheless, the risk does not pass to the buyer until the goods are clearly identified to the contract, whether by markings on the goods, by shipping documents, by notice given to the buyer or otherwise.

Article 68

The risk in respect of goods sold in transit passes to the buyer from the time of the conclusion of the contract. However, if the circumstances so indicate, the risk is assumed by the buyer from the time the goods were handed over to the carrier who issued the documents embodying the contract of carriage. Nevertheless, if at the time of the conclusion of the contract of sale the seller knew or ought to have known that the goods had been lost or damaged and did not disclose this to the buyer, the loss or damage is at the risk of the seller.

Article 69

(1) In cases not within articles 67 and 68, the risk passes to the buyer when he takes over the goods or, if he does not do so in due time, from the time when the goods are placed at his disposal and he commits a breach of contract by failing to take delivery.

(2) However, if the buyer is bound to take over the goods at a place other than a place of business of the seller, the risk passes when delivery is due and the buyer is aware of the fact that the goods are placed at his disposal at that place.

(3) If the contract relates to goods not then identified, the goods are considered not to be placed at the disposal of the buyer until they are clearly identified to the contract.

Article 70

If the seller has committed a fundamental breach of contract, articles 67, 68, and 69 do not impair the remedies available to the buyer on account of the breach.

Chapter V. Provisions Common to the
Obligations of the Seller and of the Buyer

Section I. Anticipatory Breach
and Instalment Contracts

Article 71

(1) A party may suspend the performance of his obligations if, after the conclusion of the contract, it becomes apparent that the other party will not perform a substantial part of his obligations as a result of:

(a) A serious deficiency in his ability to perform or in his creditworthiness; or

(b) His conduct in preparing to perform or in performing the contract.

(2) If the seller has already dispatched the goods before the grounds described in the preceding paragraph become evident, he may prevent the handing over of the goods to the buyer even though the buyer holds a docu-

ment which entitles him to obtain them. The present paragraph relates only to the rights in the goods as between the buyer and the seller.

(3) A party suspending performance, whether before or after dispatch of the goods, must immediately give notice of the suspension to the other party and must continue with performance if the other party provides adequate assurance of his performance.

Article 72

(1) If prior to the date for performance of the contract it is clear that one of the parties will commit a fundamental breach of contract, the other party may declare the contract avoided.

(2) If time allows, the party intending to declare the contract avoided must give reasonable notice to the other party in order to permit him to provide adequate assurance of his performance.

(3) The requirements of the preceding paragraph do not apply if the other party has declared that he will not perform his obligations.

Article 73

(1) In the case of a contract for delivery of goods by instalments, if the failure of one party to perform any of his obligations in respect of any instalment constitutes a fundamental breach of contract with respect to that instalment, the other party may declare the contract avoided with respect to that instalment.

(2) If one party's failure to perform any of his obligations in respect of any instalment gives the other party good grounds to conclude that a fundamental breach of contract will occur with respect to future instalments, he may declare the contract avoided for the future, provided that he does so within a reasonable time.

(3) A buyer who declares the contract avoided in respect of any delivery may, at the same time, declare it avoided in respect of deliveries already made or of future deliveries if, by reason of their interdependence, those deliveries could not be used for the purpose contemplated by the parties at the time of the conclusion of the contract.

Section II.   Damages

Article 74

Damages for breach of contract by one party consist of a sum equal to the loss, including loss of profit, suffered by the other party as a consequence of the breach. Such damages may not exceed the loss which the party in breach foresaw or ought to have foreseen at the time of the conclusion of the contract, in the light of the facts and matters of which he then knew or ought to have known, as a possible consequence of the breach of contract.

Article 75

If the contract is avoided and if, in a reasonable manner and within a reasonable time after avoidance, the buyer has bought goods in replacement or the seller has resold the goods, the party claiming damages may recover the difference between the contract price and the price in the substitute transaction as well as any further damages recoverable under article 74.

Article 76

(1) If the contract is avoided and there is a current price for the goods, the party claiming damages may, if he has not made a purchase or resale under article 75, recover the difference between the price fixed by the contract and the current price at the time of avoidance as well as any further damages recoverable under article 74. If, however, the party claiming damages has avoided the contract after taking over the goods, the current price at the time of such taking over shall be applied instead of the current price at the time of avoidance.

(2) For the purposes of the preceding paragraph, the current price is the price prevailing at the place where delivery of the goods should have been made or, if there is no current price at that place, the price at such other place as serves as a reasonable substitute, making due allowance for differences in the cost of transporting the goods.

Article 77

A party who relies on a breach of contract must take such measures as are reasonable in the circumstances to mitigate the loss, including loss of profit, resulting from the breach. If he fails to take such measures, the party in breach may claim a reduction in the damages in the amount by which the loss should have been mitigated.

Section III. Interest

Article 78

If a party fails to pay the price or any other sum that is in arrears, the other party is entitled to interest on it, without prejudice to any claim for damages recoverable under article 74.

Section IV. Exemptions

Article 79

(1) A party is not liable for a failure to perform any of his obligations if he proves that the failure was due to an impediment beyond his control and

that he could not reasonably be expected to have taken the impediment into account at the time of the conclusion of the contract or to have avoided or overcome it or its consequences.

(2) If the party's failure is due to the failure by a third person whom he has engaged to perform the whole or a part of the contract, that party is exempt from liability only if:

(a) He is exempt under the preceding paragraph; and

(b) The person whom he has so engaged would be so exempt if the provisions of that paragraph were applied to him.

(3) The exemption provided by this article has effect for the period during which the impediment exists.

(4) The party who fails to perform must give notice to the other party of the impediment and its effect on his ability to perform. If the notice is not received by the other party within a reasonable time after the party who fails to perform knew or ought to have known of the impediment, he is liable for damages resulting from such non-receipt.

(5) Nothing in this article prevents either party from exercising any right other than to claim damages under this Convention.

Article 80

A party may not rely on a failure of the other party to perform, to the extent that such failure was caused by the first party's act or omission.

Section V. Effects of Avoidance

Article 81

(1) Avoidance of the contract releases both parties from their obligations under it, subject to any damages which may be due. Avoidance does not affect any provision of the contract for the settlement of disputes or any other provision of the contract governing the rights and obligations of the parties consequent upon the avoidance of the contract.

(2) A party who has performed the contract either wholly or in part may claim restitution from the other party of whatever the first party has supplied or paid under the contract. If both parties are bound to make restitution, they must do so concurrently.

Article 82

(1) The buyer loses the right to declare the contract avoided or to require the seller to deliver substitute goods if it is impossible for him to make restitution of the goods substantially in the condition in which he received them.

(2) The preceding paragraph does not apply:

(a) If the impossibility of making restitution of the goods or of making restitution of the goods substantially in the condition in which the buyer received them is not due to his act or omission;

(b) If the goods or part of the goods have perished or deteriorated as a result of the examination provided for in article 38; or

(c) If the goods or part of the goods have been sold in the normal course of business or have been consumed or transformed by the buyer in the course of normal use before he discovered or ought to have discovered the lack of conformity.

Article 83

A buyer who has lost the right to declare the contract avoided or to require the seller to deliver substitute goods in accordance with article 82 retains all other remedies under the contract and this Convention.

Article 84

(1) If the seller is bound to refund the price, he must also pay interest on it, from the date on which the price was paid.

(2) The buyer must account to the seller for all benefits which he has derived from the goods or part of them:

(a) If he must make restitution of the goods or part of them; or

(b) If it is impossible for him to make restitution of all or part of the goods or to make restitution of all or part of the goods substantially in the condition in which he received them, but he has nevertheless declared the contract avoided or required the seller to deliver substitute goods.

Section VI.   Preservation of the Goods

Article 85

If the buyer is in delay in taking delivery of the goods or, where payment of the price and delivery of the goods are to be made concurrently, if he fails to pay the price, and the seller is either in possession of the goods or otherwise able to control their disposition, the seller must take such steps as are reasonable in the circumstances to preserve them. He is entitled to retain them until he has been reimbursed his reasonable expenses by the buyer.

Article 86

(1) If the buyer has received the goods and intends to exercise any right under the contract or this Convention to reject them, he must take such steps to preserve them as are reasonable in the circumstances. He is entitled to retain them until he has been reimbursed his reasonable expenses by the seller.

(2) If the goods dispatched to the buyer have been placed at his disposal at their destination and he exercises the right to reject them, he must take possession of them on behalf of the seller, provided that this can be done without payment of the price and without unreasonable inconvenience or unreasonable expense. This provision does not apply if the seller or a person

authorized to take charge of the goods on his behalf is present at the destination. If the buyer takes possession of the goods under this paragraph, his rights and obligations are governed by the preceding paragraph.

Article 87

A party who is bound to take steps to preserve the goods may deposit them in a warehouse of a third person at the expense of the other party provided that the expense incurred is not unreasonable.

Article 88

(1) A party who is bound to preserve the goods in accordance with article 85 or 86 may sell them by any appropriate means if there has been an unreasonable delay by the other party in taking possession of the goods or in taking them back or in paying the price or the cost of preservation, provided that reasonable notice of the intention to sell has been given to the other party.

(2) If the goods are subject to rapid deterioration or their preservation would involve unreasonable expense, a party who is bound to preserve the goods in accordance with article 85 or 86 must take reasonable measures to sell them. To the extent possible he must give notice to the other party of this intention to sell.

(3) A party selling the goods has the right to retain out of the proceeds of sale an amount equal to the reasonable expenses of preserving the goods and of selling them. He must account to the other party for the balance.

PART IV.   FINAL PROVISIONS

Article 96

A Contracting State whose legislation requires contracts of sale to be concluded in or evidenced by writing may at any time make a declaration in accordance with article 12 that any provision of article 11, article 29, or Part II of this Convention, that allows a contract of sale or its modification or termination by agreement or any offer, acceptance, or other indication of intention to be made in any form other than in writing, does not apply where any party has his place of business in that State.

The Restatement (Second) of Contracts

EDITORS' NOTE [1]

For centuries critics of the legal system have complained of its delay, uncertainty, and complexity, and each generation has attempted to devise solutions to these problems. In the early part of the twentieth century, prominent members of the legal profession created an institution to study the legal system and to offer proposals for reform. Formed in 1923, this organization, the American Law Institute (ALI), remains today a private, nonprofit corporation, funded by grants principally from foundations.

While the Institute has undertaken a variety of projects since its formation, its best-known work has been the preparation of "Restatements" of the common law. Begun in the 1920s and 1930s, the Restatements are black-letter pronouncements, in statute-like form, of the rules of the major common law subjects, such as contracts, property, torts, and agency. The ALI appointed Professor Samuel Williston of Harvard Law School, the best-known contracts scholar of his day, as Chief Reporter for the first Restatement of Contracts. Professor Arthur Corbin of Yale Law School acted as a special advisor for the Remedies section of that Restatement.

Adopted by the ALI in 1932, the first Restatement of Contracts has generated both respect and ridicule. Thousands of courts have cited provisions of the Restatement to support their decisions. Yet some scholars, particularly those associated with the movement in law known as "legal realism," have attacked the Restatements. Writing in 1933, one year after the publication of the first

---

1. For further material on the history of the Restatements, see Grant Gilmore, The Death of Contract (1974); John Honnold, The Life of the Law 144-180 (1964); Nathan M. Crystal, Codification and the Rise of the Restatement Movement, 54 Wash. L. Rev. 239 (1979).

Restatement of Contracts, Dean Charles Clark of the Yale Law School remarked that the drafters of the Restatement had tried to simplify contract law by preparing an authoritative statement of rules. He was extremely critical of this approach:

> Actually the resulting statement is the law nowhere and in its unreality only deludes and misleads. It is either a generality so obvious as immediately to be accepted, or so vague as not to offend, or of such antiquity as to be unchallenged as a statement of past history.
>
> . . . There are a large number of purely bromidic sections, such as section 3 ("An agreement is a manifestation of mutual assent by two or more persons to one another."). . . . No one would wish to dissent from them. They cannot be used in deciding cases; nor are they now useful in initiating students into contract law, for the present teaching mode is to start with case study, not abstract definition. They may afford convenient citations to a court, but that is all.

Charles E. Clark, The Restatement of the Law of Contracts, 42 Yale L.J. 643, 654-655 (1933).

When the American Law Institute began preparing the Restatements, it recognized that the project would be a continuing one, requiring periodic reexamination. In the 1950s and 1960s the Institute began work on the second generation of Restatements. The ALI chose Professor Robert Braucher of Harvard Law School as Chief Reporter for the Restatement (Second) of Contracts. After Professor Braucher's appointment to the Supreme Judicial Court of Massachusetts in 1971, Professor Allan Farnsworth of Columbia Law School was designated Chief Reporter. Originally issued in 14 installments labeled "tentative drafts," the final version (revised and renumbered) was adopted by the ALI in 1979.

While the revised Restatement continues the black-letter approach of the first Restatement, it also represents a shift in several respects. Stylistically, the black-letter text has been rewritten and supplemented with extensive commentary and case citations. Substantively, influenced by the publication of the Uniform Commercial Code, the drafters of the Restatement (Second) have added a number of new provisions not found in the first Restatement. These include §205, which imposes on each party to a contract a duty of good faith and fair dealing, and §208, which provides that a court may refuse to enforce an agreement or any of its terms that the court finds to be unconscionable. Many other rules carried forward from the original Restatement have been modified to reflect the Code's influence. E.g., Restatement (Second) §33 (requirement of certainty of contractual terms reformulated based on UCC §2-204); Restatement (Second) §222 (concept of usage of trade modeled on UCC §1-205).

Unlike a statute or a court decision, the provisions of the Restatements do not have the force of law. They are generally regarded, however, as authoritative by courts and commentators. Judge Herbert Goodrich, former Director of the Institute, characterized the Restatements as "common law 'persuasive authority' with a high degree of persuasion." Restatement and Codification, in John Honnold, The Life of the Law 173 (1964). Indeed, many recent cases have used the Restatement (Second) provisions as the framework for analysis of contract problems. See, e.g., Gaglidari v. Denny's Restaurants, Inc., 815 P.2d 1362 (Wash.

1991) (en banc) (relying on text and comments of Restatement §353 to determine if damages for emotional distress should be allowed in an action for breach of contract); Lenawee County Board of Health v. Messerly, 331 N.W.2d 203 (Mich. 1982) (adopting Restatement (Second) §152 to analyze the issue of unilateral mistake). Courts are zealous in protecting their independence, however, and they are likely to bristle at the suggestion that they should blindly follow the Restatement. For example, in Rowe v. Montgomery Ward & Co., 473 N.W.2d 268 (Mich. 1990), the Michigan Supreme Court (the court that eight years earlier in *Lenawee* had relied on the Restatement) had this to say in response to the argument that it should follow the provisions of Restatement (Second) §33, which deals with contractual certainty:

> While we acknowledge the Restatement as persuasive authority on the subject of contracts, this Court is not, nor is any other court, bound to follow any of the rules set out in the Restatement. Moreover, even assuming . . . that our ruling is inconsistent with the Restatement, the writings of the American Law Institute do not control the rulings of this Court, nor is the contract law of this state necessarily written to be consistent with the Restatement.

Id. at 278.

The selections from the Restatement (Second) contained in this supplement consist only of the black-letter provisions. In the unabridged version of the Restatement published by the American Law Institute, each section is followed by comments and illustrations. Some of these are cited or quoted in the Editors' casebook, Problems in Contract Law. In addition, Reporter's Notes, which follow the comments and illustrations, refer the reader to cases and commentary. The most complete treatment of the revised Restatement to date can be found in E. Allan Farnsworth, Contracts (2d ed. 1990).

The following provisions are reprinted with the permission of the American Law Institute. Copyright 1981 by the American Law Institute.

CHAPTER 1. MEANING OF TERMS

§1.　Contract Defined

CHAPTER 2. FORMATION OF CONTRACTS — PARTIES
AND CAPACITY

§14.　Infants
§15.　Mental Illness or Defect

CHAPTER 3. FORMATION OF
CONTRACTS — MUTUAL ASSENT

Topic 1.　In General

§17.　Requirement of a Bargain

Topic 2.　Manifestation of Assent in General

§22.　Mode of Assent: Offer and Acceptance

CHAPTER 4.   FORMATION OF CONTRACTS — CONSIDERATION

Topic 1.   The Requirement of Consideration

CHAPTER 5.   THE STATUTE OF FRAUDS

CHAPTER 1.   MEANING OF TERMS

§1.   Contract Defined

A contract is a promise or a set of promises for the breach of which the law gives a remedy, or the performance of which the law in some way recognizes as a duty.

CHAPTER 2.   FORMATION OF CONTRACTS — PARTIES AND CAPACITY

§14.   Infants

Unless a statute provides otherwise, a natural person has the capacity to incur only voidable contractual duties until the beginning of the day before the person's eighteenth birthday.

§15.   Mental Illness or Defect

(1) A person incurs only voidable contractual duties by entering into a transaction if by reason of mental illness or defect

(a) he is unable to understand in a reasonable manner the nature and consequences of the transaction, or

(b) he is unable to act in a reasonable manner in relation to the transaction and the other party has reason to know of his condition.

(2) Where the contract is made on fair terms and the other party is without knowledge of the mental illness or defect, the power of avoidance under Subsection (1) terminates to the extent that the contract has been so performed in whole or in part or the circumstances have so changed that avoidance would be unjust. In such a case a court may grant relief as justice requires.

CHAPTER 3. FORMATION OF CONTRACTS — MUTUAL ASSENT

Topic 1. In General

§17. Requirement of a Bargain

(1) Except as stated in Subsection (2), the formation of a contract requires a bargain in which there is a manifestation of mutual assent to the exchange and a consideration.

(2) Whether or not there is a bargain a contract may be formed under special rules applicable to formal contracts or under the rules stated in §§82-94.

Topic 2. Manifestation of Assent in General

§22. Mode of Assent: Offer and Acceptance

(1) The manifestation of mutual assent to an exchange ordinarily takes the form of an offer or proposal by one party followed by an acceptance by the other party or parties.

(2) A manifestation of mutual assent may be made even though neither offer nor acceptance can be identified and even though the moment of formation cannot be determined.

Topic 3. Making of Offers

§24. Offer Defined

An offer is the manifestation of willingness to enter into a bargain, so made as to justify another person in understanding that his assent to that bargain is invited and will conclude it.

§26. Preliminary Negotiations

A manifestation of willingness to enter into a bargain is not an offer if the person to whom it is addressed knows or has reason to know that the person making it does not intend to conclude a bargain until he has made a further manifestation of assent.

§27. Existence of Contract Where Written Memorial Is Contemplated

Manifestations of assent that are in themselves sufficient to conclude a contract will not be prevented from so operating by the fact that the parties also manifest an intention to prepare and adopt a written memorial thereof; but the circumstances may show that the agreements are preliminary negotiations.

§33. Certainty

(1) Even though a manifestation of intention is intended to be understood as an offer, it cannot be accepted so as to form a contract unless the terms of the contract are reasonably certain.

(2) The terms of a contract are reasonably certain if they provide a basis for determining the existence of a breach and for giving an appropriate remedy.

(3) The fact that one or more terms of a proposed bargain are left open or uncertain may show that a manifestation of intention is not intended to be understood as an offer or as an acceptance.

Topic 4. Duration of the Offeree's Power of Acceptance

§36. Methods of Termination of the Power of Acceptance

(1) An offeree's power of acceptance may be terminated by
    (a) rejection or counter-offer by the offeree, or
    (b) lapse of time, or
    (c) revocation by the offeror, or
    (d) death or incapacity of the offeror or offeree.

(2) In addition, an offeree's power of acceptance is terminated by the non-occurrence of any condition of acceptance under the terms of the offer.

§38. Rejection

(1) An offeree's power of acceptance is terminated by his rejection of the offer, unless the offeror has manifested a contrary intention.

(2) A manifestation of intention not to accept an offer is a rejection unless the offeree manifests an intention to take it under further advisement.

§39. Counter-offers

(1) A counter-offer is an offer made by an offeree to his offeror relating to the same matter as the original offer and proposing a substituted bargain differing from that proposed by the original offer.

(2) An offeree's power of acceptance is terminated by his making of a counter-offer, unless the offeror has manifested a contrary intention or unless the counter-offer manifests a contrary intention of the offeree.

§40. Time When Rejection or Counter-offer
Terminates the Power of Acceptance

Rejection or counter-offer by mail or telegram does not terminate the power of acceptance until received by the offeror, but limits the power so that a letter or telegram of acceptance started after the sending of an otherwise effective rejection or counter-offer is only a counter-offer unless the acceptance is received by the offeror before he receives the rejection or counter-offer.

§43. Indirect Communication of Revocation

An offeree's power of acceptance is terminated when the offeror takes definite action inconsistent with an intention to enter into the proposed contract and the offeree acquires reliable information to that effect.

§45. Option Contract Created by Part
Performance or Tender

(1) Where an offer invites an offeree to accept by rendering a performance and does not invite a promissory acceptance, an option contract is created when the offeree tenders or begins the invited performance or tenders a beginning of it.

(2) The offeror's duty of performance under any option contract so created is conditional on completion or tender of the invited performance in accordance with the terms of the offer.

Topic 5.   Acceptance of Offers

§50.   Acceptance of Offer Defined; Acceptance by Performance; Acceptance by Promise

(1) Acceptance of an offer is a manifestation of assent to the terms thereof made by the offeree in a manner invited or required by the offer.

(2) Acceptance by performance requires that at least part of what the offer requests be performed or tendered and includes acceptance by a performance which operates as a return promise.

(3) Acceptance by a promise requires that the offeree complete every act essential to the making of the promise.

§58.   Necessity of Acceptance Complying with Terms of Offer

An acceptance must comply with the requirements of the offer as to the promise to be made or the performance to be rendered.

§59.   Purported Acceptance Which Adds Qualifications

A reply to an offer which purports to accept it but is conditional on the offeror's assent to terms additional to or different from those offered is not an acceptance but is a counter-offer.

§60.   Acceptance of Offer Which States Place, Time, or Manner of Acceptance

If an offer prescribes the place, time or manner of acceptance its terms in this respect must be complied with in order to create a contract. If an offer merely suggests a permitted place, time or manner of acceptance, another method of acceptance is not precluded.

§63.   Time When Acceptance Takes Effect

Unless the offer provides otherwise,

(a) an acceptance made in a manner and by a medium invited by an offer is operative and completes the manifestation of mutual assent as soon as put out of the offeree's possession, without regard to whether it ever reaches the offeror; but

(b) an acceptance under an option contract is not operative until received by the offeror.

§69. Acceptance by Silence or Exercise of Dominion

(1) Where an offeree fails to reply to an offer, his silence and inaction operate as an acceptance in the following cases only:

(a) Where an offeree takes the benefit of offered services with reasonable opportunity to reject them and reason to know that they were offered with the expectation of compensation.

(b) Where the offeror has stated or given the offeree reason to understand that assent may be manifested by silence or inaction, and the offeree in remaining silent and inactive intends to accept the offer.

(c) Where because of previous dealings or otherwise, it is reasonable that the offeree should notify the offeror if he does not intend to accept.

(2) An offeree who does any act inconsistent with the offeror's ownership of offered property is bound in accordance with the offered terms unless they are manifestly unreasonable. But if the act is wrongful as against the offeror it is an acceptance only if ratified by him.

CHAPTER 4. FORMATION OF CONTRACTS — CONSIDERATION

Topic 1. The Requirement of Consideration

§71. Requirement of Exchange; Types of Exchange

(1) To constitute consideration, a performance or a return promise must be bargained for.

(2) A performance or return promise is bargained for if it is sought by the promisor in exchange for his promise and is given by the promisee in exchange for that promise.

(3) The performance may consist of

(a) an act other than a promise, or

(b) a forbearance, or

(c) the creation, modification, or destruction of a legal relation.

(4) The performance or return promise may be given to the promisor or to some other person. It may be given by the promisee or by some other person.

§73. Performance of Legal Duty

Performance of a legal duty owed to a promisor which is neither doubtful nor the subject of honest dispute is not consideration; but a similar performance is consideration if it differs from what was required by the duty in a way which reflects more than a pretense of bargain.

§74. Settlement of Claims

(1) Forbearance to assert or the surrender of a claim or defense which proves to be invalid is not consideration unless
    (a) the claim or defense is in fact doubtful because of uncertainty as to the facts or the law, or
    (b) the forbearing or surrendering party believes that the claim or defense may be fairly determined to be valid.
(2) The execution of a written instrument surrendering a claim or defense by one who is under no duty to execute it is consideration if the execution of the written instrument is bargained for even though he is not asserting the claim or defense and believes that no valid claim or defense exists.

§77. Illusory and Alternative Promises

A promise or apparent promise is not consideration if by its terms the promisor or purported promisor reserves a choice of alternative performances unless
    (a) each of the alternative performances would have been consideration if it alone had been bargained for; or
    (b) one of the alternative performances would have been consideration and there is or appears to the parties to be a substantial possibility that before the promisor exercises his choice events may eliminate the alternatives which would not have been consideration.

§79. Adequacy of Consideration; Mutuality of Obligation

If the requirement of consideration is met, there is no additional requirement of
    (a) a gain, advantage, or benefit to the promisor or a loss, disadvantage, or detriment to the promisee; or
    (b) equivalence in the values exchanged; or
    (c) "mutuality of obligation."

§81. Consideration as Motive or Inducing Cause

(1) The fact that what is bargained for does not of itself induce the making of a promise does not prevent it from being consideration for the promise.
(2) The fact that a promise does not of itself induce a performance or

return promise does not prevent the performance or return promise from being consideration for the promise.

Topic 2. *Contracts Without Consideration*

§82. Promise to Pay Indebtedness; Effect on the Statute of Limitations

(1) A promise to pay all or part of an antecedent contractual or quasi-contractual indebtedness owed by the promisor is binding if the indebtedness is still enforceable or would be except for the effect of a statute of limitations.

(2) The following facts operate as such a promise unless other facts indicate a different intention:

(a) A voluntary acknowledgment to the obligee, admitting the present existence of the antecedent indebtedness; or

(b) A voluntary transfer of money, a negotiable instrument, or other thing by the obligor to the obligee, made as interest on or part payment of or collateral security for the antecedent indebtedness; or

(c) A statement to the obligee that the statute of limitations will not be pleaded as a defense.

§83. Promise to Pay Indebtedness Discharged in Bankruptcy

An express promise to pay all or part of an indebtedness of the promisor, discharged or dischargeable in bankruptcy proceedings begun before the promise is made, is binding.

§86. Promise for Benefit Received

Material Benefit Rule

(1) A promise made in recognition of a benefit previously received by the promisor from the promisee is binding to the extent necessary to prevent injustice.

(2) A promise is not binding under Subsection (1)

(a) if the promisee conferred the benefit as a gift or for other reasons the promisor has not been unjustly enriched; or

(b) to the extent that its value is disproportionate to the benefit.

§87. Option Contract

(1) An offer is binding as an option contract if it

(a) is in writing and signed by the offeror, recites a purported consideration for the making of the offer, and proposes an exchange on fair terms within a reasonable time; or

✓ (b) is made irrevocable by statute.

(2) An offer which the offeror should reasonably expect to induce action or forbearance of a substantial character on the part of the offeree before acceptance and which does induce such action or forbearance is binding as an option contract to the extent necessary to avoid injustice.

§89. Modification of Executory Contract

A promise modifying a duty under a contract not fully performed on either side is binding

Unanticipated Difficulties

(a) if the modification is fair and equitable in view of circumstances not anticipated by the parties when the contract was made; or

(b) to the extent provided by statute; or

(c) to the extent that justice requires enforcement in view of material change of position in reliance on the promise.

§90. Promise Reasonably Inducing Action or Forbearance

(1) A promise which the promisor should reasonably expect to induce action or forbearance on the part of the promisee or a third person and which does induce such action or forbearance is binding if injustice can be avoided only by enforcement of the promise. The remedy granted for breach may be limited as justice requires.

(2) A charitable subscription or a marriage settlement is binding under Subsection (1) without proof that the promise induced action or forbearance.

CHAPTER 5.   THE STATUTE OF FRAUDS

§110. Classes of Contracts Covered

(1) The following classes of contracts are subject to a statute, commonly called the Statute of Frauds, forbidding enforcement unless there is a written memorandum or an applicable exception:

(a) a contract of an executor or administrator to answer for a duty of his decedent (the executor-administrator provision);

(b) a contract to answer for the duty of another (the suretyship provision);

(c) a contract made upon consideration of marriage (the marriage provision);

(d) a contract for the sale of an interest in land (the land contract provision);

(e) a contract that is not to be performed within one year from the making thereof (the one-year provision).

(2) The following classes of contracts, which were traditionally subject to the Statute of Frauds, are now governed by Statute of Frauds provisions of the Uniform Commercial Code:

(a) a contract for the sale of goods for the price of $500 or more (Uniform Commercial Code §2-201);

(b) a contract for the sale of securities (Uniform Commercial Code §8-319);

(c) a contract for the sale of personal property not otherwise covered, to the extent of enforcement by way of action or defense beyond $5,000 in amount or value of remedy (Uniform Commercial Code §1-206).

(3) In addition the Uniform Commercial Code requires a writing signed by the debtor for an agreement which creates or provides for a security interest in personal property or fixtures not in the possession of the secured party.

(4) Statutes in most states provide that no acknowledgment or promise is sufficient evidence of a new or continuing contract to take a case out of the operation of a statute of limitations unless made in some writing signed by the party to be charged, but that the statute does not alter the effect of any payment of principal or interest.

(5) In many states other classes of contracts are subject to a requirement of a writing.

Topic 6. Satisfaction of the Statute by a Memorandum

§131. General Requisites of a Memorandum

Unless additional requirements are prescribed by the particular statute, a contract within the Statute of Frauds is enforceable if it is evidenced by any writing, signed by or on behalf of the party to be charged, which

(a) reasonably identifies the subject matter of the contract,

(b) is sufficient to indicate that a contract with respect thereto has been made between the parties or offered by the signer to the other party, and

(c) states with reasonable certainty the essential terms of the unperformed promises in the contract.

§132. Several Writings

The memorandum may consist of several writings if one of the writings is signed and the writings in the circumstances clearly indicate that they relate to the same transaction.

e. g. Elizabeth Arden

143

§133. Memorandum Not Made as Such

Except in the case of a writing evidencing a contract upon consideration of marriage, the Statute may be satisfied by a signed writing not made as a memorandum of a contract.

§134. Signature

The signature to a memorandum may be any symbol made or adopted with an intention, actual or apparent, to authenticate the writing as that of the signer.

Topic 7.   Consequences of Non-Compliance

§139. Enforcement by Virtue of Action in Reliance

(1) A promise which the promisor should reasonably expect to induce action or forbearance on the part of the promisee or a third person and which does induce the action or forbearance is enforceable notwithstanding the Statue of Frauds if injustice can be avoided only by enforcement of the promise. The remedy granted for breach is to be limited as justice requires.

(2) In determining whether injustice can be avoided only by enforcement of the promise, the following circumstances are significant:

(a) the availability and adequacy of other remedies, particularly cancellation and restitution;

(b) the definite and substantial character of the action or forbearance in relation to the remedy sought;

(c) the extent to which the action or forbearance corroborates evidence of the making and terms of the promise, or the making and terms are otherwise established by clear and convincing evidence;

(d) the reasonableness of the action or forbearance;

(e) the extent to which the action or forbearance was forseeable by the promisor.

CHAPTER 6.   MISTAKE

§152. When Mistake of Both Parties Makes a *mutual mistake* Contract Voidable

(1) Where a mistake of both parties at the time a contract was made as to a basic assumption on which the contract was made has a material effect on

the agreed exchange of performances, the contract is voidable by the adversely affected party unless he bears the risk of the mistake under the rule stated in §154.

(2) In determining whether the mistake has a material effect on the agreed exchange of performances, account is taken of any relief by way of reformation, restitution, or otherwise.

§153. When Mistake of One Party Makes a Contract Voidable

Unilateral mistake

Where a mistake of one party at the time a contract was made as to a basic assumption on which he made the contract has a material effect on the agreed exchange of performances that is adverse to him, the contract is voidable by him if he does not bear the risk of the mistake under the rule stated in §154, and

(a) the effect of the mistake is such that enforcement of the contract *(so grave)* would be unconscionable, or

(b) the other party had reason to know of the mistake or his fault caused the mistake.

§154. When a Party Bears the Risk of a Mistake

A party bears the risk of a mistake when

(a) the risk is allocated to him by agreement of the parties, or

(b) he is aware, at the time the contract is made, that he has only limited knowledge with respect to the facts to which the mistake relates but treats his limited knowledge as sufficient, or *"Conscious ignorance"*

(c) the risk is allocated to him by the court on the ground that it is reasonable in the circumstances to do so. *"Catch all"*

§157. Effect of Fault of Party Seeking Relief

A mistaken party's fault in failing to know or discover the facts before making the contract does not bar him from avoidance or reformation under the rules stated in this Chapter, unless his fault amounts to a failure to act in good faith and in accordance with reasonable standards of fair dealing.

§158. Relief Including Restitution

(1) In any case governed by the rules stated in this Chapter, either party may have a claim for relief including restitution under the rules stated in §§240 and 376.

(2) In any case governed by the rules stated in this Chapter, if those rules together with the rules stated in Chapter 16 will not avoid injustice, the court may grant relief on such terms as justice requires including protection of the parties' reliance interests.

CHAPTER 7. MISREPRESENTATION, DURESS AND UNDUE INFLUENCE

Topic 1. Misrepresentation

§161. When Non-Disclosure Is Equivalent to an Assertion

A person's non-disclosure of a fact known to him is equivalent to an assertion that the fact does not exist in the following cases only:

(a) where he knows that disclosure of the fact is necessary to prevent some previous assertion from being a misrepresentation or from being fraudulent or material.

(b) where he knows that disclosure of the fact would correct a mistake of the other party as to a basic assumption on which that party is making the contract and if non-disclosure of the fact amounts to a failure to act in good faith and in accordance with reasonable standards of fair dealing.

(c) where he knows that disclosure of the fact would correct a mistake of the other party as to the contents or effect of a writing, evidencing or embodying an agreement in whole or in part.

(d) where the other person is entitled to know the fact because of a relation of trust and confidence between them.

§162. When a Misrepresentation Is Fraudulent or Material

(1) A misrepresentation is fraudulent if the maker intends his assertion to induce a party to manifest his assent and the maker

(a) knows or believes that the assertion is not in accord with the facts, or

(b) does not have the confidence that he states or implies in the truth of the assertion, or

(c) knows that he does not have the basis that he states or implies for the assertion.

(2) A misrepresentation is material if it would be likely to induce a reasonable person to manifest his assent, or if the maker knows that it would be likely to induce the recipient to do so.

§163. When a Misrepresentation Prevents Formation of a Contract

If a misrepresentation as to the character or essential terms of a proposed contract induces conduct that appears to be a manifestation of assent by one who neither knows nor has reasonable opportunity to know of the character or essential terms of the proposed contract, his conduct is not effective as a manifestation of assent.

§164. When a Misrepresentation Makes a Contract Voidable

(1) If a party's manifestation of assent is induced by either a fraudulent or a material misrepresentation by the other party upon which the recipient is justified in relying, the contract is voidable by the recipient.

(2) If a party's manifestation of assent is induced by either a fraudulent or a material misrepresentation by one who is not a party to the transaction upon which the recipient is justified in relying, the contract is voidable by the recipient, unless the other party to the transaction in good faith and without reason to know of the misrepresentation either gives value or relies materially on the transaction.

§168. Reliance on Assertions of Opinion

(1) An assertion is one of opinion if it expresses only a belief, without certainty, as to the existence of a fact or expresses only a judgment as to quality, value, authenticity, or similar matters.

(2) If it is reasonable to do so, the recipient of an assertion of a person's opinion as to facts not disclosed and not otherwise known to the recipient may properly interpret it as an assertion

(a) that the facts known to that person are not incompatible with his opinion, or

(b) that he knows facts sufficient to justify him in forming it.

§169. When Reliance on an Assertion of Opinion Is Not Justified

To the extent that an assertion is one of opinion only, the recipient is not justified in relying on it unless the recipient

(a) stands in such a relation of trust and confidence to the person whose opinion is asserted that the recipient is reasonable in relying on it, or

(b) reasonably believes that, as compared with himself, the person whose opinion is asserted has special skill, judgment or objectivity with respect to the subject matter, or

(c) is for some other special reason particularly susceptible to a misrepresentation of the type involved.

§173. When Abuse of a Fiduciary Relation Makes a Contract Voidable

If a fiduciary makes a contract with his beneficiary relating to matters within the scope of the fiduciary relation, the contract is voidable by the beneficiary, unless

(a) it is on fair terms, and

(b) all parties beneficially interested manifest assent with full understanding of their legal rights and of all relevant facts that the fiduciary knows or should know.

Topic 2.   Duress and Undue Unfluence

§174. When Duress by Physical Compulsion Prevents Formation of a Contract

If conduct that appears to be a manifestation of assent by a party who does not intend to engage in that conduct is physically compelled by duress, the conduct is not effective as a manifestation of assent.

§175. When Duress by Threat Makes a Contract Voidable

(1) If a party's manifestation of assent is induced by an improper threat by the other party that leaves the victim no reasonable alternative, the contract is voidable by the victim.

(2) If a party's manifestation of assent is induced by one who is not a party to the transaction, the contract is voidable by the victim unless the other party to the transaction in good faith and without reason to know of the duress either gives value or relies materially on the transaction.

§176. When a Threat Is Improper

(1) A threat is improper if

(a) what is threatened is a crime or a tort, or the threat itself would be a crime or a tort if it resulted in obtaining property,

(b) what is threatened is a criminal prosecution,

(c) what is threatened is the use of civil process and the threat is made in bad faith, or

(d) the threat is a breach of the duty of good faith and fair dealing under a contract with the recipient.

(2) A threat is improper if the resulting exchange is not on fair terms, and

(a) the threatened act would harm the recipient and would not significantly benefit the party making the threat,

(b) the effectiveness of the threat in inducing the manifestation of assent is significantly increased by prior unfair dealing by the party making the threat, or

(c) what is threatened is otherwise a use of power for illegitimate ends.

§177. When Undue Influence Makes a Contract Voidable

(1) Undue influence is unfair persuasion of a party who is under the domination of the person exercising the persuasion or who by virtue of the relation between them is justified in assuming that that person will not act in a manner inconsistent with his welfare.

(2) If a party's manifestation of assent is induced by undue influence by the other party, the contract is voidable by the victim.

(3) If a party's manifestation of assent is induced by one who is not a party to the transaction, the contract is voidable by the victim unless the other party to the transaction in good faith and without reason to know of the undue influence either gives value or relies materially on the transaction.

CHAPTER 8. UNENFORCEABILITY ON GROUNDS OF PUBLIC POLICY

Topic 1. Unenforceability in General

§178. When a Term Is Unenforceable on Grounds of Public Policy

(1) A promise or other term of an agreement is unenforceable on grounds of public policy if legislation provides that it is unenforceable or the interest in its enforcement is clearly outweighed in the circumstances by a public policy against the enforcement of such terms.

(2) In weighing the interest in the enforcement of a term, account is taken of

(a) the parties' justified expectations,

(b) any forfeiture that would result if enforcement were denied, and

(c) any special public interest in the enforcement of the particular term.

(3) In weighing a public policy against enforcement of a term, account is taken of

 (a) the strength of that policy as manifested by legislation or judicial decisions,

 (b) the likelihood that a refusal to enforce the term will further that policy,

 (c) the seriousness of any misconduct involved and the extent to which it was deliberate, and

 (d) the directness of the connection between that misconduct and the term.

§181. Effect of Failure to Comply with Licensing or Similar Requirement

If a party is prohibited from doing an act because of his failure to comply with a licensing, registration or similar requirement, a promise in consideration of his doing that act or of his promise to do so it is unenforceable on grounds of public policy if

 (a) the requirement has a regulatory purpose, and

 (b) the interest in the enforcement of the promise is clearly outweighed by the public policy behind the requirement.

Topic 2. Restraint of Trade

§187. Non-Ancillary Restraints on Competition

A promise to refrain from competition that imposes a restraint that is not ancillary to an otherwise valid transaction or relationship is unreasonably in restraint of trade.

§188. Ancillary Restraints on Competition

(1) A promise to refrain from competition that imposes a restraint that is ancillary to an otherwise valid transaction or relationship is unreasonably in restraint of trade if

 (a) the restraint is greater than is needed to protect the promisee's legitimate interest, or

 (b) the promisee's need is outweighed by the hardship to the promisor and the likely injury to the public.

(2) Promises imposing restraints that are ancillary to a valid transaction or relationship include the following:

 (a) a promise by the seller of a business not to compete with the buyer in such a way as to injure the value of the business sold;

(b) a promise by an employee or other agent not to compete with his employer or other principal;

(c) a promise by a partner not to compete with the partnership.

Topic 5. Restitution

§198. Restitution in Favor of Party Who Is Excusably Ignorant or Is Not Equally in the Wrong

A party has a claim in restitution for performance that he has rendered under or in return for a promise that is unenforceable on grounds of public policy if

(a) he was excusably ignorant of the facts or of legislation of a minor character, in the absence of which the promise would be enforceable, or

(b) he was not equally in the wrong with the promisor.

CHAPTER 9. THE SCOPE OF CONTRACTUAL OBLIGATIONS

Topic 1. The Meaning of Agreements

§201. Whose Meaning Prevails

[handwritten: Modified Objective Approach to interpretation]

(1) Where the parties have attached the same meaning to a promise or agreement or a term thereof, it is interpreted in accordance with that meaning. *[handwritten: (subjective)]*

(2) Where the parties have attached different meanings to a promise or agreement or a term thereof, it is interpreted in accordance with the meaning attached by one of them if at the time the agreement was made

(a) that party did not know of any different meaning attached by the other, and the other knew the meaning attached by the first party; or

(b) that party had no reason to know of any different meaning attached by the other, and the other had reason to know the meaning attached by the first party.

(3) Except as stated in this Section, neither party is bound by the meaning attached by the other, even though the result may be a failure of mutual assent.

§202. Rules in Aid of Interpretation

(1) Words and other conduct are interpreted in the light of all the circumstances, and if the principal purpose of the parties is ascertainable it is given great weight.

(2) A writing is interpreted as a whole, and all writings that are part of the same transaction are interpreted together.

(3) Unless a different intention is manifested,

(a) where language has a generally prevailing meaning, it is interpreted in accordance with that meaning;

(b) technical terms and words of art are given their technical meaning when used in a transaction within their technical field.

(4) Where an agreement involves repeated occasions for performance by either party with knowledge of the nature of the performance and opportunity for objection to it by the other, any course of performance accepted or acquiesced in without objection is given great weight in the interpretation of the agreement.

(5) Wherever reasonable, the manifestations of intention of the parties to a promise or agreement are interpreted as consistent with each other and with any relevant course of performance, course of dealing, or usage of trade.

§203. Standards of Preference in Interpretation

In the interpretation of a promise or agreement or a term thereof, the following standards of preference are generally applicable:

(a) an interpretation which gives a reasonable, lawful, and effective meaning to all the terms is preferred to an interpretation which leaves a part unreasonable, unlawful, or of no effect;

(b) express terms are given greater weight than course of performance, course of dealing, and usage of trade, course of performance is given greater weight than course of dealing or usage of trade, and course of dealing is given greater weight than usage of trade;

(c) specific terms and exact terms are given greater weight than general language;

(d) separately negotiated or added terms are given greater weight than standardized terms or other terms not separately negotiated.

§204. Supplying an Omitted Essential Term

When the parties to a bargain sufficiently defined to be a contract have not agreed with respect to a term which is essential to a determination of their rights and duties, a term which is reasonable in the circumstances is supplied by the court.

Topic 2. Considerations of Fairness and the Public Interest

§205. Duty of Good Faith and Fair Dealing

Every contract imposes upon each party a duty of good faith and fair dealing in its performance and its enforcement.

§206. Interpretation Against the Draftsman

In choosing among the reasonable meanings of a promise or agreement or a term thereof, that meaning is generally preferred which operates against the party who supplies the words or from whom a writing otherwise proceeds.

§207. Interpretation Favoring the Public

In choosing among the reasonable meanings of a promise or agreement or a term thereof, a meaning that serves the public interest is generally preferred.

§208. Unconscionable Contract or Term

If a contract or term thereof is unconscionable at the time the contract is made a court may refuse to enforce the contract, or may enforce the remainder of the contract without the unconscionable term, or may so limit the application of any unconscionable term as to avoid any unconscionable result.

Topic 3. Effect of Adoption of a Writing

§209. Integrated Agreements

(1) An integrated agreement is a writing or writings constituting a final expression of one or more terms of an agreement.

(2) Whether there is an integrated agreement is to be determined by the court as a question preliminary to determination of a question of interpretation or to application of the parol evidence rule.

✓(3) Where the parties reduce an agreement to a writing which in view of its completeness and specificity reasonably appears to be a complete agreement, it is taken to be an integrated agreement unless it is established by other evidence that the writing did not constitute a final expression.

§210. Completely and Partially Integrated Agreements

(1) A completely integrated agreement is an integrated agreement adopted by the parties as a complete and exclusive statement of the terms of the agreement.

(2) A partially integrated agreement is an integrated agreement other than a completely integrated agreement.

(3) Whether an agreement is completely or partially integrated is to be determined by the court as a question preliminary to determination of a question of interpretation or to application of the parol evidence rule.

§211. Standardized Agreements

(1) Except as stated in Subsection (3), where a party to an agreement signs or otherwise manifests assent to a writing and has reason to believe that like writings are regularly used to embody terms of agreements of the same type, he adopts the writing as an integrated agreement with respect to the terms included in the writing.

(2) Such a writing is interpreted wherever reasonable as treating alike all those similarly situated, without regard to their knowledge or understanding of the standard terms of the writing.

(3) Where the other party has reason to believe that the party manifesting such assent would not do so if he knew that the writing contained a particular term, the term is not part of the agreement.

§213. Effect of Integrated Agreement on Prior Agreements (Parol Evidence Rule)

(1) A binding integrated agreement discharges prior agreements to the extent that it is inconsistent with them.

(2) A binding completely integrated agreement discharges prior agreements to the extent that they are within its scope.

(3) An integrated agreement that is not binding or that is voidable and avoided does not discharge a prior agreement. But an integrated agreement, even though not binding, may be effective to render inoperative a term which would have been part of the agreement if it had not been integrated.

§214. Evidence of Prior or Contemporaneous Agreements and Negotiations

Agreements and negotiations prior to or contemporaneous with the adoption of a writing are admissible in evidence to establish

(a) that the writing is or is not an integrated agreement;

(b) that the integrated agreement, if any, is completely or partially integrated;

(c) the meaning of the writing, whether or not integrated;

(d) illegality, fraud, duress, mistake, lack of consideration, or other invalidating cause;

(e) ground for granting or denying rescission, reformation, specific performance, or other remedy.

§215. Contradiction of Integrated Terms

Except as stated in the preceding Section, where there is a binding agreement, either completely or partially integrated, evidence of prior or contemporaneous agreements or negotiations is not admissible in evidence to contradict a term of the writing.

§216. Consistent Additional Terms

(1) Evidence of a consistent additional term is admissible to supplement an integrated agreement unless the court finds that the agreement was completely integrated.

(2) An agreement is not completely integrated if the writing omits a consistent additional agreed term which is

(a) agreed to for separate consideration, or

(b) such a term as in the circumstances might naturally be omitted from the writing.

§217. Integrated Agreement Subject to Oral Requirement of a Condition

Where the parties to a written agreement agree orally that performance of the agreement is subject to the occurrence of a stated condition, the agreement is not integrated with respect to the oral condition.

Topic 4. Scope as Affected by Usage

§222. Usage of Trade

(1) A usage of trade is a usage having such regularity of observance in a place, vocation, or trade as to justify an expectation that it will be observed with respect to a particular agreement. It may include a system of rules regularly observed even though particular rules are changed from time to time.

(2) The existence and scope of a usage of trade are to be determined as questions of fact. If a usage is embodied in a written trade code or similar writing the interpretation of the writing is to be determined by the court as a question of law.

(3) Unless otherwise agreed, a usage of trade in the vocation or trade in which the parties are engaged or a usage of trade of which they know or have reason to know gives meaning to or supplements or qualifies their agreement.

§223. Course of Dealing

(1) A course of dealing is a sequence of previous conduct between the parties to an agreement which is fairly to be regarded as establishing a common basis of understanding for interpreting their expressions and other conduct.

(2) Unless otherwise agreed, a course of dealing between the parties gives meaning to or supplements or qualifies their agreement.

Topic 5. Conditions and Similar Events

§224. Condition Defined

A condition is an event, not certain to occur, which must occur, unless its non-occurrence is excused, before performance under a contract becomes due.

§225. Effects of the Non-Occurrence of a Condition

(1) Performance of a duty subject to a condition cannot become due unless the condition occurs or its non-occurrence is excused.

(2) Unless it has been excused, the non-occurrence of a condition discharges the duty when the condition can no longer occur.

(3) Non-occurrence of a condition is not a breach by a party unless he is under a duty that the condition occur.

§226. How an Event May Be Made a Condition

An event may be made a condition either by the agreement of the parties or by a term supplied by the court.

§227. Standards of Preference with Regard to Conditions

(1) In resolving doubts as to whether an event is made a condition of an obligor's duty, and as to the nature of such an event, an interpretation is

preferred that will reduce the obligee's risk of forfeiture, unless the event is within the obligee's control or the circumstances indicate that he has assumed the risk.

(2) Unless the contract is of a type under which only one party generally undertakes duties, when it is doubtful whether

(a) a duty is imposed on an obligee that an event occur, or

(b) the event is made a condition of the obligor's duty, or

(c) the event is made a condition of the obligor's duty and a duty is imposed on the obligee that the event occur,

the first interpretation is preferred if the event is within the obligee's control.

(3) In case of doubt, an interpretation under which an event is a condition of an obligor's duty is preferred over an interpretation under which the non-occurrence of the event is a ground for discharge of that duty after it has become a duty to perform.

§228. Satisfaction of the Obligor as a Condition

When it is a condition of an obligor's duty that he be satisfied with respect to the obligee's performance or with respect to something else, and it is practicable to determine whether a reasonable person in the position of the obligor would be satisfied, an interpretation is preferred under which the condition occurs if such a reasonable person in the position of the obligor would be satisfied.

§229. Excuse of a Condition to Avoid Forfeiture

To the extent that the non-occurrence of a condition would cause disproportionate forfeiture, a court may excuse the non-occurrence of that condition unless its occurrence was a material part of the agreed exchange.

CHAPTER 10. PERFORMANCE AND NON-PERFORMANCE

Topic 1. Performances to Be Exchanged under an Exchange of Promises

§234. Order of Performances

(1) Where all or part of the performances to be exchanged under an exchange of promises can be rendered simultaneously, they are to that extent due simultaneously, unless the language or the circumstances indicate the contrary.

(2) Except to the extent stated in Subsection (1), where the performance of only one party under such an exchange requires a period of time, his performance is due at an earlier time than that of the other party, unless the language or the circumstances indicate the contrary.

Topic 2.   *Effect of Performance and Non-Performance*

§235.   Effect of Performance as Discharge and of Non-Performance as Breach

(1) Full performance of a duty under a contract discharges the duty.

(2) When performance of a duty under a contract is due any non-performance is a breach.

§237.   Effect on Other Party's Duties of a Failure to Render Performance

Except as stated in §240, it is a condition of each party's remaining duties to render performances to be exchanged under an exchange of promises that there be no uncured material failure by the other party to render any such performance due at an earlier time.   *Can suspend performance*

§240.   Part Performances as Agreed Equivalents

If the performances to be exchanged under an exchange of promises can be apportioned into corresponding pairs of part performances so that the parts of each pair are properly regarded as agreed equivalents, a party's performance of his part of such a pair has the same effect on the other's duties to render performance of the agreed equivalent as it would have if only that pair of performances had been promised.

§241.   Circumstances Significant in Determining Whether a Failure Is Material   *Material Breach*

In determining whether a failure to render or to offer performance is material, the following circumstances are significant:

(a) the extent to which the injured party will be deprived of the benefit which he reasonably expected;

(b) the extent to which the injured party can be adequately compensated for the part of that benefit of which he will be deprived; *damages sufficient?*

(c) the extent to which the party failing to perform or to offer to perform will suffer forfeiture;

(d) the likelihood that the party failing to perform or to offer to perform will cure his failure, taking account of all the circumstances including any reasonable assurances;

(e) the extent to which the behavior of the party failing to perform or to offer to perform comports with standards of good faith and fair dealing. *) new*

§242. Circumstances Significant in Determining When Remaining Duties are Discharged *Total Breach*

In determining the time after which a party's uncured material failure to render or to offer performance discharges the other party's remaining duties to render performance under the rules stated in §§237 and 238, the following circumstances are significant:

(a) those stated in §241; *material breach*

(b) the extent to which it reasonably appears to the injured party that delay may prevent or hinder him in making reasonable substitute arrangements; *timing*

(c) the extent to which the agreement provides for performance without delay, but a material failure to perform or to offer to perform on a stated day does not of itself discharge the other party's remaining duties unless the circumstances, including the language of the agreement, indicate that performance or an offer to perform by that day is important. *Stated in K* *(boilerplate or negotiated)*

§246. Effect of Acceptance as Excusing the Non-Occurrence of a Condition

(1) Except as stated in Subsection (2), an obligor's acceptance or his retention for an unreasonable time of the obligee's performance, with knowledge of or reason to know of the non-occurrence of a condition of the obligor's duty, operates as a promise to perform in spite of that non-occurrence, under the rules stated in §84.

(2) If at the time of its acceptance or retention the obligee's performance involves such attachment to the obligor's property that removal would cause material loss, the obligor's acceptance or retention of that performance operates as a promise to perform in spite of the non-occurrence of the condition, under the rules stated in §84, only if the obligor with knowledge of or reason to know of the defects manifests assent to the performance.

§247. Effect of Acceptance of Part Performance as Excusing the Subsequent Non-Occurrence of a Condition

An obligor's acceptance of part of the obligee's performance, with knowledge or reason to know of the non-occurrence of a condition of the obligor's duty, operates as a promise to perform in spite of a subsequent non-occurrence of the condition under the rules stated in §84 to the extent that it justifies the obligee in believing that subsequent performances will be accepted in spite of that non-occurrence.

§248. Effect of Insufficient Reason for Rejection as Excusing the Non-Occurrence of a Condition

Where a party rejecting a defective performance or offer of performance gives an insufficient reason for rejection, the non-occurrence of a condition of his duty is excused only if he knew or had reason to know of that non-occurrence and then only to the extent that the giving of an insufficient reason substantially contributes to a failure by the other party to cure.

Topic 3. Effect of Prospective Non-Performance

§250. When a Statement or an Act is a Repudiation

A repudiation is
 (a) a statement by the obligor to the obligee indicating that the obligor will commit a breach that would of itself give the obligee a claim for damages for total breach under §243, or
 (b) a voluntary affirmative act which renders the obligor unable or apparently unable to perform without such a breach.

§251. When a Failure to Give Assurance May Be Treated as a Repudiation

 (1) Where reasonable grounds arise to believe that the obligor will commit a breach by non-performance that would of itself give the obligee a claim for damages for total breach under §243, the obligee may demand adequate assurance of due performance and may, if reasonable, suspend any performance for which he has not already received the agreed exchange until he receives such assurance.

 (2) The obligee may treat as a repudiation the obligor's failure to provide within a reasonable time such assurance of due performance as is adequate in the circumstances of the particular case.

§253. Effect of a Repudiation as a Breach and on Other Party's Duties

 (1) Where an obligor repudiates a duty before he has committed a breach by non-performance and before he has received all of the agreed exchange

for it, his repudiation alone gives rise to a claim for damages for total breach.

(2) Where performances are to be exchanged under an exchange of promises, one party's repudiation of a duty to render performance discharges the other party's remaining duties to render performance.

CHAPTER 11. IMPRACTICABILITY OF PERFORMANCE AND FRUSTRATION OF PURPOSE

§261. Discharge by Supervening Impracticability

Where, after a contract is made, a party's performance is made impracticable without his fault by the occurrence of an event the non-occurrence of which was a basic assumption on which the contract was made, his duty to render that performance is discharged, unless the language or the circumstances indicate the contrary.

§262. Death or Incapacity of Person Necessary for Performance

If the existence of a particular person is necessary for the performance of a duty, his death or such incapacity as makes performance impracticable is an event the non-occurrence of which was a basic assumption on which the contract was made.

§263. Destruction, Deterioration or Failure to Come into Existence of Thing Necessary for Performance

If the existence of a specific thing is necessary for the performance of a duty, its failure to come into existence, destruction, or such deterioration as makes performance impracticable is an event the non-occurrence of which was a basic assumption on which the contract was made.

§264. Prevention by Governmental Regulation or Order

If the performance of a duty is made impracticable by having to comply with a domestic or foreign governmental regulation or order, that regulation or order is an event the non-occurrence of which was a basic assumption on which the contract was made.

§265. Discharge by Supervening Frustration

Where, after a contract is made, a party's principal purpose is substantially frustrated without his fault by the occurrence of an event the non-occurrence of which was a basic assumption on which the contract was made, his remaining duties to render performance are discharged, unless the language or the circumstances indicate the contrary.

§272. Relief Including Restitution

(1) In any case governed by the rules stated in this Chapter, either party may have a claim for relief including restitution under the rules stated in §§240 and 377.

(2) In any case governed by the rules stated in this Chapter, if those rules together with the rules stated in Chapter 16 will not avoid injustice, the court may grant relief on such terms as justice requires including protection of the parties' reliance interests.

CHAPTER 14. CONTRACT BENEFICIARIES

§302. Intended and Incidental Beneficiaries

(1) Unless otherwise agreed between promisor and promisee, a beneficiary of a promise is an intended beneficiary if recognition of a right to performance in the beneficiary is appropriate to effectuate the intention of the parties and either

(a) the performance of the promise will satisfy an obligation of the promisee to pay money to the beneficiary; or

(b) the circumstances indicate that the promisee intends to give the beneficiary the benefit of the promised performance.

(2) An incidental beneficiary is a beneficiary who is not an intended beneficiary.

§309. Defenses Against the Beneficiary

(1) A promise creates no duty to a beneficiary unless a contract is formed between the promisor and the promisee; and if a contract is voidable or

unenforceable at the time of its formation the right of any beneficiary is subject to the infirmity.

(2) If a contract ceases to be binding in whole or in part because of impracticability, public policy, non-occurrence of a condition, or present or prospective failure of performance, the right of any beneficiary is to that extent discharged or modified.

(3) Except as stated in Subsections (1) and (2) and in §311 or as provided by the contract, the right of any beneficiary against the promisor is not subject to the promisor's claims or defenses against the promisee or to the promisee's claims or defenses against the beneficiary.

(4) A beneficiary's right against the promisor is subject to any claim or defense arising from his own conduct or agreement.

§311. Variation of a Duty to a Beneficiary

(1) Discharge or modification of a duty to an intended beneficiary by conduct of the promisee or by a subsequent agreement between promisor and promisee is ineffective if a term of the promise creating the duty so provides.

(2) In the absence of such a term, the promisor and promisee retain power to discharge or modify the duty by subsequent agreement.

(3) Such a power terminates when the beneficiary, before he receives notification of the discharge or modification, materially changes his position in justifiable reliance on the promise or brings suit on it or manifests assent to it at the request of the promisor or promisee.

(4) If the promisee receives consideration for an attempted discharge or modification of the promisor's duty which is ineffective against the beneficiary, the beneficiary can assert a right to the consideration so received. The promisor's duty is discharged to the extent of the amount received by the beneficiary.

§313. Government Contracts

(1) The rules stated in this Chapter apply to contracts with a government or governmental agency except to the extent that application would contravene the policy of the law authorizing the contract or prescribing remedies for its breach.

(2) In particular, a promisor who contracts with a government or governmental agency to do an act for or render a service to the public is not subject to contractual liability to a member of the public for consequential damages resulting from performance or failure to perform unless

    (a) the terms of the promise provide for such liability; or

    (b) the promisee is subject to liability to the member of the public for the damages and a direct action against the promisor is consistent with the terms of the contract and with the policy of the law authorizing the contract and prescribing remedies for its breach.

CHAPTER 15. ASSIGNMENT AND DELEGATION

Topic 1. What Can Be Assigned or Delegated

§317. Assignment of a Right

(1) An assignment of a right is a manifestation of the assignor's intention to transfer it by virtue of which the assignor's right to performance by the obligor is extinguished in whole or in part and the assignee acquires a right to such performance.

(2) A contractual right can be assigned unless

(a) the substitution of a right of the assignee for the right of the assignor would materially change the duty of the obligor, or materially increase the burden or risk imposed on him by his contract, or materially impair his chance of obtaining return performance, or materially reduce its value to him, or

(b) the assignment is forbidden by statute or is otherwise inoperative on grounds of public policy, or

(c) assignment is validly precluded by contract.

§318. Delegation of Performance of Duty

(1) An obligor can properly delegate the performance of his duty to another unless the delegation is contrary to public policy or the terms of his promise.

(2) Unless otherwise agreed, a promise requires performance by a particular person only to the extent that the obligee has a substantial interest in having that person perform or control the acts promised.

(3) Unless the obligee agrees otherwise, neither delegation of performance nor a contract to assume the duty made with the obligor by the person delegated discharges any duty or liability of the delegating obligor.

§321. Assignment of Future Rights

(1) Except as otherwise provided by statute, an assignment of a right to payment expected to arise out of an existing employment or other continuing business relationship is effective in the same way as an assignment of an existing right.

(2) Except as otherwise provided by statute and as stated in Subsection (1), a purported assignment of a right expected to arise under a contract not in existence operates only as a promise to assign the right when it arises and as a power to enforce it.

§322. Contractual Prohibition of Assignment

(1) Unless the circumstances indicate the contrary, a contract term prohibiting assignment of "the contract" bars only the delegation to an assignee of the performance by the assignor of a duty or condition.

(2) A contract term prohibiting assignment of rights under the contract, unless a different intention is manifested,

(a) does not forbid assignment of a right to damages for breach of the whole contract or a right arising out of the assignor's due performance of his entire obligation;

(b) gives the obligor a right to damages for breach of the terms forbidding assignment but does not render the assignment ineffective;

(c) is for the benefit of the obligor, and does not prevent the assignee from acquiring rights against the assignor or the obligor from discharging his duty as if there were no such prohibition.

Topic 2. Mode of Assignment or Delegation

§328. Interpretation of Words of Assignment; Effect of Acceptance of Assignment

(1) Unless the language or the circumstances indicate the contrary, as in an assignment for security, an assignment of "the contract" or of "all my rights under the contract" or an assignment in similar general terms is an assignment of the assignor's rights and a delegation of his unperformed duties under the contract.

(2) Unless the language or the circumstances indicate the contrary, the acceptance by an assignee of such an assignment operates as a promise to the assignor to perform the assignor's unperformed duties, and the obligor of the assigned rights is an intended beneficiary of the promise.

Caveat: The Institute expresses no opinion as to whether the rule stated in Subsection (2) applies to an assignment by a purchaser of his rights under a contract for the sale of land.

Topic 4. Effect on the Obligor's Duty

§336. Defenses Against an Assignee

(1) By an assignment the assignee acquires a right against the obligor only to the extent that the obligor is under a duty to the assignor; and if the right of the assignor would be voidable by the obligor or unenforceable against him if no assignment had been made, the right of the assignee is subject to the infirmity.

(2) The right of an assignee is subject to any defense or claim of the obligor which accrues before the obligor receives notification of the assignment, but not to defenses or claims which accrue thereafter except as stated in this Section or as provided by statute.

(3) Where the right of an assignor is subject to discharge or modification in whole or in part by impracticability, public policy, non-occurrence of a condition, or present or prospective failure of performance by an obligee, the right of the assignee is to that extent subject to discharge or modification even after the obligor receives notification of the assignment.

(4) An assignee's right against the obligor is subject to any defense or claim arising from his conduct or to which he was subject as a party or a prior assignee because he had notice.

CHAPTER 16.   REMEDIES

Topic 1.   In General

§344.   Purposes of Remedies — *General*

Judicial remedies under the rules stated in this Restatement serve to protect one or more of the following interests of a promisee:

(a) his "expectation interest," which is his interest in having the benefit of his bargain by being put in as good a position as he would have been in had the contract been performed,

(b) his "reliance interest," which is his interest in being reimbursed for loss caused by reliance on the contract by being put in as good a position as he would have been in had the contract not been made, or

(c) his "restitution interest," which is his interest in having restored to him any benefit that he has conferred on the other party.

Topic 2.   Enforcement by Award of Damages

§347.   Measure of Damages in General

Subject to the limitations stated in §§350–53, the injured party has a right to damages based on his expectation interest as measured by

(a) the loss in the value to him of the other party's performance caused by its failure or deficiency, plus

(b) any other loss, including incidental or consequential loss, caused by the breach, less

(c) any cost or other loss that he has avoided by not having to perform.

§348. Alternatives to Loss in Value of Performance

(1) If a breach delays the use of property and the loss in value to the injured party is not proved with reasonable certainty, he may recover damages based on the rental value of the property or on interest on the value of the property.

(2) If a breach results in defective or unfinished construction and the loss in value to the injured party is not proved with sufficient certainty, he may recover damages based on

(a) the diminution in the market price of the property caused by the breach, or

(b) the reasonable cost of completing performance or of remedying the defects if that cost is not clearly disproportionate to the probable loss in value to him.

(3) If a breach is of a promise conditioned on a fortuitous event and it is uncertain whether the event would have occurred had there been no breach, the injured party may recover damages based on the value of the conditional right at the time of breach.

§349. Damages Based on Reliance Interest

As an alternative to the measure of damages stated in §347, the injured party has a right to damages based on his reliance interest, including expenditures made in preparation for performance or in performance, less any loss that the party in breach can prove with reasonable certainty the injured party would have suffered had the contract been performed.

§350. Avoidability as a Limitation on Damages

(1) Except as stated in Subsection (2), damages are not recoverable for loss that the injured party could have avoided without undue risk, burden or humiliation.

(2) The injured party is not precluded from recovery by the rule stated in Subsection (1) to the extent that he has made reasonable but unsuccessful efforts to avoid loss.

§351. Unforeseeability and Related Limitations on Damages

(1) Damages are not recoverable for loss that the party in breach did not have reason to foresee as a probable result of the breach when the contract was made.

(2) Loss may be foreseeable as a probable result of a breach because it follows from the breach.

(a) in the ordinary course of events, or

(b) as a result of special circumstances, beyond the ordinary course of events, that the party in breach had reason to know.

(3) A court may limit damages for foreseeable loss by excluding recovery for loss of profits, by allowing recovery only for loss incurred in reliance, or otherwise if it concludes that in the circumstances justice so requires in order to avoid disproportionate compensation.

§352. Uncertainty as a Limitation on Damages

Damages are not recoverable for loss beyond an amount that the evidence permits to be established with reasonable certainty.

§353. Loss Due to Emotional Disturbance

Recovery for emotional disturbance will be excluded unless the breach also caused bodily harm or the contract or the breach is of such a kind that serious emotional disturbance was a particularly likely result.

§355. Punitive Damages

Punitive damages are not recoverable for a breach of contract unless the conduct constituting the breach is also a tort for which punitive damages are recoverable.

§356. Liquidated Damages and Penalties

(1) Damages for breach by either party may be liquidated in the agreement but only at an amount that is reasonable in the light of the anticipated or actual loss caused by the breach and the difficulties of proof of loss. A term fixing unreasonably large liquidated damages is unenforceable on grounds of public policy as a penalty.

(2) A term in a bond providing for an amount of money as a penalty for non-occurrence of the condition of the bond is unenforceable on grounds of public policy to the extent that the amount exceeds the loss caused by such non-occurrence.

Topic 3. Enforcement by Specific Performance and Injunction

§359. Effect of Adequacy of Damages

(1) Specific performance or an injunction will not be ordered if damages would be adequate to protect the expectation interest of the injured party.

(2) The adequacy of the damage remedy for failure to render one part of the performance due does not preclude specific performance or injunction as to the contract as a whole.

(3) Specific performance or an injunction will not be refused merely because there is a remedy for breach other than damages, but such a remedy may be considered in exercising discretion under the rule stated in §357.

§360. Factors Affecting Adequacy of Damages

In determining whether the remedy in damages would be adequate, the following circumstances are significant:
   (a) the difficulty of proving damages with reasonable certainty,
   (b) the difficulty of procuring a suitable substitute performance by means of money awarded as damages, and
   (c) the likelihood that an award of damages could not be collected.

§361. Effect of Provision for Liquidated Damages

Specific performance or an injunction may be granted to enforce a duty even though there is a provision for liquidated damages for breach of that duty.

§362. Effect of Uncertainty of Terms

Specific performance or an injunction will not be granted unless the terms of the contract are sufficiently certain to provide a basis for an appropriate order.

§364. Effect of Unfairness

(1) Specific performance or an injunction will be refused if such relief would be unfair because
   (a) the contract was induced by mistake or by unfair practices,
   (b) the relief would cause unreasonable hardship or loss to the party in breach or to third persons, or

(c) the exchange is grossly inadequate or the terms of the contract are otherwise unfair.

(2) Specific performance or an injunction will be granted in spite of a term of the agreement if denial of such relief would be unfair because it would cause unreasonable hardship or loss to the party seeking relief or to third persons.

§365.   Effect of Public Policy

Specific performance or an injunction will not be granted if the act or forbearance that would be compelled or the use of compulsion is contrary to public policy.

§366.   Effect of Difficulty in Enforcement or Supervision

A promise will not be specifically enforced if the character and magnitude of the performance would impose on the court burdens in enforcement or supervision that are disproportionate to the advantages to be gained from enforcement and to the harm to be suffered from its denial.

§367.   Contracts for Personal Service or Supervision

(1) A promise to render personal service will not be specifically enforced.

(2) A promise to render personal service exclusively for one employer will not be enforced by an injunction against serving another if its probable result will be to compel a performance involving personal relations the enforced continuance of which is undesirable or will be to leave the employee without other reasonable means of making a living.

Topic 4.   Restitution

§370.   Requirement That Benefit Be Conferred

A party is entitled to restitution under the rules stated in this Restatement only to the extent that he has conferred a benefit on the other party by way of part performance or reliance.

§371.   Measure of Restitution Interest

If a sum of money is awarded to protect a party's restitution interest, it may as justice requires be measured by either

(a) the reasonable value to the other party of what he received in terms of what it would have cost him to obtain it from a person in the claimant's position, or

(b) the extent to which the other party's property has been increased in value or his other interests advanced.

§373. Restitution When Other Party Is in Breach

(1) Subject to the rule stated in Subsection (2), on a breach by non-performance that gives rise to a claim for damages for total breach or on a repudiation, the injured party is entitled to restitution for any benefit that he has conferred on the other party by way of part performance or reliance.

(2) The injured party has no right to restitution if he has performed all of his duties under the contract and no performance by the other party remains due other than payment of a definite sum of money for that performance.

§374. Restitution in Favor of Party in Breach

(1) Subject to the rule stated in Subsection (2), if a party justifiably refuses to perform on the ground that his remaining duties of performance have been discharged by the other party's breach, the party in breach is entitled to restitution for any benefit that he has conferred by way of part performance or reliance in excess of the loss that he has caused by his own breach.

(2) To the extent that, under the manifested assent of the parties, a party's performance is to be retained in the case of breach, that party is not entitled to restitution if the value of the performance as liquidated damages is reasonable in the light of the anticipated or actual loss caused by the breach and the difficulties of proof of loss.

§375. Restitution When Contract Is Within Statute of Frauds

A party who would otherwise have a claim in restitution under a contract is not barred from restitution for the reason that the contract is unenforceable by him because of the Statute of Frauds unless the Statute provides otherwise or its purpose would be frustrated by allowing restitution.

§376. Restitution When Contract Is Voidable

A party who has avoided a contract on the ground of lack of capacity, mistake, misrepresentation, duress, undue influence or abuse of a fiduciary relation is entitled to restitution for any benefit that he has conferred on the other party by way of part performance or reliance.

§377. Restitution in Cases of Impracticability, Frustration, Non-Occurrence of Condition or Disclaimer by Beneficiary

A party whose duty of performance does not arise or is discharged as a result of impracticability of performance, frustration of purpose, non-occurrence of a condition or disclaimer by a beneficiary is entitled to restitution for any benefit that he has conferred on the other party by way of part performance or reliance.

Topic 5. Preclusion by Election and Affirmance

§384. Requirement That Party Seeking Restitution Return Benefit

(1) Except as stated in Subsection (2), a party will not be granted restitution unless

(a) he returns or offers to return, conditional on restitution, any interest in property that he has received in exchange in substantially as good condition as when it was received by him, or

(b) the court can assure such return in connection with the relief granted.

(2) The requirement stated in Subsection (1) does not apply to property

(a) that was worthless when received or that has been destroyed or lost by the other party or as a result of its own defects,

(b) that either could not from the time of receipt have been returned or has been used or disposed of without knowledge of the grounds for restitution if justice requires that compensation be accepted in its place and the payment of such compensation can be assured, or

(c) as to which the contract apportions the price if that part of the price is not included in the claim for restitution.

Contract Drafting:
A Sample Problem

I. THE PROBLEM

Memorandum

To: File of Owens Chemical, Inc.
From: Attorney
Date: September 1, 1993

Tom Owens, owner of Owens Chemical, Inc., one of our clients, called me today. He wants me to draft a contract for his sales personnel.

The company sells cleaning chemicals to hotels, restaurants, and other businesses through commission salespeople. In the past the company has relied on oral agreements, but for several reasons Tom has now decided to have a written contract. He wants the contract to cover several points.

First, the company treats its sales force as independent contractors for tax purposes. This is important so that the company will not be responsible for withholding, social security, and other employment taxes. His accountant has said that it would be desirable to have this arrangement reflected in writing. Second, the company has had some problems with salespeople selling outside their territories. He says that the agreement should specify that salespeople are limited to certain territories.

I asked Tom about other provisions of the agreement. He said that sales personnel are paid a commission of 6 percent of gross sales each month and are responsible for paying all of their own automobile and other expenses. The company does not provide them with retirement or other employment benefits. I asked about duration of the contract, and he said that a one-year term would be fine.

Tom also said to keep it simple. He doesn't want a 20-page agreement and doesn't want a big bill.

II. THE LAWYER'S ROLE AND ETHICAL OBLIGATIONS IN CONTRACT DRAFTING

Contract drafting is a significant service that lawyers provide for their clients. Situations in which clients call on their lawyers to draft contracts typically fall in two categories. In the most common case, like the one involving Owens Chemical, the client asks the lawyer to draft a contract that the client will use in transactions with one or more other people. Examples of such contracts include leases of real property, contracts of purchase and sale of goods or real estate, and employment agreements.

In this first type of drafting situation, the lawyer does not have an attorney-client relationship with the other party, but only with the client for whom the lawyer drafted the contract. In fact, the lawyer may never even meet the other party to the contract. The other party may be represented by counsel, but it is often the case that this person will be unrepresented. If the lawyer does have any contact with an unrepresented party, the lawyer should be careful to make it clear that the lawyer does not represent that person. American Bar Association, Model Rules of Professional Conduct, Rule 4.3.

In the second type of drafting situation, a lawyer may be called on to serve as an intermediary between two or more persons, all of whom will be clients. For example, a lawyer might be asked to form a corporation and to prepare various agreements (such as employment and buy/sell contracts) between the shareholders. The lawyer could, of course, refuse to represent all the parties in this transaction and instead represent only one of the parties. In that case, the other participants would need to retain independent counsel or be unrepresented. To reduce legal fees and to facilitate the transaction, the parties to a business venture may prefer that one lawyer represent all their interests. Ethically, an attorney may do so, but the attorney must proceed with caution. The lawyer must fully advise all parties of the advantages and risks of multiple representation, must obtain their informed consent (preferably in writing), must treat all clients equally, and must withdraw from representation should an actual conflict of interest develop. See Model Rule 2.2 dealing with the lawyer as an intermediary.

The Owens Chemical situation involves the first type of transaction. Owens Chemical wants the lawyer to draft a standard form contract to be used to employ its sales personnel. Owens Chemical is the lawyer's client; the lawyer does not have an attorney-client relationship with the company's sales representatives. Since Owens is the client, the attorney has an ethical obligation to draft the

174

contract to protect its interests. This does not mean, however, that the attorney has no ethical obligations to the sales personnel. Under the ABA Model Rules of Professional Conduct, a lawyer "shall not counsel a client to engage, or assist a client, in conduct that the lawyer knows is criminal or fraudulent." Model Rule 1.2(d). On occasion a client may ask a lawyer to draft a contract that would violate the criminal law, such as a price-fixing agreement.

Even if not criminal, some contractual provisions that a client might want to include would clearly be unenforceable. Some state statutes, for example, prohibit a seller of goods from disclaiming the implied warranty of merchantability in the sale of goods. E.g., Mass. Gen. Laws Ann. ch. 106, §2-316A (West 1990). See generally Peter Millspaugh & Richard Coffinberger, Sellers' Disclaimers of Implied Warranties: The Legislatures Strike Back, 13 U.C.C.L.J. 160 (1980). Drafting a clearly unenforceable disclaimer would be tantamount to fraud on the other person. If a client demands that a lawyer draft a contract that includes a clearly illegal or fraudulent provision, the lawyer should refuse to do so and should withdraw from representation if necessary. Model Rule 1.16(a)(1) (lawyer must withdraw if "representation will result in violation of the rules of professional conduct"). In addition, as discussed below in the comments to the model agreement, the lawyer often must consider the fairness of provisions being drafted. See generally Lee A. Pizzimenti, Prohibiting Lawyers from Assisting in Unconscionable Transactions: Using an Overt Tool, 72 Marq. L. Rev. 151 (1989).

III. THE DRAFTING PROCESS

How does one begin the process of drafting a contract? The client will have given the lawyer some major points to include in the contract, as Mr. Owens has done for an agreement with his sales representatives. These include the following:

— independent contractor status
— definition of territory
— 6 percent commission
— responsibility for all expenses
— no retirement or other benefits
— one-year duration

Can the lawyer simply reduce to written form the points that the client wishes to include in the contract? Clearly not. Attorneys have a duty to represent their clients competently. Model Rule 1.1. Indeed, attorneys have been subject to professional discipline when they purported to do nothing more than act as a mere scrivener. See In re Solomon, 413 S.E.2d 808 (S.C. 1992) (rejecting "mere scrivener" defense to charge of representing conflicting interests). The lawyer's duty of competency in drafting a contract requires that the lawyer determine whether the client's expressed desires can be legally effectuated. Mr. Owens says that his company treats sales personnel as independent contractors for tax purposes, but is it proper for it to do so under federal and state tax law? The attorney or a specialist in tax law must research this point. See Horne v. Peckham, 158 Cal. Rptr. 714 (Cal. App. 1979) (in specialized area like tax law, lawyer must either refer matter to specialist or handle matter with degree of care and skill that would be exercised by specialist).

The duty of competency also means, however, that the lawyer cannot simply focus on the provisions that the client wishes to include in the agreement. The lawyer must determine whether other matters should be covered by the agreement or at least discussed with the client for possible addition to the contract.

Here the lawyer's duty of competency may encounter the economic realities of law practice. Owens says that he does not want a long contract; he wants to keep it simple and does not want a big bill. Yet, to adequately research and draft the contract may require considerable time. In some cases this may mean that the lawyer simply cannot bill the client for the actual time spent on the case. An attorney can view this unbilled time either as an investment in good client relations or as a cost that must be incurred along with the benefits of being a professional. What the attorney must *not* do, however, is consider the obligation to prepare the contract competently as somehow reduced because the client will not pay a full fee. It would be better to refuse the matter to begin with than to "cut corners."

How does a lawyer proceed to determine other provisions to consider including in the agreement? Experience and discussion with other lawyers can suggest some provisions that the agreement should contain. Usually, an attorney must turn to previously prepared agreements and checklists for guidance. Law offices typically maintain form files that an attorney can consult. In addition, commercial publishers offer form books of various types that normally include checklists, sample agreements, and commentary. Comprehensive sets of forms include the following:

American Jurisprudence, Legal Forms (2d ed.)
Nichols Cyclopedia of Legal Forms Annotated
Rabkin & Johnson, Current Legal Forms with Tax Analysis
West's Legal Forms (2d ed.)

After consulting these various sources, the lawyer should be able to prepare an outline of provisions to include in the agreement, along with suggested language for a number of these terms. The lawyer is now ready to prepare a draft of the contract.

IV. MODEL CONTRACT WITH COMMENTS

Independent Contractor Agreement[1]

Agreement entered into this _____ day of _____ , 19____ , between Owens Chemical, Inc. (the "Company"), of _____ , and _____ ("Contractor") of _____ .[2]

Recitals[3]

Company operates an industrial chemical business and wishes to hire Contractor as an independent contractor to sell chemicals on behalf of the Company.

Contractor is willing to perform sales services for the Company as an independent contractor.

In consideration[4] of the mutual covenants set forth below, the parties hereby agree as follows:

1. *Description of Work.*[5] Contractor shall devote his[6] full time and use his best efforts[7] to make sales of chemical products to the Company's customers.

---

1. The Contract is titled "Independent Contractor Agreement" both for ease of identification and to bolster one of the client's major goals, to clarify the status of the sales personnel for tax purposes.

2. Contracts typically begin with an introduction that includes date, names of the parties, and the city in which they reside or do business. Shorthand references like "Company" and "Contractor" eliminate the need to fill in blanks. Avoid terms like "party of the first part," which are cumbersome and hard to follow.

3. Recitals are background facts and statements of the purposes of the agreement. Both may be useful should an issue of interpretation later develop. Older forms usually began the recitals with "Witnesseth." The trend in drafting is to use plain English whenever possible. Archaic language usually serves no useful purpose and should generally be eliminated. However, some "magic" phrases ("heirs and assigns," for example) have such an established meaning that it would be difficult and probably counterproductive to attempt to develop a modern equivalent.

4. The consideration clause is not strictly necessary since the contract contains mutual promises, but it is customary to include and serves as a transition to the body of the contract.

5. The drafter should strive to have a logical order to the substantive provisions. In the Model Contract, paragraphs 1 and 2 deal with the duties of the contractor. Paragraph 3 sets forth the compensation paid by the company. Paragraphs 4 through 6 focus on the various aspects of the independent contractor relationship. Paragraph 7 deals with termination of the relationship. Paragraph 8 is a merger clause. Contracts, particularly long ones, should include headings for easy reference.

6. In some contracts the use of gender-specific pronouns may be appropriate, but most standard form contracts apply to transactions with both men and women. Use of the plural rather than the singular can avoid the problem of choice of gender, but the plural does not always fit the context. (In the Owens Chemical contract, for example, it would be inappropriate to use the plural to refer to contractors since the agreement is with an individual salesperson.) Some contracts use the male pronoun with a general statement that the male form is intended to include the female, but this form can give the impression of male dominance.

7. The obligation of sales personnel to devote full time and to use their best efforts on behalf of the company was not mentioned by the client but was included by the drafter on the assumption that these provisions reflect the client's desires. Any provision that the drafter includes based on the drafter's view of what the client probably wants should be discussed with the client before the agreement is executed. See the letter to the client that follows the Model Contract.

2. *Territory*.[8] Contractor shall contact only customers whose principal place of business is located in the following territory:

In case of doubt Contractor shall notify the Company and obtain permission to contact a customer. If Contractor learns of customers in other territories who are interested in purchasing the Company's products, Contractor shall promptly notify the Company of the names of these customers.

3. *Commission.* Company shall pay to Contractor a commission of six percent (6%) of gross sales.[9] Payment shall be made on the 15th of each month for sales made during the previous month.[10]

4. *Relationship of Parties.* The parties intend that an independent contractor-employer relationship will be created by this contract. The Company is interested only in the results to be achieved, and the conduct and control of the work will lie solely with the Contractor.[11]

5. *Expenses and Benefits.* Contractor shall be responsible for all expenses involved in performing duties under this agreement and shall not be entitled to any employee benefits, such as social security, workers' compensation, or insurance.

6. *Liability.* The work to be performed under this contract will be performed entirely at Contractor's risk. For the duration of this contract, Contractor will carry public liability insurance naming Company as an additional insured in the following amount: _____ . Contractor agrees to indemnify and hold the company harmless against any liability or loss arising from Contractor's negligence.[12]

8. Owens has said that the Company has a problem with sales representatives selling outside their territories. Drafting a clause to deal with this issue may appear to be a simple task, but it is not. Owens's customers may have more than one place of business; companies may also move or open additional places of business. How should the agreement deal with the fact that a customer may be physically located in more than one territory? Your tasks as a drafter are first to identify the problem and then to draft a solution that is compatible with the client's desires and business operation.

The agreement uses blanks for provisions that vary among the sales personnel. It is also common to group individual variations in an appendix to the standard form agreement.

9. Is the meaning of "gross sales" clear or is a definition needed? For example, are returns or credits deducted in determining the amount of gross sales to which the commission applies? This point should be raised with the client. The more general point is that operative terms in the agreement often needed to be defined. When the agreement contains a number of definitions, the contract should contain a separate definitional paragraph.

10. Is the date for payment consistent with company practice?

11. Under federal income tax law a salesperson will be treated as an independent contractor not subject to social security tax, unemployment tax, or withholding when the employer is interested only in the results obtained and does not control or have the right to control the day-to-day activities of the sales person. Employment Tax Reg. §31-3121(d)-1; Employee Defined, Tax Management Portfolio (BNA) No. 391 (1987).

12. Paragraph 6 raises the issues of the lawyer's role in drafting and of the fairness of the agreement. The client has not mentioned the need for sales personnel to carry insurance or for indemnification against liability. The lawyer certainly has an ethical obligation to raise the issue of insurance with the client because the absence of such insurance could pose a substantial legal risk to the client and because it would not be unreasonable for sales personnel to be required to carry insurance.

The indemnification clause, however, is a different matter. Does the client really need the additional protection of an indemnification clause from the sales personnel? If so, how broadly should

7. *Duration and Termination.* This contract shall continue for one year from its execution. It shall be automatically renewed for additional one-year periods unless either party gives written notice of termination at least three (3) months before the anniversary of the execution of this agreement.[13] Provided, however, either party may terminate this agreement at any time for good cause.

8. *Entire Agreement.* This document constitutes the entire agreement between the parties. No agreements between the parties are binding on them unless incorporated in a writing signed by both parties. This agreement may be modified only in writing signed by both parties.[14]

In witness whereof,[15] the parties have executed[16] this agreement on the day and year first written above.

CONTRACTOR: OWENS CHEMICAL, INC.

_____   By: _____
                                          Authorized Agent[17]

---

the clause be drafted? Should it indemnify the Company against any loss resulting from the negligence of the salesperson, or should it protect the Company against any liability arising from the actions of the salesperson, whether negligent or not? As noted above, a lawyer may not draft a clause that is illegal or fraudulent, but this broad clause clearly does not violate those restrictions. Should the lawyer, therefore, include any provision that protects the client's interests, or should the lawyer strive to draft an agreement that reasonably protects the client's interests without being overreaching?

One possible answer to this question is that the lawyer should draft the agreement to protect the client to the maximum extent possible but also should discuss with the client the advantages and disadvantages of the provisions in question so that the client can make an informed decision. The difficulty with this approach is that the client will often turn to the lawyer for advice about what should be included. In addition, human inertia being what it is, the provision that the lawyer initially drafts will be more likely to remain in the agreement.

The drafter of this agreement has included an indemnification clause that the drafter believes reasonably protects the client's interest but without being overreaching. The clause, therefore, is limited to negligence by the salesperson. Do you agree with this approach? Or do you consider it inconsistent with the lawyer's fiduciary obligations to his client?

13. The automatic renewal clause avoids the necessity of additional paperwork to renew the contract each year, but the Company should be made aware of the requirement to give three months' written notice if it wishes to terminate a salesperson at the end of any year.

14. This merger clause is intended to invoke the application of the parol evidence rule and to prevent oral modifications.

15. This is a standard conclusion to a contract but could easily be eliminated.

16. Witnesses to a contract are not required for the validity of a contract but may be desirable if there is any possibility of a later dispute about execution or terms of the contract. Given the nature of this contract, witnesses seem unnecessary.

Certain contracts, particularly contracts involving real estate, may be recorded in public records if one of the parties wishes to give public notice of the existence of the contract. To be recorded, however, a contract must meet statutory requirements regarding number of witnesses, one of whom must be a "notary public" or other similar officer legally authorized to witness the execution of documents under oath. Since this contract will not be recorded, notarization is unnecessary.

Many older contracts stated that they were executed "under seal" or "L.S." (*locus sigilli*). The significance of the seal has largely disappeared in modern times. In some jurisdictions, execution under seal may have the benefit of lengthening the statute of limitations for suit for breach of the agreement, but this is a fairly minor point.

17. Whenever a corporation or other business entity is a party to an agreement, the authority of

V. *COUNSELING THE CLIENT*

Once the attorney has prepared a draft of the contract, the attorney will then submit the draft to the client for review. Typically, the lawyer will do this with an accompanying cover letter pointing out the principal provisions in the agreement along with questions that the attorney would like the client to consider.

September 15, 1993

Mr. Tom Owens
Owens Chemical, Inc.
218 Local Street
Your Town, YS 91128

Dear Tom:

I enclose for your review a draft Independent Contractor Agreement for your sales personnel. Please consider the following points and questions as you review the agreement:

1. *Description of Work.* I included a provision stating that salespeople will devote their "full time" to Company sales. Is this satisfactory? Do you have or expect to have any part-timers? Do you have any sales representatives who also represent other chemical companies?

The provision also states that sales personnel will use their best efforts on behalf of the company. Under paragraph 7 you can terminate any salesperson for good cause, which would include failure to use best efforts. You can also terminate a salesperson at the end of any year for any reason provided you give three months' written notice.

2. *Territory.* I drafted the territory clause to try to deal with the problem you mentioned about salespeople who contact customers outside their territories. A possible difficulty is that your customers may have places of business in several territories. This clause uses the principal place of business of a customer to define the territory in which the customer is located. Let's discuss this to determine if it meets your needs.

---

the agent who is signing the agreement on its behalf should be verified. This may be done by a certification from the Secretary of the entity that the official has authority to act on behalf of the entity either under the bylaws or other governing document of the entity, or by virtue of a resolution adopted by the governing body of the entity (the board of directors of a corporation, for example). The president of a corporation normally has implied or inherent authority to execute contracts that are reasonably necessary for the operation of the business, Restatement (Second) of Agency §73, so it is probably unnecessary for the Company to take any formal action to authorize Owens to sign these contracts.

3. *Commission.* As you mentioned, this is based on 6 percent of gross sales. Do we need to define "gross sales"? Are there any deductions that should be made from gross sales, like returns or credits, for the purpose of determining commissions? Is payment of the commission on the 15th of the month for the previous month's sales consistent with your practice?

4. *Relationship of Parties.* This paragraph confirms that sales personnel are independent contractors. Under federal and state law, a salesperson will be treated as an independent contractor if the employer is concerned only about results and does not control the day-to-day activities of the sales personnel. This is a factual question. Despite what the agreement says, if you do try to control or direct the day-to-day activities of your personnel, they will no longer be independent contractors. Be aware of this fact as you conduct your business.

5. *Expenses and Benefits.* This confirms that the Company has no obligation to reimburse sales personnel for expenses or to provide any benefits.

6. *Liability.* We did not discuss the question of liability but I have drafted a clause requiring sales personnel to carry insurance and also providing that sales personnel must indemnify the company for any liability arising from their negligence. Do you need or want this protection, or do you simply want to rely on your own insurance? In any event, you need to check with your insurance company to make sure your insurance covers the Company for any actions of its sales personnel.

7. *Duration and Termination.* The term of the agreement is one year, and the agreement automatically renews for additional one-year periods unless written notice of termination is given by either party three months before the end of any one-year period. The agreement may be terminated at any time for good cause. Are there any specific forms of misconduct that the agreement should specify as grounds for discharge?

8. *Entire Agreement.* This is a standard provision requiring that any modifications or additions to the agreement be in writing. The purpose of this clause is to reduce or eliminate disputes about the terms of the agreement. If you decide that change or modification of the agreement is necessary, you should reduce the provision to writing and have it signed by both the Company and the Contractor.

Other points to consider.

I did not include in the agreement a covenant not to compete. Do you want to consider including such a clause? For example, the agreement might prohibit a salesperson who leaves the Company from contacting any customer of the Company on behalf of a competitor of the Company for a designated period, such as one year. Courts sometimes refuse to enforce covenants not to compete, so if you wish to pursue this idea, we will need to discuss it further.

The agreement provides that if a salesperson learns of a potential customer outside the salesperson's territory, the salesperson will promptly notify the company. Do you want to give sales personnel an incentive to make such contacts, such as giving them a referral fee if a sale results?

After you have had a chance to review the draft, give me a call so that we can discuss revisions and consider any suggestions you may have.

Best regards,

Helen T. Partner, Esq.

VI. BIBLIOGRAPHY

Given the importance of drafting, law schools are devoting increasing attention to the subject. In the past few years a number of fine books on drafting have been published. These include the following:

Scott Burnham, Drafting Contracts (1987)
Barbara Child, Drafting Legal Documents (2d ed. 1992)
Reed Dickerson, The Fundamentals of Legal Drafting (2d ed. 1986) (with bibliography)

SAMPLE EXAMINATION QUESTIONS AND ANSWERS

EDITORS' NOTE

The two sample examination questions and model answers that follow deal with issues covered in most contracts casebooks, although the order of their presentation may differ. Students using casebooks other than Knapp & Crystal, Problems in Contract Law (3d ed. 1993), should have little difficulty following the analysis. We have also included several questions without model answers, to be used by students for review or by instructors for class discussion.

CONTRACT FORMATION, DEFENSES, AND REMEDIES

You are an attorney practicing in a small midwestern town. One Monday morning you are consulted in your office by Karen Mackenzie, a local resident whom you know slightly but have not represented before. She tells you the following story:

"As you may know, my husband died several years ago. Our children were nearly grown then, and since I have a well-paying position at the hospital and he left a substantial estate, I haven't had severe financial worries. Now that our children are all through school and supporting themselves, I have moved into a smaller, less expensive apartment. As a result I find myself in quite comfortable circumstances, financially.

"Last week I got in the mail one of those promotional letters that said I had won a 'valuable prize' (you probably know the kind I mean), either a Jeep or a diamond ring or a set of luggage or $10,000 in cash. All I had to do to claim my prize, the letter said, was to come to Fairgate Hills, a new condominium development some 10 miles west of town, near the lake, and visit the 'prize redemption center.' Well, I knew there would be a sales pitch involved, but I was sort of curious to see the place, having heard about it from some friends of mine who live near there. And in fact I had thought a little about investing in some sort of vacation home where the kids could come and stay with me for a while. Now that they're all having families of their own, it's too crowded for them to visit my apartment in town.

"So last Saturday I took my 'Winner's Certificate' and drove out to Fairgate Hills. When I arrived I was met by a young woman named Abby something-or-other (I never did get her last name) who told me that before she could authorize my picking up the prize she would have to take me on a tour of Fairgate Hills and tell me about the terms on which condominium units were available there. I said I realized something like that would be involved, and that was okay with me — she should know I had no intention of buying anything, I said, but I did have some time to kill. So we walked around, and looked through some of the units, and I was pretty impressed, in spite of myself. There were tennis courts, too, and picnic areas, and the whole thing was very attractive. The more she talked the better it all seemed, and by the time we were finished, I had signed something and given her a check for $5000."

At this point, you ask Ms. Mackenzie if she has a copy of the paper she signed. She produces the following for your inspection:

Offer to Purchase

The undersigned, <u>Karen Mackenzie</u> , hereby offers to purchase condominium unit <u>54</u> in Fairgate Hills, a <u>three</u> bedroom unit with <u>two</u> baths and <u>carport adjoining</u> . I agree that the seller, Fairgate Hills, Inc. (the "Seller"), may investigate my credit before accepting this offer, and I agree to provide such information and sign such consents as Seller may request for this purpose. I also agree that should this Offer be accepted, I will enter into the standard form of Sale and Mortgage Agreement used by the Seller for its sales of condominium units in Fairgate Hills (a copy of which has been made available for my inspection), with such changes therein as Seller and I may mutually agree to.

In earnest of my intention to perform all of my obligations hereunder, I have today paid to Seller the sum of <u>$5000.00</u> , which sum will be applied toward my total purchase price of <u>$165,000</u> should Seller accept this Offer. If my Offer is not accepted within sixty days of the date below, that sum will be refunded to me (subject to deduction of Seller's reasonable expenses incurred in connection with the processing of this Offer), and this Offer will thereupon terminate.

I understand and agree that this Offer is made for valuable consideration, and is irrevocable by me. I further understand and agree that the payment made by me today will not be refundable for any reason except the failure of the Seller to accept my Offer, and may in the event of my non-performance of any obligation hereunder be retained by the Seller as damages for my nonperformance, without limitation of the Seller's right to any other remedy instead of, or in addition to, such sum.

December 16, 1993	(signed) Karen Mackenzie
Date	Purchaser

Karen Mackenzie's story continues: "After she had my check, Abby walked me over to the 'prize redemption center,' where they gave me my prize — a set of cheap plastic luggage, worth $50 at the most — and I left for home.

"All the way home, I kept having second thoughts. Even if I did want a vacation home, this one was too big for me, and too expensive. By the time I got home, I was sure I'd made a mistake. So right away I telephoned the office at Fairgate Hills, and asked to speak to Abby. As soon as she was on the phone, I identified myself and said I'd changed my mind, that I didn't want to buy a unit at Fairgate Hills after all. She said I must have misunderstood our conversation, that the paper I signed committed me to make the purchase, that it was an enforceable contract, and that if I tried to back out I'd not only lose my $5000, I'd be liable for damages, too. Is she right? Do I have to go through with this, or else lose a lot of money?"

You have some reason to think there may be provisions of federal or state statutory law that would be helpful to someone in Ms. Mackenzie's situation, and you resolve to do research in that area. First, however, you consider her position under traditional contract law. Is she legally bound to Fairgate Hills? Or can she freely terminate any potential obligation she may have incurred under the "Offer to Purchase" quoted above? If she is indeed bound by some sort of obligation, what kinds of liability might she face, should Fairgate Hills elect to enforce it? Finally, in light of your answers to these questions, what course of action would you advise her now to follow? If you need more facts in order to answer these questions, indicate what those facts might be and why they would be relevant to your conclusions.

OUTLINE OF ANSWER

1. Has Karen Mackenzie made an offer?
   a. Sufficiently definite and certain
   b. Finality of commitment
2. If offer was made, can it be revoked?
   a. Traditional rule of free revocability
   b. Presence of consideration
   c. Effectiveness of recital of consideration
   d. Application of statute

  e. Reliance by offeree
  f. Offer already revoked
  g. Offer already accepted (mailbox rule)
3. If offer accepted, enforceable contract?
  a. Sufficiently complete agreement
  b. Satisfaction of Statute of Frauds
  c. Possibility of avoidance for fraud or mistake
  d. Capacity to contract
  e. Unconscionability
4. Remedies of Seller
  a. Damages
  b. Specific performance
  c. Retention of down payment (vs. buyer's claim to restitution)

MODEL ANSWER

In order to counsel my client Karen Mackenzie (to whom I will refer for convenience as "Mackenzie"), I will first need to address several questions:

(1) Did Mackenzie make an offer to Fairgate Hills, Inc. ("Fairgate"), in the writing she signed during her Saturday visit to the condominium development?

(2) If Mackenzie did make an effective offer, is it one that she has the power to revoke?

(3) If Mackenzie has indeed made an offer, and does not effectively revoke that offer before Fairgate accepts it, will a contract enforceable against her be created?

(4) If Mackenzie is (or comes to be) bound to Fairgate by an enforceable contract, to what remedy would Fairgate be entitled if Mackenzie should refuse to perform?

These questions will be addressed below in the order stated above.

1. Has Mackenzie made an offer?

For a communication to reach the level of an "offer," creating in the one to whom it is addressed the power to bring a contract into being by making an acceptance, it must be such as to reasonably create in the mind of the (potential) "offeree" the belief that the person making it has stated a definite proposal for exchange, with sufficient commitment on the part of the "offeror" that no further expression of assent from her is necessary in order to complete the bargain. (See Restatement (Second) of Contracts §24 — offeree's "assent to that bargain is invited and will conclude it.")

In this case the writing signed by Mackenzie was clearly designed by Fairgate to be an offer, although one to be made by the potential purchasers of its condos, *not* by Fairgate itself. It uses the language of offer, and, with the incorporation by reference of Fairgate's standard form purchase agreement, probably has sufficient detail and certainty to satisfy that requirement as well. (The latter point is discussed further below.) As Mackenzie told her story to me, she did not seem to have been ignorant of the possibility that the writing she signed could in effect commit her to the purchase of a condo; rather, she apparently had assumed that she could back out if she chose before Fairgate had committed itself. (This goes more to the issue of irrevocability, discussed below.) Unless Mackenzie maintains that she was in fact deceived about the nature of the paper she was signing (she was told it was merely a receipt for her luggage "prize," for instance), it seems unlikely that she can successfully deny making an offer to purchase. (Her delivery to Abby of a $5000 check would undercut any "I thought I was only signing a receipt" argument — clearly one doesn't blithely hand over a check that large unless some substantial transaction is in process.) Before reaching a definite conclusion on this first point, however, I would quiz Mackenzie further as to just what Abby said to her about the writing she signed, and whether Mackenzie read it before signing (or at all).

2. If Mackenzie made an offer, can she revoke it?

This issue raises several questions: Was Mackenzie's offer (assuming for the moment it was indeed an offer) irrevocable when made? If not, has she revoked it already? If she has not, can she do so now? How?

Under the traditional common law of contract, an offeror may freely revoke her offer at any time before an effective acceptance is made, *even if* the offer expressly states that it is irrevocable. This rule sometimes appears to produce unjust results when used by a knowledgeable offeror against an unsophisticated offeree, who may have relied in various ways on the continuing availability of what was assumed to be in fact an irrevocable, or "firm," offer. In this case, however, the traditional rule could enable Mackenzie to escape from a bargain that she does not want and that, apparently, she believed she could avoid. A variety of exceptions to the general common law rule, however, might cause Mackenzie's offer to be irrevocable: She might be bound by a consideration-supported "option contract"; her offer might be irrevocable because of its form; the offeree might have reasonably relied on her apparent intention to make an irrevocable offer. It is even possible that her offer, even if it was in effect a revocable one from the start, has already been accepted by Fairgate and thus is no longer capable of being revoked. These possibilities will be explored in order below.

Even the most "classical" form of contract law allows for the possibility that an offer will be irrevocable for some period of time because the offeree has given "consideration" for its remaining open — has purchased an "option contract." Consideration was traditionally defined as a "detriment to the promisor" (who in the case of an option contract would be the offeror, promising to keep her offer open) or a "benefit to the promisee" (in this case, the offeree). The "benefit" or "detriment" involved may be of slight value, however, as shown by Hamer v. Sidway. Under the more modern definition of consideration, virtually anything may serve as consideration if it was bargained for and given in exchange for the promise. (Restatement (Second) of Contracts §71).

In Mackenzie's case, it is difficult to find anything in the facts as related which could serve the function of consideration to keep her offer open. Mackenzie did in fact suffer a variety of "detriments," some quite substantial (the $5000) and some less so (driving out to Fairgate Hills, taking the tour and enduring Abby's sales pitch). These are also "benefits" to Fairgate, in varying degrees. But they move the wrong way — Mackenzie in this case would be the "promisor" (promising to keep her offer open), so the benefit must move *to* her, not *from* her; similarly, the detriment must be suffered by Fairgate, not by Mackenzie.

On the facts as related, the only thing that might serve as consideration for the making of an irrevocable offer by Mackenzie is the set of luggage she received at the end of her Saturday visit. The modest value of the luggage is no obstacle — clearly $50 or the equivalent in goods could be sufficient consideration for an option contract, *if bargained for*. This latter point appears crucial, however. If the luggage was indeed given to Mackenzie by Fairgate as the "exchange" or the "price" for anything at all (rather than being just a "gift," which is what "prize" connotes, probably), it was the price for Mackenzie's willingness to travel several miles to Fairgate Hills, or perhaps for that plus her willingness to sit through a sales pitch. Although the presentation of the luggage was not characterized by Fairgate as an exchange, the luggage may have served in effect to purchase the presence of a potential buyer. Thus, if Fairgate had not come through with the luggage at the end of her tour, Mackenzie might in theory have had a cause of action against Fairgate for the luggage or its value. (Note that this scenario is different from Williston's "tramp" hypothetical, because Mackenzie's presence at the condo development, unlike the tramp's trip to obtain the overcoat, could have been — and in fact was — of benefit to Fairgate.) But to call the luggage consideration for the making of an irrevocable offer by Mackenzie seems to stretch the facts too far. It was never so characterized, and Mackenzie never understood that the luggage was given in exchange for anything other than, perhaps, her presence at the condo long enough for the sales pitch to be made.

If no consideration was in fact given for Mackenzie's offer, can Fairgate claim the benefit of the suggested rule of Restatement (Second) of Contracts §87(1)(a)? This rule applies to an offer that meets certain specific requirements: It is in writing and signed (which Mackenzie's is), recites a "purported consideration" for the making of the offer, and "proposes an exchange on fair terms within a reasonable time." Applying this rule to Mackenzie's situation could create problems. The "offer" Mackenzie signed recites that it is made for consideration, but doesn't otherwise identify that consideration. Must it do so to satisfy §87(1)(a)? That's not clear from the statement of the rule. Does her offer propose an exchange "on fair terms"? Until I conduct some investigation of the facts, I have no idea whether the $165,000 price is a reasonable one. Is the proposed exchange one that will take place "within a reasonable time"? Again, I can't know this from reading the offer itself; the form it refers to may have a provision governing the time by which the sale is to be closed. (It seems unlikely, however, that the seller would draft a form unreasonably *delaying* the closing.)

The proposed rule of §87(1)(a) has not been embraced by the courts; not all courts have addressed it, and not all that have done so have adopted it. I would have to examine the case law of my jurisdiction to know whether a mere recital of consideration would be given this effect. If our courts have not yet adopted the rule of §87(1)(a), we can in good faith take the position that it is not good law (and unlikely to become so). Moreover, there is also room to argue that this is not an appropriate case for the application of that rule. If I understood her correctly, Mackenzie did not in fact believe that she was making an offer that she could not revoke, and did not know that the "recital of consideration" could have that effect. This by itself may not be persuasive, however, since a court might not believe her or might conclude that she *should* have understood the writing to have that effect.

A clearer rebuttal can be given to another possible argument in favor of irrevocability. The Uniform Commercial Code in §2-205 provides that written, signed "firm" offers may be binding without consideration. That section applies only to sales of goods, however, and only to offers made by "merchants." Fairgate might be considered a "merchant," as Article 2 uses that rather broad term, but *Mackenzie* probably is not. Moreover, the condo is not "goods" as defined in the Code. UCC §2-205 thus does not directly apply, and in view of Mackenzie's nonmerchant status should not be applied even "by analogy." (Note also that §2-205 calls for separate signing, or at least initialing, when a "firm offer" is made on a form supplied by the *offeree*, another reason why that section should have no relevance here.) A few states, such as New York, have broader statutes making "firm" offers irrevocable, a point that also needs research. (For the moment, I will assume that my jurisdiction does not have such a statute.)

Since the decision in Drennan v. Star Paving Co., courts have been willing to consider the possibility that reliance on an offer by the offeree may be sufficient to deprive the offeror at least temporarily of the power to revoke. Despite its incorporation in Restatement (Second) of Contracts §87(2), however, this application of "promissory estoppel" seems unlikely to help Fairgate, even if the courts of my jurisdiction would be willing to apply the *Drennan* principle in non-construction-bidding cases, as the Restatement suggests. According to Mackenzie's story, she called Abby as soon as she returned home from her trip to Fairgate Hills; the facts we know suggest that the time lag cannot have been more than a few hours, at most. It is difficult to imagine any actions Fairgate might have taken during that brief interval other than to initiate a credit check on Mackenzie, an action that by itself seems unlikely to be viewed by the court as the sort of "substantial" action that under §87(2) might result in injustice if the offer were freely revocable. Once Mackenzie notified Fairgate that she did not wish to proceed with the transaction, it seems that any further reliance on her willingness to honor an apparent promise of irrevocability would be unreasonable and thus should have no effect on her power to revoke. Moreover, when Abby told Mackenzie the offer could not be withdrawn, she did not mention any change of position on Fairgate's part to justify that conclusion; she seemed to be arguing simply on the strength of the language of the offer. This by itself is not conclusive, of course, but it strengthens our argument that any reliance on Fairgate's part was insubstantial at that point.

This leads logically to another, related question. Assuming that Mackenzie's offer is not in legal effect an irrevocable one, has she already revoked it? Her telephone call, as she recounted it, seems to have been sufficient to give Abby notice that Mackenzie no longer wanted to make the purchase, and it may have had the effect suggested above on Fairgate's power to reasonably rely. Whether it also served effectively as a revocation is less clear. Abby took the strong position that Mackenzie simply had no power to withdraw from the transaction, and it may be that Mackenzie's response to that assertion was sufficiently equivocal to leave her offer on the table. In any event, recollections of a conversation (and the credibility of those recollections) may differ. Since it is at least possible that Mackenzie has the power to revoke, she should do so immediately in a written letter to Fairgate. (This point is explored further at the end of the discussion.)

It should be noted here that, although perhaps unlikely, one other factor could make it impossible for Mackenzie now to revoke her offer. That is the possibility that Fairgate has already accepted it. Mackenzie wrote her offer and left it with Abby for Fairgate to consider; clearly the offer did not call only for an immediate acceptance. Under these circumstances, the offer is probably susceptible of acceptance by mail, under the traditional "deposited acceptance," or "mailbox," rule. Conceivably Mackenzie's call to Abby triggered an immediate mailing of such an acceptance (if only for the purpose of giving Fairgate an even stronger claim to retention of Mackenzie's $5000 payment). At this point we don't know whether that happened. In case it did, we should take the position (which on the facts we can, in good faith) that Mackenzie's telephone call was itself a revocation sufficient to terminate any power of acceptance. Any letter of revocation sent now by Mackenzie should therefore take the position that revocation has already been effected orally and that the letter is simply to confirm that fact.

3. If Fairgate does accept before Mackenzie effectively revokes her offer, will an enforceable contract result?

This general question raises a number of distinct issues: Would a mere acceptance by Fairgate without further assent by Mackenzie conclude an effective contract? Would Mackenzie have the ability to avoid that contract, or have a defense against its enforcement, under some applicable rule of law?

In discussing the "offer" status of Mackenzie's signed writing, it was suggested that the incorporation by reference of Fairgate's standard form could satisfy the requisite certainty of terms that common law courts (with varying degrees of scrutiny) look for in a contract. Not actually having seen the form, I cannot be sure of that, but for the moment I can assume it, given the nature of Fairgate and the likelihood that the form was drafted by a competent attorney. (If a dispute with Fairgate develops, at some point we will demand and get a copy of that form, of course.) The offer refers to the possibility of amending the terms of that standard form, to the extent that the parties may both agree. The possibility of such modifications probably would not undercut the agreement so greatly as to make it ineffective for vagueness or "agreement to agree" character, however, whether or not we hypothesize some degree of obligation on Fairgate's part to bargain in good faith over possible amendments to the form.

A second rule of law that can make an agreement unenforceable is the Statute of Frauds. A condominium is an interest in land (as contrasted with a "cooperative," which technically is a shareholder's interest in a land-owning corporation), and clearly the Statute of Frauds could — at least at this point — be a defense to any enforcement by Mackenzie *against* Fairgate. But Mackenzie has signed an offer, and the offer coupled with the incorporated-by-reference terms of the standard agreement probably satisfies the writing requirement of the Statute of Frauds, as against her. (Some research again is called for, to see whether our courts have imposed an unusually high threshold for completeness or land-description.) Traditionally the Statute of Frauds only requires a writing signed by the "party to be charged," and in this case that's Mackenzie.

If Mackenzie's offer once accepted is sufficient in form and content to satisfy the ordinary rules of contract law, are there any grounds on which she might seek to avoid its enforcement? One set of rules focuses on possible misconduct by the other party. Did Fairgate misrepresent any material fact, intentionally or otherwise? Here again, a more searching conversation with Mackenzie is needed to determine precisely what Mackenzie was and was not told during her visit to Fairgate Hills. Nothing Mackenzie has said so far suggests any misrepresentation by Abby, other than her assertion that Mackenzie cannot now withdraw her offer. That assertion was made after the offer was signed, however, and therefore played no role in inducing Mackenzie's entry into this transaction. Moreover, it was at worst a misrepresentation by one party of the other party's legal position, which is the sort of assertion that is not likely to be actionable fraud, if only because — like "puffing" — it's not an assertion on which the other party should reasonably rely. It should also be noted that although Mackenzie quickly concluded that this purchase was for her a "mistake," this is not the sort of mistake that provides a legal power of avoidance. That requires a later-discovered material fact that at the time of contracting was unknown either to both parties or at least to the one seeking to avoid. Absent more facts, we have nothing like that here.

Although we know that Mackenzie is old enough to have grown children with families of their own, she sounds too vigorous (physically as well as mentally) to be able to make a viable claim of legal incompetence to contract (even if she wanted to, which seems doubtful). Could she have been the victim of undue influence? Presumably Abby is a well-trained, high-pressure salesperson, and an effective one, too; by itself, however, this is not enough. Mackenzie seems to have understood from the start that she was letting herself in for a sales talk. The sales pitch seems to have had real substance, and the condos to have been attractive, but nothing (other than the lure of her "prize") appears to have kept Mackenzie at any point from just picking up her marbles and walking away.

Can this agreement be "unconscionable," and for that reason unenforceable? To answer this, I need to see the standard Sale and Mortgage Agreement referred to in the offer. Even if the price itself is a fair one, other terms in that form may appear shocking to the conscience of a court, such as stronger-than-ordinary rights for the seller upon buyer's default. I also need to ask Mackenzie whether she even saw that form, whether she was given an opportunity to study it, and (if so) whether she did. If the price is shockingly high or the terms unusually onerous, the transaction is one — sophisticated seller, unsophisticated and un-counseled buyer, hasty decision — that could qualify for unconscionability treatment. (This is not confined to sales of goods, of course, even though the modern law of unconscionability can be traced in large part to UCC §2-302.) For a number of reasons, however, the unconscionability defense is best as a backstop. First, courts are often reluctant to apply it; second, Mackenzie may not be an ideal candidate. (She is hardly a poor or illiterate person — did she have an "absence of meaningful choice"?) Even if successful, it might result only in staving off further liability, not in a refund of Mackenzie's $5000.

4. If Mackenzie is bound by an enforceable contract, what remedies might be available to Fairgate if she refuses to perform?

The potential remedies for Fairgate fall into three categories: money damages, specific performance, and liquidated damages (retention of the down payment).

The vendor's money damages for breach of a contract to purchase real estate are traditionally computed as the excess of the purchase price over the value of the property, plus incidental and consequential damages occasioned by the breach. The first question here is one we have already raised above: What is the market value of the condo at issue? If it is worth about what Mackenzie agreed to pay for it, then Fairgate's money damages for her breach could consist only of the "incidental" damages involved in finding another buyer. The chance of consequential damages to Fairgate appears nil — nothing Mackenzie has told me suggests she had any reason at the time of her meeting with Abby to foresee any unusual damages to Fairgate from a buyer's refusal to perform, so the traditional Hadley v. Baxendale rule would protect her. (As an analogy, consider that the UCC doesn't even expressly contemplate the recovery of consequential damages by a *seller*.) Suppose, however, that the condos Fairgate is selling are in fact worth much less on the market than the price stated to Mackenzie. (If so, this could also be a first step — but *only* a first step — toward an argument that material misrepresentations were made to her.) In this case, Fairgate's money damages for a breach by Mackenzie could range from little or nothing to quite a lot of money. (Note that even if the clause providing for Fairgate's retention of the down payment is valid and effective as in effect a liquidated remedy, the clause itself is specific on the point that retention of the deposit is not necessarily the *only* remedy to which Fairgate might be entitled.)

Could Fairgate succeed in an action for specific performance? Traditionally this remedy has been available in land cases, to sellers as well as to buyers. We might well argue, however, that money damages here would certainly be adequate; some courts would accept that argument by a defendant-buyer where the property is readily resaleable and the plaintiff-seller's damages can be fixed with sufficient accuracy. Specific performance is also sometimes withheld because the exchange appears to be an unfair one; thus, the greater the disparity between contract and market prices, the less likely it is that specific performance will be granted. (Paradoxically, this disparity would also *increase* the likelihood of substantial money damages unless the court found the contract to be unenforceable for some other reason, such as fraud or mistake.)

Assuming the money damages available to Fairgate would in fact be small, can we successfully claim the right to a refund of Mackenzie's $5000? If the contract is not otherwise vulnerable to our defense or avoidance, Mackenzie's right (as a party in breach) to restitution will depend on our jurisdiction's attitude toward the retention-of-deposit clause in the offer form. Traditionally such provisions have been regarded as valid and enforceable, the breaching party being considered ineligible for restitution. More recently, however, many courts have been disposed to recognize in principle the possibility that even a breaching party might be entitled to restitution of benefits conferred. Once that position is taken, the validity of clauses like this will be judged under the broader rules governing liquidated damages in general. Under that approach, the breaching party may be granted restitution of all or part of her down payment where the other party has not been damaged at all by the breach, or where the injury from breach is demonstrably less than the amount being retained as damages. Research into the case law of our jurisdiction is again called for here. In the end, Mackenzie might (with my counsel) decide to surrender her claim to all or part of the $5000 in order to obtain a release from further liability to Fairgate.

5. What counsel should I give to Mackenzie?

Besides communicating to Mackenzie my conclusions about her legal position, as set forth above, I should in light of those conclusions counsel her to do two things without further delay.

First, she should send a letter to Fairgate, confirming her previous declaration that she does not wish to purchase the condo and asserting that any offer she may have made to that effect was withdrawn by her and is no longer open for acceptance. That letter should also state that Mackenzie demands prompt return of her $5000 payment to Fairgate and that she intends to pursue legal action if Fairgate does not comply. It should also assert that Mackenzie's attorney is ready to discuss the matter if Fairgate does not simply accede to Mackenzie's position. This letter should be sent in such a manner as to arrive reliably and speedily at Fairgate's offices. (Q.: Does Fairgate have a fax number?)

Second, I would urge Mackenzie to stop payment immediately on the check she gave to Abby. Of course, it may be too late to prevent Mackenzie's bank from honoring the check, and in any event merely stopping the check will not improve Mackenzie's substantive position vis-à-vis liability to Fairgate. It can, however, tremendously improve her *tactical* position: The burden of suing to change the status quo would then be on Fairgate, rather than on Mackenzie (as it otherwise would be, with respect to restitution of the $5000 payment). It is important to caution here that some state statutes make it a crime to obtain property or services by giving a check that is later dishonored. It is unlikely, however, that such a statute would apply to Mackenzie's situation since she didn't receive anything from Fairgate for her check. Still, before advising her to stop payment, I would research statutory law dealing with dishonored checks to determine whether this step would pose any risk to Mackenzie.

As suggested earlier, statutory rules may regulate either the substance or the form of contracts like this one (rules mandating written disclosure of interest rates, for instance, or giving the purchaser a "cooling-off period" within which free withdrawal is permitted). In the absence of such more specialized rules, however, the above analysis would apply.

JUSTIFICATIONS FOR NONPERFORMANCE AND REMEDIES

John Sanders owns Sanders's Steak and Ale, a local restaurant. Several months ago Sanders decided to sell his restaurant and retire to Florida. In response to one of Sanders's advertisements in the newspaper, Leyman Boyle approached Sanders about purchasing the business. Boyle told Sanders that he had recently retired from the military and was looking for a business that he could operate. After inspecting Sanders's operation, Boyle expressed interest in engaging in serious negotiations.

One of the first questions that Boyle asked was about Sanders's license to sell alcoholic beverages. Sanders told him that the sale of his restaurant included his rights to the liquor license. He told Boyle that Boyle would be required to obtain approval from the Alcoholic Beverages Commission to have the license transferred to him.

Boyle hired an accountant who reviewed the books and records of the restaurant and gave him advice about the value of the business. Based on this advice Boyle made an offer to Sanders to purchase the restaurant, including the land and building, for $300,000. During the negotiations, Boyle informed Sanders that he had not actually retired from the military but had been dishonorably discharged because he had been convicted of distributing drugs. Sanders knew that this would cause Boyle a problem in obtaining transfer of the liquor license, but he did not say anything to Boyle about this.

After some lengthy negotiations Sanders and Boyle agreed on a price of $310,000 for the sale of the business. The parties executed a written contract calling for a closing of the sale within 60 days. Boyle gave Sanders a check for $60,000 as a deposit for purchase of the business. Paragraphs 16 and 17 of the contract provided as follows:

16. *Transfer of License to Sell Alcoholic Beverages.* Sanders agrees to transfer to Boyle all right, title, and interest in his license to sell alcoholic beverages at the restaurant. Sanders agrees to cooperate fully with Boyle to obtain the approval of the Alcoholic Beverages Commission to transfer the liquor license to Boyle.

17. *No Warranties.* This document constitutes the entire agreement between the parties. The seller makes no representations or warranties other than those specifically contained in this document. The restaurant is being sold "AS IS."

After execution of the contract Boyle contacted the Alcoholic Beverages Commission to apply for a transfer of the license. He received several forms to complete. One question asked whether the applicant had ever been convicted of a crime or subject to court martial. Boyle disclosed his conviction on his application. When members of the Commission staff reviewed the application, they informed Boyle that his application for transfer of the license would be denied because state law prohibited ownership of a liquor license by anyone convicted of a serious crime. Boyle asked whether he could form a corporation to own the license, but he was told that the law applied not only to individuals but to any entity, whether a corporation or a partnership, in which one of the principals had been convicted of a crime.

Boyle immediately contacted Sanders, told him of his problem with the Commission, and indicated that he would be unable to go forward with the purchase of the restaurant. Sanders said that he was sorry that Boyle had this problem, but that he expected Boyle to go ahead with the purchase. Boyle responded that the restaurant was worthless without the license. Sanders pointed out that the restaurant would still be profitable, even without a liquor license. The parties ended their meeting without any resolution of the matter.

A few days before the scheduled closing, Sanders's attorney wrote Boyle to remind him of the upcoming closing and to insist on performance of the contract. Boyle hired his own lawyer, who wrote a letter to Sanders stating that his client took the position that his obligations under the contract were discharged because of his inability to obtain transfer of the liquor license. He demanded return of the $60,000 deposit.

When Boyle did not appear at the closing, Sanders's lawyer wrote another letter informing Boyle that Sanders was giving him thirty days to complete purchase of the business. Sanders's lawyer informed Boyle that his failure to complete the purchase would cause Sanders to be unable to acquire an interest in a real estate limited partnership at a very favorable price. (The price of the interest was $250,000 and its value was $350,000.) Boyle's attorney wrote back protesting that his client had been discharged from any obligations under the contract and again demanding return of the $60,000 deposit. Because Boyle failed to complete the purchase, Sanders was unable to acquire the limited partnership interest.

Sanders's lawyer responded that Sanders was holding Boyle to his obligations under the contract. Sanders then proceeded to hire a manager to operate the business while he moved to Florida. He agreed to pay the manager a salary of $2,500 per month. Sanders also employed a broker to try to sell the business, but he was unable to find a purchaser.

Sanders has continued operating the restaurant through a manager (he has paid the manager $20,000 to date) and has now brought suit against Boyle seeking to enforce the contract or to obtain damages for breach. An expert is prepared to testify that the fair market value of the restaurant was $300,000 at the date set for performance, but the value has now declined to $225,000. Discuss fully (a) the defenses that Boyle could raise in an action by Sanders for breach of contract and (b) Sanders's remedies if Boyle is found to have breached the contract. Assume that a court would apply general common law principles rather than the UCC.[1]

OUTLINE OF ANSWER

I. Boyle's defenses
    A. Failure of condition
        1. Was obtaining license a condition? Question of interpretation.
        2. Consider language, preliminary negotiations, antiforfeiture maxim. Restatement (Second) §227.
    B. Nondisclosure
        1. Was there a duty? Restatement (Second) §161.
        2. Effect of disclaimer.
    C. Mistake
        1. Unilateral rather than mutual. Restatement (Second) §153.
        2. Does Boyle bear risk? Restatement (Second) §154. Effect of "AS IS" clause.
    D. Impossibility/impracticability/frustration of purpose
        1. Performance not impossible. Could still buy restaurant.
        2. Impracticability and frustration require Boyle to act without fault. Restaurant may still be profitable. Also, "as is" clause may bar relief.
    E. Restitution
        1. If not in breach, can obtain restitution. Restatement (Second) §§376, 377. Would get deposit back.

---

1. Article 2 of the UCC might apply in whole or in part to this transaction, depending on how the sale was structured and the assets involved in the sale. Tangible assets, such as equipment and inventory, constitute "goods" subject to Article 2 of the Code. Intangible assets, such as common stock or real property, are not subject to the Code.

    2. If in breach, could still seek restitution but subject to damages. Restatement (Second) §374.

II. Sanders's remedies

  A. Specific performance

    1. Must show damage remedy inadequate. May be difficult to do because can compute damages. Restatement (Second) §360.

    2. Question of whether this is unfair under Restatement (Second) §364. Involves mistake and perhaps nondisclosure.

  B. Expectation damages

    1. General measure is difference between contract price and market price.

    2. Normally measure at time of breach, but would not fully compensate. Could measure by market value now.

  C. Incidental and consequential damages

    1. Cost of manager. Recoverable as part of mitigation. Restatement (Second) §350(2).

    2. Consequential damages. Lost profit on investment. Subject to *Hadley* rule. Generally must determine at time of contract, not later.

  D. Attorney fees, punitive damages, and damages for emotional distress

    1. Generally no recovery of attorney fees unless contract provision or statute.

    2. No recovery of punitive damages unless breach also a tort.

    3. No recovery of damages for emotional distress unless bodily harm or emotional distress particularly likely to result.

MODEL ANSWER

I. *Boyle's Defenses*

The first issue to address is whether Boyle breached the contract by failing to complete the purchase of the restaurant. Boyle's failure to perform amounts to a breach unless Boyle has a justification for nonperformance. See Restatement (Second) of Contracts §235, Comment *b.* Boyle can argue that his nonperformance was justified because of failure of condition, nondisclosure by Sanders, mistake, and impossibility/impracticability/frustration of purpose.

A. Failure of Condition

Boyle can argue that transfer of the liquor license to him was an express condition and that the failure of this condition to occur discharged his obligation to purchase the restaurant. Whether an event is a condition of a party's duty to perform is a question of interpretation. A court will examine a variety of factors in making this determination, including the language of the agreement, preliminary notifications, and maxims of interpretation.

The language of the agreement points against Boyle's position. The agreement provides in paragraph 16 that Sanders agrees to transfer his interest in the liquor license to Boyle and "to cooperate fully with Boyle to obtain the approval of the Alcoholic Beverages Commission to transfer the liquor license to Boyle." The agreement does not, however, specifically state that transfer of the license is a condition to Boyle's duty to perform.

The preliminary negotiations between the parties also are against Boyle's position. Boyle raised the issue of transfer of the license when he first discussed purchasing the business with Sanders, but Sanders immediately told him that he would be required to obtain Commission approval. While Sanders later learned that Boyle had been dishonorably discharged, he said nothing that could have misled Boyle. (The issue of nondisclosure is discussed below.)

Restatement (Second) of Contracts §227 sets forth certain maxims of interpretation regarding conditions. A crucial factor in the application of these maxims is whether the event in question is one within the control of the obligee (Sanders). Since obtaining a liquor license was not within Sanders's control, the maxims do not appear to favor Boyle.

Based on the language of the agreement, preliminary negotiations, and maxims of interpretation, it appears likely that a court would find that obtaining a liquor license is not a condition to Boyle's duty to perform the contract.

B. Nondisclosure

A contract may be rescinded by a party because of a material misrepresentation made by the other party. Restatement (Second) of Contracts §164(1). Here Sanders does not appear to have made any actual misrepresentations. Nondisclosure by one party is the equivalent of a misrepresentation if that party has a "duty" to disclose. A party has a duty to disclose when (a) disclosure is necessary to prevent a previous representation from being a misrepresentation; (b) disclosure would correct a mistake about a basic assumption about the contract and the failure to disclose amounts to a "failure to act in good faith and in accordance with reasonable standards of fair dealing"; (c) disclosure is necessary to correct a mistake about the contents or effect of a writing evidencing an agreement between the parties; or (d) a fiduciary relationship exists between the parties, Restatement (Second) of Contracts §161.

Only (b) is potentially applicable here. (Note that no fiduciary relationship exists between the parties since this is an arm's-length business transaction.) Because Boyle appears to have labored under a mistake about a basic assumption regarding the contract — his ability to obtain a transfer of the liquor license — the analysis must focus on whether Sanders failed to act in good faith and in accordance with reasonable standards of fair dealing. Sanders originally told Boyle of his need to check with the Commission about transfer of the license, but when he learned of Boyle's dishonorable discharge, he said nothing even though he knew this was a problem. Good faith means, at a minimum, "honesty in fact." It seems that Sanders was not acting honestly when he allowed Boyle to proceed with the transaction even though he knew that Boyle placed great importance on obtaining the license and even though he knew that Boyle would have difficulty obtaining a transfer of the license because of his military record. The issue is probably a question of fact for the jury to decide.

One problem that Boyle will face, however, in trying to avoid the contract on the ground of nondisclosure is the presence in the contract of a disclaimer of all warranties and representations and a statement that the restaurant is being sold "as is." A party may not rescind a contract because of nondisclosure unless the party would be "justified in relying" on the other party's failure to disclose. Restatement (Second) of Contracts §§161, 164. On the one hand, the presence of the disclaimer arguably makes any reliance by Boyle unjustified. On the other hand, some courts have held that "fraud vitiates any transaction," and a court might treat an intentional nondisclosure as fraudulent.

C. Mistake

Boyle can argue that his nonperformance is excused because he labored under a mistake of fact regarding his ability to obtain a transfer of the restaurant's liquor license. Since Sanders knew that Boyle had been dishonorably discharged and that this would cause Boyle problems in obtaining a transfer of the license, the mistake is unilateral rather than mutual. Under Restatement (Second) of Contracts §153, a unilateral mistake is a basis for avoiding enforcement of a contract if the following requirements are met:

— a mistake by one party deals with a basic assumption on which that party made the contract;
— the mistake has a material effect on the agreed exchange;
— enforcement of the contract would be unconscionable, or the other party knew of the mistake;
— the party attempting to avoid the contract does not bear the risk of the mistake.

Boyle should be able to meet each of the first three elements, but the fourth requirement, that he not bear the risk of the mistake, will cause him problems.

Under Restatement (Second) of Contracts §154, a party bears the risk of a mistake when:

— the mistake is allocated to the party by the agreement;
— the party acts on the basis of limited knowledge; or

— the court allocates the risk to the party because under the circumstances it is reasonable to do so.

All three of these, but especially the first, could apply. The agreement itself provides that Sanders made no representations or warranties other than those specifically contained in the document and that the restaurant was being sold "as is." Sanders told Boyle that he would need to obtain permission from the Beverage Commission to transfer the license, but Boyle apparently did not check with the Commission until after he signed the contract. Finally, the court might well conclude that it is reasonable to allocate the risk to Boyle because he was informed about the need to obtain Commission approval.

Boyle could counter that under the Restatement a party's fault does not bar avoidance unless the party failed to act in good faith and in accordance with reasonable standards of fair dealing. Restatement (Second) of Contracts §157. Although Boyle may have been negligent in not obtaining information from the Commission before signing the contract, there is no evidence that he acted in bad faith. In addition, the common understanding of "as is" clauses is that they relate to the condition of the property. Boyle might argue that the "as is" clause does not reasonably apply to a situation that involves the legality of operating the business rather than the condition of the premises.

D. Impossibility/Impracticability/Frustration of Purpose

Performance by Boyle is not literally impossible — he could still buy the restaurant — so the classical doctrine of impossibility is inapplicable. Boyle could argue, however, that his nonperformance should be justified under the doctrine of impracticability because the restaurant without a liquor license is substantially less valuable than a restaurant with a license. Restatement (Second) of Contracts §261. He could also rely on the doctrine of frustration of purpose, contending that his principal purpose in entering into the contract has been substantially frustrated. Restatement (Second) of Contracts §265. Boyle faces difficulties in convincing a court to apply these doctrines. First, both impracticability and frustration require the party seeking relief to act "without fault." Boyle knew that he had a problem in his background, and Sanders had told him that he must seek Commission approval to transfer the license. Second, Sanders has claimed that the restaurant would still be profitable even without a liquor license. (It might be quite difficult to prove whether the restaurant would be profitable or unprofitable without a liquor license. How could a court determine whether customers would continue to come to the restaurant if it could no longer serve alcoholic beverages?) The burden of proof on the issue probably rests with Boyle, however, since he is trying to avoid enforcement of the contract. Unless Boyle could show that the restaurant would be unprofitable without a liquor license, he is unlikely to succeed in his claim that his performance is impracticable or that his principal purpose has been substantially frustrated. Finally, under the

Restatement formulation of both doctrines a court can refuse relief if "language or the circumstances indicate the contrary." As with nondisclosure and mistake, the disclaimer and "as is" clauses could prevent Boyle from obtaining relief.

E. Restitution

If the court accepts Boyle's claim that his nonperformance was justified, Boyle will be able to obtain restitution from Sanders. See Restatement (Second) of Contracts §§376, 377. The amount of his claim for restitution would be the $60,000 deposit that he paid to Sanders. If the court finds that Boyle has breached the contract, Boyle would still be entitled to restitution of his deposit as a breaching party, less any damages that Sanders can establish. Restatement (Second) of Contracts §374(1).

II. Sanders's Remedies

A. Specific Performance

To obtain specific performance of the contract, Sanders must establish that a damage remedy is "inadequate," Restatement (Second) of Contracts §359(1), and that neither equitable nor practical factors, Restatement (Second) of Contracts §§364, 366, should prevent such relief. Sanders will have some difficulty meeting these requirements. Boyle can argue that specific performance should be denied because expectation damages can be established with reasonable certainty. The expectation measure of damages for breach of a contract of sale by the buyer is the difference between the contract price and the market price. An expert is prepared to testify regarding the value of the business both at the date set for performance and now, so there should be no difficulty in proving expectation damages with reasonable certainty. Sanders can argue, however, that a damage remedy may be inadequate even if damages can be proven with reasonable certainty. See Restatement (Second) of Contracts §360. Sanders has moved to Florida; to award him expectation damages means that he will need to make arrangements either for the continued operation of the business or for its resale. Further, the business has declined in value since Boyle has refused to perform, and Sanders has been unable to find a purchaser. Under these circumstances, a court might conclude that an expectation measure of damages would be inadequate because it would not fully compensate Sanders.

While it would be practical to enter an award of specific performance because this contract does not involve supervision, a court might find that such a holding would be unfair. Evidence shows that Sanders was acting in bad faith by not disclosing to Boyle that his dishonorable discharge would cause him problems in obtaining transfer of the liquor license. Although this factor might not be sufficient to amount to a defense on Boyle's behalf (see the discussion of nondisclosure above), a court could consider this conduct in deciding whether to order specific performance. In addition, a court might find that specifically enforcing the contract would cause hardship to Boyle because he cannot obtain a liquor license, while Sanders already has one. At the same time, denial of specific performance will impose a hardship on Sanders because of his move to Florida and the decline in value of the business.

B. Expectation Damages

As discussed previously, the formula normally used to measure expectation damages for breach of a contract of sale by the buyer is the difference between the contract price and the market price plus incidental and consequential damages. The contract price was $310,000. Sanders's expert is prepared to testify that the value of the business at the date set for performance was $300,000 but that the business has now declined in value to $225,000. Normally expectation damages are measured at the date set for performance on the theory that the nonbreaching party can then take steps to mitigate damages. If this traditional approach is used, Sanders's expectation damages would be $10,000 (increased by any incidental and consequential damages, discussed below) but reduced by Boyle's claim for restitution (see above). Sanders might be able to convince a court to use the $225,000 figure, however, since he took reasonable (albeit unsuccessful) steps to mitigate damages. To award him any less would be inconsistent with the compensation principle on which expectation damages are based.

C. Incidental and Consequential Damages

In addition to "loss in value" of the contract, the nonbreaching party is also entitled to recover "other loss," including incidental and consequential damages. See Restatement (Second) of Contracts §347. Incidental damages consist of expenses reasonably incurred to deal with the consequences of breach, including reasonable expenses in mitigation of damages. The $20,000 expense incurred by Sanders to hire a manager to run the restaurant after Boyle's breach seems to be a reasonable expense in mitigation.

Consequential damages refer to losses incurred in other contracts as a result of the breach of the principal contract. Sanders lost the benefit of a favorable real estate contract ($100,000) because of Boyle's breach. The problem that Sanders will face in recovering this amount is that consequential damages must pass the foreseeability test of Hadley v. Baxendale. The *Hadley* test provides that consequential damages are recoverable only if they either arise in the ordinary course of events or result from special circumstances of which the breaching party had reason to know. Loss of a favorable real estate contract would not arise in the ordinary course of events from breach of a contract to sell a business, and there is no evidence that Boyle had "reason to know of this contract" when he entered into the contract with Sanders. While Boyle was informed of the real estate contract prior to his breach, the *Hadley* test is applied at the date of the formation of the contract, not at the date of breach. (The breaching party could have protected itself against liability for the consequential damages if that party had reason to know of those damages at the time the contract was formed.)

D. Attorney Fees, Punitive Damages, and Damages for Emotional Distress

According to the "American Rule," a litigant may not recover legal fees unless a contract, statute, or court rule provides for recovery of fees. There is no indication that the contract provided for recovery of attorney fees. The dispute appears to be an ordinary breach of contract action that is not governed by any statute. There is also no evidence of bad faith or other improper conduct that would justify an award of attorney fees under court rule.

Punitive damages are normally not awarded in an action for breach of contract but may be allowed when the conduct that constitutes the breach also amounts to a tort. Restatement (Second) of Contracts §355. Even if a court finds that Boyle breached the contract, it is doubtful that his breach also amounts to a tort.

Damages for emotional distress are also generally unavailable in an action for breach of contract unless the breach also caused bodily injury or emotional disturbance was a "particularly likely result." Restatement (Second) of Contracts §353. Sanders has not suffered any bodily injury. Since this is a commercial contract, emotional disturbance is not likely.

MUTUAL ASSENT AND THE STATUTE OF FRAUDS

Lance Anderson owns 25 acres of lakefront property. Through Army Reserve meetings Lance has come to know Ronald Bending, a young, aggressive businessman. Several years ago Anderson mentioned to Bending that he owned lakefront property, and Bending expressed an interest in purchasing the property both for himself personally and for development. Anderson said he might be willing to sell at the right price, but Bending did not pursue the matter. From time to time Bending has raised the possibility of purchasing the property. Anderson always responded by saying to Bending, "Make me an offer." But Bending never made an offer.

About six months ago Bending again asked Anderson whether he would be willing to sell the property. Anderson responded: "Ron, how many times have we gone through this song and dance? I tell you what, I'll make you an offer you can't refuse. I'll sell you the property for $100,000. I know I'll hear from you soon, probably about the time the Falcons win the Super Bowl. Haw! Haw! Haw!"

Anderson was surprised when a week later he received a letter from Bending. The letter read as follows:

Dear Lance:

This letter is my formal acceptance of your offer to sell me your property on Lake Jones. The price is $100,000. I have arranged for financing with the First National Bank. To approve the loan the bank requires a formal contract of purchase and sale. I am enclosing the contract for your signature. I have already signed the contract. I understand that it contains the standard provisions for the sale of real estate.

I look forward to living on the property, watching the sun go down over Lake Jones, while my big screen TV shows the Falcons winning the Super Bowl.

Your friend,

Ron

Anderson immediately wrote back to Bending as follows:

Dear Ron:

All right. You proved your point and called my bluff. You win. But let's not let this get out of hand. No way am I selling the property for that price. The property is worth twice that amount. Maybe more. The whole thing was a big joke, so let's forget it.

Lance

But Bending wasn't willing to forget the sale or to treat the transaction as a joke. He told Anderson that he had signed a contract with a general contractor to construct a home on the property. Bending said that he had paid the contractor a nonrefundable deposit of $5000.

Anderson was shocked that matters had gone this far. He told Bending that he had acted totally unreasonably. This only added fuel to Bending's fire. Bending has now brought suit against Anderson. Discuss fully Bending's rights against Anderson under contract law.

BATTLE OF THE FORMS: UCC §2-207

On May 1, the Roberts County School Board submitted a purchase order to the Sealy Desk Company for 1000 school desks for a new elementary school that was to open in the fall. The order was based on the price stated in Sealy's published catalogue. The purchase order provided that delivery was to be made by July 15 and that the School Board reserved the right to cancel the order and to return the desks within 15 days of delivery if "the desks were not satisfactory to the Board in any respect."

On May 10, Sealy responded to the Board's order by sending a document entitled "Sales Contract." The document confirmed that Sealy would deliver 1000 school desks at its catalogue price by July 15. The contract also contained the following clause:

Sealy warrants that its products will be free from defects in materials or workmanship for a period of one year from the date of delivery. Except as provided in this document, there are no warranties, representations, or agreements whatsoever with respect to the products. Sealy hereby DISCLAIMS THE IMPLIED WARRANTIES OF MERCHANTABILITY AND FITNESS FOR A PARTICULAR PURPOSE.

If a defect in any product occurs during the one-year period after the date of delivery, Sealy will replace the product free of charge. Replacement of any defective product shall be the buyer's sole remedy under this contract. SEALY SHALL NOT BE LIABLE FOR INCIDENTAL OR CONSEQUENTIAL DAMAGES OF ANY TYPE WHATSOEVER.

Sealy delivered the desks on July 7. On July 15 the Board notified Sealy that it was returning the desks because they were unsatisfactory. When Sealy asked the Board to specify the problem with the desks, it learned that the Board had found another desk supplier who was willing to sell desks at a cheaper price. Attempts to resolve the matter without litigation were unsuccessful, and Sealy has now brought suit against the Board for damages for breach of contract. Discuss Sealy's right to recover from the Board for breach of contract. You may assume that the School Board would be subject to the same rules of contract law (common law or statutory) that would apply to a private party.

INTERPRETATION

Samantha Eaden owns one of the country's largest collections of Japanese art. For some time a number of museums had been trying to convince Eaden to sell her collection. In the past Eaden had rejected all offers because she wished to have her collection maintained as a whole. About a year ago, the relatively new, up-and-coming Southwestern Museum indicated a willingness to purchase Eaden's collection and to house it in a new wing that the museum had added.

On September 1, Eaden received the following letter from Ronald Hildebrand, the Director of the Southwestern Museum.

Dear Ms. Eaden:

This letter is a formal offer from the Southwestern Museum to purchase your collection of Japanese art. As I indicated in my discussions with you, the collection will be housed in a large gallery in the recently added Jawinski

Wing of the museum. The gallery will be named "The Herbert Eaden Collection of Japanese Art" in honor of your late father.

The purchase price for the collection will be negotiated between you and the museum once the collection is inventoried and appraised. After we complete the inventory and agree on price, we will have our lawyers prepare a written contract of sale. You reserve the right to cancel the contract if our plans for your collection are unsatisfactory.

The opportunity to purchase your collection is an exciting prospect for the museum. I believe that the arrangements we can make to house your collection are second to none in the world. I hope that you will decide to place your collection with the Southwestern.

Sincerely,

Ronald Hildebrand
Director

One week later, after consulting with her family and advisers, Eaden telephoned Hildebrand to inform him that she had decided to accept the Southwestern's offer. That same day, September 8, Hildebrand wrote Eaden the following letter:

Dear Ms. Eaden:

On behalf of the Southwestern Museum I wish to express my appreciation to you for accepting our offer to purchase your collection of Japanese art. We look forward to presenting your collection to the world.

Most sincerely,

Ronald Hildebrand
Director

A short time later, Hildebrand's staff members began to inventory the collection. Hildebrand also hired two noted experts in Japanese art to appraise the works in the collection. With Eaden's approval he also held a press conference to announce the acquisition of the Eaden collection.

Unfortunately, during inventory a dispute developed over five paintings by artist Winston Ambrose. Ambrose was born and educated in the United States but spent a number of years living and working in Japan. (Indeed, while retaining his American citizenship, Ambrose exhibited his art under the name of Winston Oh.) Ambrose's art focuses on the impact of industrialization on Japanese culture. Eaden considers Ambrose's art an important part of her collection and wants it prominently displayed. The Southwestern's curator of Japanese art does not classify Ambrose's work as Japanese art, but rather as art about Japan by an American. In addition, the curator's opinion is that Ambrose's work is far inferior to the other work in Eaden's collection. This opinion is shared by other noted experts on Japanese art.

The dispute now threatens the entire purchase. Eaden says that she will not go through with the transaction unless the Southwestern purchases Ambrose's art and displays it prominently as part of the collection. The Southwestern contends that it has an enforceable contract for the collection excluding the Ambrose paintings.

Discuss fully the issues of contract law raised by this fact situation.

BREACH AND REMEDIES

On April 11, 1992, the Collins Construction Company (Contractor) entered into a contract with the Oswald Development Company for the construction of an office building. The contract included the pertinent provisions summarized below:

1. *Contract Price.* $30 million. (Collins estimated the cost of construction at $28 million, producing an anticipated profit of $2 million.)

2. *Construction Schedule.* Construction was to begin by June 1, 1992, with final completion scheduled for December 1, 1993. The contract also included a detailed progress schedule for the work.

3. *Contract Documents.* The "contract documents" consisted of the agreement between Collins and Oswald, along with designs and specifications prepared by Aaron & Aaron, architects employed by Oswald, who would act as Oswald's agent in supervising the construction.

4. *Progress Payments.* Collins could apply for progress payments for work done on the building. Payment was to be made by Oswald to the extent the architect certified that the work complied with the contract documents. Oswald was allowed to withhold up to 10 percent of all progress payments as retainage until completion of the project.

5. *Substantial Completion.* When Collins had substantially completed the work, it was to notify the architect, who would inspect the work done and prepare a "punch list" of defects that Collins was required to correct.

6. *Final Payment.* When Collins had corrected all defects, the architect would issue a certificate of completion, at which time Oswald was required to make final payment to Collins.

7. *Use of Retainage.* Oswald was required to deposit the retainage in a separate interest-bearing account. Oswald could use the retainage to correct any defects in the work that Collins was unable or unwilling to correct after notification from the architect. When the architect issued the certificate of completion, Oswald was required to pay the balance in the retainage account to Collins.

8. *Termination.* Oswald could terminate the contract for a variety of causes, including violation by Collins of the contract documents in "any substantial way."

9. *Delays.* The contract provided that time was of the essence. It also stated that time for performance would be extended if delay resulted from "causes beyond the control of the contractor."

10. *Subcontractors.* Collins had responsibility for selection and performance of all subcontractors.

11. *Liquidated Damages.* If the project was not completed by December 15, 1993, Collins would be required to pay liquidated damages of $10,000 per day, the amount estimated to be the profit lost for each day of delay in occupancy of the building.

12. *Litigation.* The contract provided that "in the event either party recovers damages from the other for breach of this contract, the prevailing party shall be entitled to recover its reasonable attorney fees not to exceed 1/3 of the amount recovered."

Work began on time, and for the first few months progressed in accordance with the schedule. By January 1993, however, Collins had fallen 15 days behind schedule. On January 12, 1993, Aaron wrote Collins to complain about its failure to adhere to the construction schedule; the letter demanded strict compliance with the schedule. Collins responded that the delay had been caused by subcontractors, but that it expected to be able to make up the time as the work progressed. By March Collins was 20 days behind schedule. On March 15, 1993, Aaron wrote a letter to Collins stating that Oswald insisted on compliance with the construction schedule. The letter warned Collins that "unless your performance of the contract improves, you run the risk that the owner will elect to terminate the contract." In a letter written in response, Collins objected to the threat. The contractor claimed that Oswald did not have the right to terminate the contract because the delay was caused by subcontractors and was, in any event, too short to justify termination of the contract. On April 15, 1993, writing on behalf of Oswald, Aaron notified Collins that Oswald had elected to terminate the contract because of Collins's failure to honor the construction schedule. At that time Collins was 30 days behind schedule.

When Oswald terminated the contract, Collins had submitted requests for progress payments totaling $15 million. The architect had approved these requests and Oswald had made full payment, less $1.5 million held in retainage. Collins had also completed an additional $500,000 of work for which a request for payment had not yet been submitted. Oswald quickly employed a new contractor who was able to complete the project by January 1, 1994, 30 days late, for a contract price of $16 million.

Collins has brought suit against Oswald for breach of contract, and Oswald has counterclaimed for damages. Discuss the rights of the parties.